Can A Single Bible Study Do All This?

Creates Enthusiasm!

"*Through the Bible in One Year* has maintained more interest and better attendance for Sunday school than any other study we've found."
Cecil Hall
Faith Center

"Never seen so much excitement about a Bible study by so many people."
Fines Marcham
First Baptist Church

"Have had greater response to this course than anything else in the line of study in this church's history. Most impressive study of its kind I've taught in my 13 years of pastoral experience."
John Crawford
Christian Church

"*Through the Bible in One Year* has increased overall participation and giving by approximately 20%."
James B. Carter
First Presbyterian Church

Expands Outreach!

"Helped our Sunday School dramatically. Have many, many who have never studied the Bible before coming every Sunday morning and evening."
Rev. Troy M. Long
Airline Baptist Church

"An invaluable help. Have people of all ages attending. Some belong to other churches. Some drive over 30 miles. What an investment!"
Rev. W. W. Story
First United Methodist Church

"It's a great outreach tool for adults who have never felt confident in Biblical knowledge."
Rev. William S. Troutman
John Knox Presbyterian Church

Increases Attendance!

"Our Sunday School attendance jumped 500 in one Sunday. I've never been more excited about Bible study in the Sunday School."
Jess Moody
First Baptist Church

"Our average attendance is 150. Ordered 100 copies of *Through the Bible In One Year*. They were devoured! Went from no adult classes to four classes with 85 in attendance! Our junior high has 27 students. Now have 130 in the study. Best of all our church is beginning to grow!"
Rev. Carter W. Preston
Wesley United Methodist

"Attendance has doubled during the Wednesday evening service family night program. Every department has had substantial growth. Our Thursday morning study is multi-denominational. Dynamic!"
Rev. Don M. Brown
Bethel Church of the Assemblies of God

Creates Devoted Bible Students!

"*Through the Bible in One Year* is an excellent overview of scriptures. It has increased the students' appreciation for the Old Testament and has brought a deepening commitment."
Dr. Allen C. Ridenour
First United Methodist Church

"Excellent! *Through the Bible in One Year* stimulated commitment, exploration, and better personal study habits of the Word."
Captain Gregg Hartshorn
The Salvation Army

"The most dynamic, interesting study that we have had on the entire Bible. Extremely valuable for encouraging people to study their Bible regularly."
B. R. Burnside
First Church of the Nazarene

Encourages Spiritual Growth!

"Outstanding! I learned more about the Bible in one year of concentrated cover-to-cover study than years of topical study."
Bill Burgess
Bedford United Methodist Church

"This course can be the one most important element in beginning revival our country so desperately needs."
Norman Shaw
Church of the Nazarene

"I have personally searched for and examined a large number of Bible study curriculum for potential use in my church, and I really believe that *Through the Bible in One Year* is the best available. *Through the Bible* has given us a greater understanding of Scripture, a greater desire to study Scripture, and has helped our church to grow."
Rev. Mike Claunch
Skelly Drive Baptist

"'Wonderful!' comments one of our participants, 'just what we've needed for so long. I've hesitated to be a teacher because I haven't understood the Bible. That will change!'"
Dr. Stephen E. Kirtley
First Christian Church

Is An Outstanding Teaching Tool!

"This is one of the finest instruments God could use to reach our minds and hearts."
Dr. W. A. Criswell
First Baptist Church

"*Through the Bible in One Year* is one of the best resources I have ever used. It is easy to use and the materials are easy to understand. Excellent material"
Rev. Craig Zumbrunnan
St. Andrew Presbyterian Church

"One of the greatest programs for getting people not only to read the Bible but also to study it."
Daniel P. Gallagher
Church of Christ

"Our adult attendance doubled. People are really being ministered to. A great blessing to our church."
Rev. Neville Gritt
The Tabernacle Church

Through The Bible In One Year

A 52-Lesson Introduction
to the 66 Books of the Bible

ALAN B. STRINGFELLOW

Virgil Hensley Publishing

Since 1965

6116 East 32nd Street, Tulsa, Oklahoma 74135, (918) 664-8520

FOREWORD

"Through The Bible In One Year" was originally prepared to be taught in a local church. The need was for a short, yet a comprehensive study of the Bible so that the people could experience the thrill of having a greater understanding of all of God's Word.

The notes and outlines are designed to relate the Old Testament to the New — to relate one Book to another — and to find Christ in all the Scriptures.

The preparation of these lessons was written with the pupil in mind — under the teaching of a lay teacher — who in turn should be taught by the Holy Spirit. This is not a theological course but a Bible Study.

The teaching of these lessons has been one of the joys of my ministry. The writing of the lessons has given me many precious hours in the Word of God. The lay people have delighted in the Word of God. The pace may be fast for some students, but they will comprehend so much more than the average pastor or teacher would think. The course was taught successfully for all age groups from the fourth grade up through the oldest adult.

These outlines were written out of a vast background of teaching and learning I have reaped from great Bible scholars and wonderful friends. I have used thoughts, suggestions, helps from the sermons and the pens of people such as Dr. W. A. Criswell, Dr. J. Vernon McGee, Irving L. Jensen, Henrietta Mears, and Dr. J. Sidlow Baxter. The lessons are printed as they were presented in class. My prayer is that God will graciously use "Through The Bible In One Year" to make His Book come alive in the hearts and lives of hungry souls who need to know the Word of God.

Alan B. Stringfellow

DEDICATION

This work is dedicated to my wife, Bette — the most gifted teacher of the Word I know — a beloved partner in the work of the Master — a devoted and loving co-laborer. She is God's precious gift to me.

A.B.S.

ISBN 1-56322-014-8

THROUGH THE BIBLE IN ONE YEAR

What This Study Will Do For You

You are about to begin an exciting trip through the Bible. If you're like others who have made this journey, guided by THROUGH THE BIBLE IN ONE YEAR, you'll find it one of the most thrilling experiences of your Christian life.

With THROUGH THE BIBLE IN ONE YEAR you will learn the major themes of all the books, the key verses, the central messages, what God is saying. You will also learn how each book is organized, how it came into being, its role in the Bible story.

Still more, you will learn how to analyze all 66 books, which are the most significant chapters, where to find the central purpose, which chief verses to copy and remember. When you have completed this study, you join a long list of Bible lovers who credit THROUGH THE BIBLE IN ONE YEAR with bringing them greater insight into the Scriptures and more knowledge of God's Word than they ever thought possible.

That's because THROUGH THE BIBLE IN ONE YEAR takes you book by book through God's Word, enabling you to see the progressive step-by-step revelation of His will as perhaps never before. You will see God's Word evolve from the Pentatuech to the Revelation, 66 books written by 40 authors covering approximately 1600 years.

Studying God's Word from beginning to end is basic to knowing it well, yet most literature about the Bible skips from place to place often resulting in confusion and misunderstanding. You never read a story this way, and the Bible is a narrative telling of God's plan of redemption through Jesus Christ from Genesis through Revelation.

So you are about to see the Bible unfold as a beautiful, divinely inspired true story, with a beginning, a middle and an end yet to come.

Introduction For Students And Teachers

To receive maximum knowledge and inspiration during the next 52 weeks, heed the following suggestions. They are designed to help you become a disciplined disciple of God's Word.

"MUSTS" FOR THE STUDENT
— Attend every class session for 52 weeks.
— Read the assigned portion at the end of each lesson. (It's best to read the entire Book assigned; if you can't, then read the key chapters.)
— Review your notes from the previous week's study.
— Mark your Bible with key references from one Scripture to another.
— Take notes in class.
— Search the Scripture and mark references in class. Write in the Scriptures in this notebook where lines are provided.
— Promise the Lord at least two or three hours each week for reading the assigned Scripture for the lesson and doing your homework.

Why these "musts?" Because we have expected too little from our Bible students the past several years. The time has come for Christians who mean business for the Lord to devote themselves to the study of His Word and to learning the basic principles that we all should know. Promise yourself and promise God you will live up to these "musts."

PUBLISHER'S STUDY NOTE

It is important to note the author's premise in developing this course of study; namely, that *the Bible is the divinely inspired Word of God.* Nothing can take it's place.

Thus, THROUGH THE BIBLE IN ONE YEAR should be read neither *in place of* the Bible nor as a study *about* the Bible. Rather you should use it as a guide that takes you *into* the Bible and involves you in the study of God's Word, resulting in your understanding it better and appreciating it more.

You will also note that the text of this manual appears in outline rather than exposition. This permits quick coverage of the controlling thoughts of the book under study along with the key verses, the central message and the major themes.

Because your manual is in this form, you will get maximum benefit if your study is under the direc-

"MUSTS" FOR THE TEACHER

First you must prepare yourself spiritually by reading —
- I Corinthians 2:12-14
- Ephesians 1:17-18
- John 14:26
- John 16:12-16

These Scriptures will assure you as the teacher that the Holy Spirit will guide you and teach you as you study His Word and impart it to your pupils.

If you are in a church, the program is best taught to teachers by the pastor, minister of education, Sunday School superintendent or a specially selected teacher. This should be done on a weekday evening prior to the coming Lord's Day.

Part of the discipline of this course of study is that you attend each evening session each week without exception.

You must read the entire Book assigned for the next lesson. The assignment is at the close of each lesson study. The author has suggested that you read the entire Book or Books to be taught the following week; he has also listed key chapters for pupils if they are unable to read a Book in its entirety.

You must take notes and search out Scripture references. You must also be prepared to answer questions, add to or take away from the questions as you feel is necessary for your age group.

What's more, you must —
- Stay with the subject of each lesson.
- Not be afraid of being too elementary for your pupils.
- Stay on the major themes, not minor ones.
- Keep the lesson teaching as simple as possible with all age groups.
- Not change the lesson outline. You may add illustrations and ideas, but do not change the major points of the outline.
- Use your own personality and let the Holy Spirit use you as you teach.
- Expect your pupils to do their part.

You should teach at least 55 minutes every lesson. Even if you have to revamp your class schedule to teach for 55 minutes, it can be done. The assembly periods can be made shorter. It isn't necessary to have a devotional before going to Bible study. One song and a prayer is sufficient for the assembly period. Class absentees and other business should be handled at class meetings. Make your Bible study period an hour of concentrated Bible study.

May God bless you, pupil or teacher, as you begin your study in THROUGH THE BIBLE IN ONE YEAR. Let the Holy Spirit teach you both.

tion of a teacher. The teacher in turn should be prepared by attending weekly teachers' meetings taught by the pastor or other capable assistant.

Another major advantage of the outline form is that it allows the teacher far more latitude than does straight exposition.

In a few instances, you may find that the text differs slightly with your own theological beliefs. Please do not allow these occasions to overshadow the overall value of this excellent course. Instead, use these differences as a point around which to further refine your own theology. This adds still more value to the program, for it enables you to see denominational differences.

In your study and discussion, always be guided by the Holy Spirit, and you will profit immensely from this work, despite differences in interpretation.

The publisher feels that THROUGH THE BIBLE IN ONE YEAR is the inspired work of a devoted man of God.

INDEX

About Photocopying This Book

Lesson 1
"The Bible As A Whole"

INTRODUCTION:

No man's education is complete if he does not know the Bible. No believer can live the full and effective life without a grasp of the Bible.

PURPOSE:

Our purpose in this course of study is to give a grounding in the Scriptures. There is no need to study these outlines and notes instead of the Bible. The Bible itself shall be read and searched and researched as one proceeds through the study.

We shall build a skeleton — the bone structure, and you should add — the second and third year — the circulatory system and some muscle to that skeleton.

METHOD:

We shall study this year — seeking a grasp of controlling thought — the outstanding meaning and message of each Book and strive to see it in relation to the whole of God's Word.

We must not become so engrossed and fascinated with a subject that we lose sight of the object — to let the big, broad meanings of the wonderful Old Book get hold of us.

Let us enter the study reverently, realizing that the Bible is inbreathed by the Holy Spirit and that He, the Holy Spirit, must be our Teacher: John 14:26.

(Where lines are provided, please look up the Scriptures and fill in the Scripture or the main Truth of the passage.)

THE BIBLE AS A WHOLE:

1. The Bible is God's written revelation of His will to man. II Timothy 3:16-17; II Peter 1:21.
2. The central theme of the Bible is Jesus Christ. I Timothy 3:16.
3. The Bible contains 66 Books, written by 40 authors covering approximately 1,600 years.
4. The Old Testament was written mostly in Hebrew (a few short passages in Aramaic). The New Testament was written in Greek. Our Bible is a translation from these languages.
5. The word "Testament" means "Covenant" or agreement. The Old Testament is the Covenant God made with man about his relationship before Christ came. The New Testament is the agreement God made with man about his relationship with the Father after Christ came.

    In the Old we have the Covenant of the Law. In the New, the Covenant of Grace through Jesus Christ. Galatians 3:19-25; Galatians 3:13-14.

_____

_____

6. **The Old Testament — The First Seventeen Books**

    (1) The first 5 Books: *Genesis*   *Numbers*

                                  Exodus   *Deuteronomy*

                                  Leviticus

1

are called the **Pentateuch** — all from the pen of Moses and are five in number. They are called "The Law" but they are redemptive and historical in nature. (Pentateuch means five.)

(2) Next 12 In number are:

Joshua	*II Samuel*	*II Chronicles*
Judges	*I Kings*	*Ezra*
Ruth	*II Kings*	*Nehemiah*
I Samuel	*I Chronicles*	*Esther*

These make up the second main group of Books in the Old Testament. Note, there are 12 in number and they are historical in nature.

So the first section of the Old Testament is 17 in number, falling into a natural subdivision of:

Five (PENTATEUCH) — LAW — REDEMPTIVE — HISTORICAL

Twelve (JOSHUA THROUGH ESTHER) — HISTORICAL

7. **The Old Testament — The Middle Five Books**

(1) These are:

Job	*Ecclesiastes*
Psalms	*Song of Solomon*
Proverbs	

(2) These five are individual and experiential. All of the former 17 were national — these are personal, dealing with human problems of the heart. All of the first 17 were *prose* — these are *poetry*.

They are five in number and they are experiential in nature.

8. **The Old Testament — Last Seventeen Books**

(1) The final seventeen books — The Prophetical Books
They are:

Isaiah	*Joel*	*Habakkuk*
Jeremiah	*Amos*	*Zephaniah*
Lamentations	*Obadiah*	*Haggai*
Ezekiel	*Jonah*	*Zechariah*
Daniel	*Micah*	*Malachi*
Hosea	*Nahum*	

(2) These 17 are also divided into two groups as the first 17 were:
The first 5 — are the "Major" Prophets"
The last 12 — are the "Minor Prophets"

9. **Summary — Old Testament**

So we see that the 39 Books of the Old Testament fall into this orderly grouping —
SEVENTEEN — subdivided into 5 and 12
FIVE
SEVENTEEN — subdivided into 5 and 12

10. **The New Testament — The First Five Books**

(1) The foundational Books are:

Matthew	John
Mark	and the historical Book of
Luke	Acts

These are foundational to all that has preceded and all that follows.

11. **The New Testament — The Next Twenty-one — The Epistles**

(1) Fourteen are the EPISTLES OF PAUL. They are divided as follows:
NINE — Church Epistles —

Romans	*Philippians*
I Corinthians	*Colossians*
II Corinthians	*I Thessalonians*
Galatians	*II Thessalonians*
Ephesians	

FIVE — Pastoral or Personal —

I Timothy	*Hebrews* (and the author-
II Timothy	ship of Hebrews
Titus	by Paul is debated,
Philemon	but we shall consider
	it as Paul's based upon
	Hebrews 13:23)

(2) Seven are GENERAL EPISTLES. The names of the seven are the same as their authors — *James*   *I, II, III John*
                                                                 I Peter   *Jude*
                                                                 II Peter

12. **The New Testament — The Last — One — Prophecy**

   The Apocalypse — the Revelation of Jesus Christ penned by John.

13. **Summary — New Testament**

   Thus the New Testament consists of 5 foundational Books — firm on which to build the 21 Epistles of instruction ending in the "glorious appearing of our Lord Jesus Christ" in the Revelation.

OLD TESTAMENT — 39 BOOKS

17 HISTORICAL		5 PERSONAL EXPERIENTIAL	17 PROPHETICAL
5 — LAW MOSES Pentateuch	12 HISTORICAL	POETRY	5 MAJOR 12 MINOR

NEW TESTAMENT — 27 BOOKS

5 FOUNDATIONAL	21 EPISTLES		1 PROPHECY
GOSPELS MATT. — MARK LUKE — JOHN ------------ ACTS OF HOLY SPIRIT	14 ARE BY PAUL — (9 TO THE CHURCH, 5 ARE PASTORAL OR PERSONAL)	7 ARE GENERAL INSTRUCTIONS	THE REVELATION OF JESUS CHRIST

HOW MUCH DO YOU REMEMBER?

Q. How many Books can you remember now?

Q. Can you grasp the divisions I have taught in your own mind?

   i.e. Old Testament (Historical ____ Personal____ Prophetic____)
        New Testament (Foundation____ Epistles____ Prophetic____)

Q. What does "Testament" mean?

Q. What does "Pentateuch" mean?

Q. Can you give the Scripture that tells how the revelation (thoughts) of God were written by man?

CONCLUSION:

   The Bible is divine. The thought and revelation is divine but the expression of the communication is human. It is the *Word of God*.

II Peter 1:21 _____

_____

I Peter 1:24-25 _____

_____

   It is a progressive revelation and one cannot learn it from reading verses or passages at random. It is a step-by-step revelation of one story, one mind (God), the Creator of all things, and the story is His great purpose moving through the ages and that story was and is to redeem mankind through Jesus, the Messiah, the Saviour of all who will believe. John 3:16.

Each Book is a Book from God. Read the Book or Key Chapters assigned for each week. If you can read the entire Book, you will be blessed. If time does not allow reading all of each Book — read the Key Chapters assigned.

FACTS ABOUT THE BIBLE:

God, man, sin, redemption, justification, sanctification. In two words — *grace, glory.* In One word — *Jesus.*

CHRIST QUOTED FROM 22 OLD TESTAMENT BOOKS:

Matthew — 19 times	Luke — 25 times
Mark — 15 times	John — 11 times

- There are 1,189 chapters in the Bible.
- There are 31,373 verses in the Bible.
- There are 775,693 words in our King James Version.
- Longest chapter is Psalm 119.
- Shortest chapter is Psalm 117.
- Longest Book in Old Testament is Psalms.
- Longest Book in New Testament is Luke.

ASSIGNMENT FOR NEXT WEEK:

1. Read Genesis — 7 chapters each day or Key Chapters 1 through 27 and 49.
2. Be present next Lord's Day with your Bible and notebook.
3. Review today's lesson at least twice.

NOTES

Lesson 2
"The Book of Genesis"

(Where lines are provided, please look up Scriptures and fill in the entire Scripture or the main Truth of the passage.)

1. **"Genesis" means origin,** source, birth. "In the beginning God . . ."

2. **Genesis is the "seed plot"** of the entire Scripture. It enters the very structure of the New Testament, in which it is quoted about sixty times in seventeen Books. Its divine revelation and the fact that Moses is the author is authenticated by the Testimony of Jesus. Look up Matthew 5:17-30 _____

   _____

   _____

   _____

   John 7:21-23 _____

   _____

   _____

Genesis tells us of the beginning of everything *except God:*

The beginning of the Created World — 1:1-25.
The beginning of Man and Woman — 1:26 and Chapter 2.
The beginning of Sin — 3:1-7.
The beginning of the Promise of Redemption — 3:8-24.
The beginning of Family Life — 4:1-15.
The beginning of Civilization — 4:16 through 9:29.
The beginning of Nations — Chapters 10 and 11.
The beginning of a Chosen People — Chapters 12 through 50
  and other beginnings, i.e. Judgment, Altars, Death, etc.

3. **The Structure of Genesis**

   (1) **THE FIRST PART** — Chapters 1 through 11.

   The First Part Covers Four Major Events

   1. The Creation — Chapters 1 and 2
   2. The Fall of Man — Chapters 3 and 4
   3. The Flood — Chapters 5 through 9
   4. The Babel Crisis — Chapters 10 and 11

   (2) **THE SECOND PART** — Chapters 12 through 50.

   The Second Part Covers Four Outstanding Persons

   1. Abraham, the man of faith — Chapters 12 through 23.
   2. Isaac, the beloved son — Chapters 24 through 26.
   3. Jacob, whose name was changed to Israel — Chapter 27 through 36.
   4. Joseph, life of suffering and glory — Chapter 37 through 50.

   (We shall look briefly at each of these events and persons.)

4. The Creation — Chapters 1 and 2

(1) This is not a human theory in this Scripture but a divine testimony — Verse 1. There is *no* definition of God, *no* description of creation, *no* declaration of date. *It is a declaration of divine truth.* Accept the first sentence in Scripture and there will be little difficulty in accepting all of God's Word.

(2) The time space between Verse 1 and Verse 2 is unknown but it does leave room for all the geologic eras. Verse 2 should read "the earth *became* without form and void . . ." The same word used here is also used in 2:7 — "Man *became* a living soul."

(3) The six days in Chapter 1 do not record the original creation for what happened in Verse 1. The six days give an account of a *new* beginning or a *re-creation*. During the first four days no creative act is recorded. Only when we come to animals in Verse 21 and man in Verse 27 is the Hebrew word for "create" used.

(4) We are the crown of His creation. Notice 1:26-27 and 2:7. Man was created in the image (representation or resemblance) and likeness (character or model) of God. No words can adequately express this but the fact that God breathed into man "the breath of life and man became a living soul" is the best expression to be found. We are then body, soul and spirit. Look up I Thessalonians 5:23 _____

_____

_____

(5) The seventh day God rested — the Sabbath — 2:2-3. Look up Hebrews 4:9-10 _____

_____

5. The Fall of Man — Chapters 3 and 4

(1) THE TEMPTING — 3:1-6 (note Satan casting doubt on God's Word in Verse 1, the first lie in Verse 4, the appeal to pride in Verse 5). Satan captured the ear, eye, inward desire. See I John 2:16 and we see the natural man. _____

_____

_____

(2) THE YIELDING — Verse 6.
Look up Romans 5:12 _____

_____

(3) THE RESULTS — Verses 7-24. Notice, now there is self conscience — Verse 7; shame and fear — Verse 10; sorrow — Verse 17; cursed — Verse 17; thorns — Verse 18; sweat — Verse 19.

(4) THE GRACE OF GOD — 3:9 and 15.
God sought out Adam — Verse 9.
The Promise of a Redeemer — Verse 15 — This verse may be translated into layman's terms as follows:

> *"And there will be intense hatred between Satan and Christ. Eventually Christ will crush the head of Satan and Satan will only bruise the heel of Christ."*

THIS IS THE FIRST DIRECT PROPHECY OF JESUS CHRIST.

Look up II Corinthians 5:21 _____

_____

Look up Isaiah 53:5_____

_____

(5) THE FRUIT OF SIN — Chapter 4 — the Cain line or "the sons of man" — the first murder, and the birth of Seth, a spiritual seed. Note Verses 3-5 and Verse 8 _____

_____

Note Verse 25 _____

_____

6. The Flood — Chapters 5 through 9

(1) The Book of the generations of Adam through Seth — 4:25 through 5:3.

(2) In Chapter 6 we see the mixing of the Godly and ungodly. Note II Corinthians 6:14.

_____

_____

(3) Judgment falls in Chapter 7 as a result of Chapter 6:5-7. (Read this again.)

One man found grace in the eyes of the Lord — Noah. Look up Genesis 6:8; Matthew 24:37-39.

_____

_____

_____

Doesn't this remind you of our day?

(4) God's Covenant with Noah — 9:8-17.

Seven times God uses the word "Covenant" in this passage. Underline the word in your Bible.

7. The Babel Crisis — Chapters 10 and 11

(1) The generations of the sons of Noah — Chapter 10.

(2) The confusion at Babel — Chapter 11.

The reason for the action of God was because the people refused to obey God in spreading abroad to replenish the earth. Note: "Let *us* make *us* a name, lest *we* be scattered" — Verse 4.

Now note Verses 7-8. God did this so they would scatter abroad.

"Babel" means confusion. It was the "capital" in Nimrod's kingdom — 10:9-10.

8. Abraham — Genesis 12 through 23 (there is some overlapping in Scriptures in this second part of Genesis):

(1) His call — 12:1 and Acts 7:2.

(2) The Abrahamic Covenant — 12:2-3; Acts 7:3.

Note the seven promises of God:

(a) I will make thee a great nation.
(b) I will bless thee.
(c) I will make thy name great.
(d) Thou shalt be a blessing.
(e) I will bless them that bless thee.
(f) I will curse them that curse thee.
(g) In thee shall all the families of the earth be blessed.

(3) This Covenant was confirmed again and again in:

| 13:14-18 | 17:6-8 | 26:1-5 |
| 15:1-21 | 22:15-18 | 28:13-15 |

(4) Abraham was a man of faith. Read Hebrews 11:8-19.

_____

_____

9. Isaac — Genesis 24 through 26 — (Read Chapter 17:15-19 first.)

   (1) The beloved and obedient son — 22:1-8.

   (2) A bride for Isaac, Rebekah — Chapter 24.

   (3) Father of Esau and Jacob — "two nations in womb" — 25:23-26.
Note Hebrews 11:17-20_____

_____

_____

   (4) The Abrahamic Covenant confirmed to Isaac — Chapter 26.

10. **Jacob — Chapters 27-36** (became "Israel")

   (1) The stolen blessing of his father, Isaac — Chapter 27.

   (2) Abrahamic Covenant confirmed to Jacob — 28:13-15.

   (3) The twelve sons of Jacob:

Reuben — 29:32	Gad — 30:13
Simeon — 29:33	Asher — 30:13
Levi — 29:34	Issachar — 30:18
Judah — 29:35	Zebulon — 30:20
(Line of Christ — Gen. 49:8-10)	Joseph — 30:24
Dan — 30:6	Benjamin — 35:18
Naphtali — 30:8	

These are the heads of the twelve tribes of Israel — 49:28.

   (4) Jacob's name changed to Israel — 32:28.
Thus we have Israel and the 12 tribes.

11. **Joseph — Chapters 37-50**

   (1) There is no word or reproof against Joseph.

   (2) He was the favored son — 37:3.
Sold for 20 pieces of silver and taken to Egypt — 37:20-36.

   (3) Humiliation and exaltation in Egypt — Chapters 39 through 48.

   (4) Jacob (Israel) enters Egypt with his entire household (46:27) which numbers 70. Acts 7:14 refers to 75 "and all his kindred," a probable reference to the five surviving wives of Jacob's sons.

In Genesis 46:26 the number is 66 "which came out of his loins."

In Verse 27 the number is 70 from "the house of Jacob" including the 66, Joseph and his two sons, Ephraim and Manasseh and Jacob himself.

   (5) Joseph is the most complete picture (type) or shadow of Christ in the Bible. Here are just a few illustrations:

    (a) Both were beloved by their fathers – Genesis 37:3; Matthew 3:17.

    (b) Both were shepherds – Genesis 37:2; John 10:11-14.

    (c) Both were severely tempted – Genesis 39:7; Matthew 4:1.

    (d) Both were taken to Egypt – Genesis 37:26; Matthew 2:14-15.

    (e) Both were sold for the price of a slave – Genesis 37:28; Matthew 26:15.

    (f) Both were highly exalted after suffering – Genesis 41:41; Phil. 2:9-10.

And many more, but this gives you the idea of a type or an example in the Old Testament of a reality in the New Testament.

   (6) The prophecy and blessing of the tribes of Israel — Chapter 49.
See Hebrews 11:22.

So we see in the Book of Genesis the supreme object of God in providing for us a family through which the promised Redeemer was to come. Read Galatians 3:14_____

_____

HOW MUCH DO YOU REMEMBER?

Q. Where is the first prophecy of Christ found in Genesis?

Q. When did the Sabbath day begin?

Q. In one word, how would you describe the fall of man?

Q. Where do we find Israel at the close of Genesis?

Q. Can you list the four outstanding events of Genesis?

1. _____

2. _____

3. _____

4. _____

Q. Can you name the four outstanding persons of Genesis?

1. _____ 3. _____

2. _____ 4. _____

YOUR ASSIGNMENT FOR NEXT WEEK

1. Read Exodus — 6 Chapters each day or Key Chapters 1 through 7; 12 through 14; 19 and 20; 25 through 33.
2. Review our study of Genesis from your notes.
3. Mark your Bible from your notes taken in class.
4. Be present next Lord's Day with your Bible and notebook.

Lesson 3
"The Book of Exodus"

(Where lines are provided, please look up Scriptures and fill in the entire Scripture or the main Truth of the passage.)

1. **"Exodus" means "the outgoing"** of the Israelites from the land of Egypt. It was written (as was Genesis) by Moses and this was confirmed by Christ in Luke 24:44. _____

   _____

2. **Exodus is the Book of Redemption.** The Israelites had been under the bondage of Egypt's ruler, Pharaoh (a ruler in Egypt). Exodus describes how God delivered them from bondage. In Genesis we saw the ruin of man through the sin (fall) of man. In Exodus we shall see the redemption by blood and power of God.

3. **Exodus continues what was begun in Genesis.** Genesis 46:27 tells the number of the family of Jacob (70) and approximately 400 years later a vast multitude, 600,000 men, plus women and children, (12:37) came out of Egypt.

   Genesis 15:13 says the seed of Abraham would spend 400 years in Egypt. Exodus 12:40 says it was 430 years and Galatians 3:16-17 confirms it. It was 430 years from the call of Abraham. Remember the vastness of the Exodus.

4. **The Structure of Exodus**
   (1) THE EXODUS — Chapters 1 through 18.
   (2) THE LAW — Chapters 19 through 24.
   (3) THE TABERNACLE — Chapters 25 through 40.
   In these three divisions we see:

THE EXODUS (CHAPTERS 1 THROUGH 18)	THE LAW (CHAPTERS 19 THROUGH 24)	THE TABERNACLE (CHAPTERS 25 THROUGH 40)
• POWER OF GOD • BROUGHT OUT TO NEW LIFE • LIBERTY	• HOLINESS OF GOD • BROUGHT UNDER LAW • RESPONSIBILITY	• WISDOM OF GOD • BROUGHT INTO A NEW LOVE AND FELLOWSHIP • PRIVILEGE

5. **The Exodus — Chapters 1-18**
   (1) A DELIVERER
       (a) Birth of Moses and 40 years in Palace — Chapter 2. (Read Hebrews 11:23-29)
       (b) Call of Moses — 40 years in Midian — Chapter 3.
       (c) Announcement of Deliverance for Israel — Chapter 4.
       (d) The Nine Plagues of Pharaoh — Chapters 5-11.
           (Note the *Assurance of* God to Israel in Chapter 6:1-8.)
   (2) DELIVERANCE BY BLOOD AND POWER
       (a) Institution of Passover — 10th plague (11:5), death of first born (blood). Chapter 12. See I Corinthians 5:7.

   _____

   _____

(b) The Crossing of Red Sea — Power — Chapters 13-14.
Read 13:21-22 — and note the power and presence of God.

_____

_____

_____

(3) MARCHING TO MT. SINAI
(a) Song of the redeemed — Chapter 15.
(b) God provided for 40 years — Verses 4, 13 and 35. Chapter 16. Read John 6:47-51.

_____

_____

(c) The Smitten Rock — Chapter 17.
Note Verses 5 through 7 — then refer to I Corinthians 10:4 and see Christ. Also John 4:13-14.

_____

_____

6. **The Law — Chapters 19 through 24**
(1) COMMANDMENTS — *governing Moral life* — Chapters 19-20.
At foot of Sinai — People agreed to the Covenant at Sinai — 19:8.
Note the Ten Commandments — 20:1-17.

_____

_____

Read Matthew 22:37-39_____

_____

(2) JUDGMENTS — *governing Social life* — Chapters 21-23.
Masters and servants — Chapter 21.
Property rights — Chapter 22.
Sabbaths and feasts — Chapter 23.
(3) ORDINANCES — *governing Religious life* — Chapter 24.
All taught in the giving of tabernacle.
(4) WHY THE LAW WAS GIVEN
To provide a standard of righteousness — Deut. 4:2,8.
It was added to Abrahamic Covenant — it was an insertion and not a deletion — because of transgression — Gal. 3:17-18.

_____

_____

Galatians 3:19-24. It was a schoolmaster.

_____

_____

To expose and identify sin — Romans 5:20.
Romans 3:20 — Romans 7:7 _____

_____

_____

To reveal the holiness and power of God — Deut. 4:32-36.
Symbol of presence and holiness of God is cloud and fire — Exodus 19:9; Exodus 19:18; Exodus 24:17.

_____

_____

_____

(5) HOW DOES THE LAW AFFECT US? Romans 8:3-4.

_____

_____

The keeping of the "rules" of the law is not *obligatory* to salvation, but the spontaneous result of salvation.

7. **The Tabernacle — Chapters 25-40**

   (1) The *Pattern* was given to Moses during his 40 days in the mountain — Chapters 25-31.

   (2) Then, Israel's lapse into idolatry — the episode of the golden calf — causes the *delay* of the building of the Tabernacle — Chapters 32-34 (temporary substitute is provided in a tent pitched "without the camp" — 33:7).

   (3) Finally the Tabernacle is *completed* and erected (exactly one year after the Exodus 40:2) and the glory of the *Presence* of God descends upon it — Chapters 35-40.

   (4) The Scriptures devote more room to the description of the Tabernacle than to any other *single* subject. It was designed in the plan of God to teach spiritual truths. To teach all the truths would take many lessons but the important thing is to remember that God taught and still teaches "according to this *Pattern*" — Hebrews 9:23. Here read Hebrews Chapter 9 and see some of the meaning for us.

   THE TABERNACLE PORTRAYS **CHRIST.** Read Hebrews 9:8-12.

_____

_____

Q. Who was the deliverer, chosen by God, to lead the Exodus?

Q. What are the three principle subjects of Exodus?

   1. _____

   2. _____

   3. _____

Q. Why was the Law given?

   1. _____

   2. _____

   3. _____

HOW MUCH DO YOU REMEMBER?

Q. How did God dwell with, and lead His people?

Q. What does the Tabernacle teach us today? I Corinthians 10:11

Q. Who is our passover? I Corinthians 5:7

Q. What does the Book of Exodus teach us?

YOUR ASSIGNMENT FOR NEXT WEEK
1. Read Leviticus — 4 chapters each day.
2. Review our study of Exodus from your own notes.
3. Mark your Bible (Exodus) from your notes and look up all references.
4. Be present next Lord's Day ready to study Leviticus. Bring your notebook and Bible.

Lesson 4
"The Book of Leviticus"

NOTES

(Where lines are provided, please look up Scriptures and fill in the entire Scripture or the main Truth of the passage.)

1. **The Book**
   Leviticus gets its name from the Levites — the priests — and it is God's plan for the detailed *walk, worship and service* of the people. In Exodus God spoke out of the Mount where the people were not allowed. In Leviticus He speaks out of the Tabernacle in which He dwells in the midst of His people.

2. **A Transition**
   In Genesis we saw the ruin of man — through the fall. In Exodus we saw the redemption and deliverance by blood and the power of God.

   In Leviticus we shall see worship and communion on the ground of atonement. Leviticus is called the Book of Atonement (see Lev. 16:30-34). _____

   _____

3. **Its Main Purpose**
   Leviticus was written to show Israel how to live in fellowship with God. Above all Israel must be taught the holiness of God and Leviticus reveals this in three ways:

   (1) *The sacrificial system* — Leviticus 17:11 — Hebrews 9:22.

   (2) *The precepts of the law* — Leviticus 18:5.

   (3) *The penalties for violations* — Leviticus 26:1-46.

   Israel was to be a separated people, just as we are today.

4. **Its Abiding Value**
   FIRST — Leviticus is a revelation of the divine character and holiness of God. God has not changed.

   SECOND — It emphasizes the exceeding sinfulness of man and his estrangement from God.

   THIRD — It prefigures the redemptive ministry of Christ and how we are restored to fellowship with God.

   FOURTH — It provides a body of civil law for a theocracy which is foundational for civil law today, i.e., land and ownership, marriage and divorce and other matters we face today.

5. **Its Author**
   Moses was the author. The internal evidence is stated no less than 56 times in Leviticus that the Lord God gave the laws to His people through Moses.

   Jesus ascribes the Book and all the Pentateuch to Moses in Luke 24:44. Christ also referred to Moses as the author in Matthew 8:2-4 (compare this with Lev. 14:1-4). _____

   _____

   _____

6. **Its Theme**

By looking at all the five Books of Moses we can see the theme of Leviticus is *"Fellowship."*

GENESIS	EXODUS	LEVITICUS	NUMBERS	DEUTER-ONOMY
ORIGIN OF THE NATION	*DELIVERANCE* OF THE NATION	*LIFE* OF THE NATION	*TEST* OF THE NATION	*REMINDERS* TO THE NATION
THEOCRACY BORN	THEOCRACY ESTABLISHED		THEOCRACY TESTED AND PREPARED FOR THE NEW HOME	
	COVENANT AMPLIFIED EX. 19:5-6	LAWS ARE PRESCRIBED LEV. 18:5		

7. **The Structure of Leviticus**

It may be divided into two broad divisions:

(1) *The Way To God* — Sacrifice — Chapters 1-17.

(2) *The Walk With God* — Separation — Chapters 18-27.

THE CENTRAL THEME IS "FELLOWSHIP." In the first division is found God's foundation of fellowship — while the second division shows man's condition of fellowship. Thus, it is the supreme Old Testament illustration of that New Testament truth expressed in I John 1:7. The first section of Leviticus says: "The blood cleanseth us." The second says: "If we walk in the light." The whole Book says: "If we walk in the light — the blood cleanseth us" and we have fellowship one with another and truly our fellowship is with the Father.

8. **The Way to God — Sacrifice — Chapters 1-17**

(1) THE OFFERINGS — Chapters 1-7.

The Burnt Offering — Chapter 1 ⎤
The Meal Offering — Chapter 2 ⎬ Sweet Savour Voluntary
The Peace Offering — Chapter 3 ⎦

The Sin Offering — Chapter 4 ⎤ Non-Sweet Savour
The Trespass Offering — Chapter 5 ⎦ Compulsory

Note: The *Burnt Offering* foreshadows Christ "offering Himself without spot to God" — Hebrews 9:14 and pictures Christ on the Cross.

The *Meal Offering* exhibits the manhood of Christ and the life that was offered. Hebrews 2:17-18

_____

_____

The *Peace Offering* speaks of restored communion with God through Christ's offering. He is our peace — Ephesians 2:14. It is a thank offering — Leviticus 7:11-12.

_____

_____

The *Sin Offering* pictures Christ as the sin bearer — "made sin for us" — II Corinthians 5:21.

_____

_____

The *Trespass Offerings* speak of *sins* (plural) against others and the injury sin does — (Lev. 5:16 — Restitution taught in the words "make amends.") This offering pictures Christ atoning for the *damage* of sin. II Corinthians 5:19 — Ephesians 2:1 — note "trespasses" and "sins."

_____

_____

_____

(Chapters 6 and 7 are the *Laws of Offerings*.)

(2) THE PRIESTS — Chapters 8-10.

  (a) The Consecration of the Priests — Chapter 8.

THE HIGH PRIEST (AARON)	THE OTHER PRIESTS (HIS SONS)
Cleansed — Verse 6	Cleansed — Verse 6
Clothed — Verses 7-8	Clothed — Verse 13
Crowned — Verse 9	Charged — Verse 35
Anointed — Verse 12	Anointed — Verse 30

Note: Aaron anointed before the blood sacrifice — Verse 12.
    His sons anointed after the blood sacrifice — Verse 30.
      (See Hebrews 2:11)
    The offerings and the blood of consecration — Verses 14-24.
    Do you see the picture?
    Hebrews 9:11-15_____

_____

  (b) The Ministry of the Priests — Chapter 9.
    Note Verses 22-24 — God blesses through leaders.

  (c) The Violation of Two Priests — Chapter 10.
    Name them — Verse 1. _____

_____

    The sin of offering "strange fire" — The sin of presumption. God punished — Verse 2.

(3) THE PEOPLE — Chapters 11-16.

God's people must be a clean people:

        Clean foods — Chapter 11

        Clean bodies — Chapter 12

        Clean clothes — Chapter 13

        Clean houses — Chapter 14

        Clean contacts — Chapter 15

        A clean nation through the blood atonement — Chapter 16.

        This is the great chapter of atonement when the High Priest entered the most holy place. This was the great day of *forgiveness* through the blood sacrificed on the altar.

        Christians are priests — I Peter 2:5 and 9.

        Christ is our High Priest — Hebrews 2:17 — Hebrews 10:12.

_____

_____

_____

_____

The Old Testament word "atonement" is used which means "to cover." In accepted theological usage today, the word "atonement" denotes the redeeming sacrifice *of Christ* — but in Leviticus the Hebrew word is used which means "to cover." The Leviticus offerings merely *covered* sin until the one real atonement was effected on Calvary. Romans 3:25. _____

_____

_____

_____

(4) THE ALTAR — Chapter 17.

Five times the *one place* of sacrifice is divinely ordained — Verses 3-9.

The meaning is clear. There is only one place where God meets sinful man —*The Cross* which the altar at the door of the Tabernacle was a type. Romans 3:23-25_____

_____

_____

The sanctity and meaning of blood sacrifice — Verse 11.

Read Hebrews 9:14 _____

_____

_____

So in the first part we have the fact — that through the blood of Calvary's Lamb, and nothing else, we find our *Way To God*.

9. **The Walk With God — Separation — Chapters 18-27** (Second Division of the Book) (Read Chapter 18:1-5)

(1) A HOLY PEOPLE — Chapters 18-20.
   Set apart people concerning sex (Chapter 18) and all forms of sin — Chapters 19 and 20.

(2) HOLY PRIESTS — Chapters 21-22 — Concerning the Levites.

(3) HOLY FEASTS — Chapter 23.
   (Set seasons God appointed Israel to observe)

   (a) THE FEAST OF PASSOVER — Verses 5-14.
      Where does the word Passover come from in a former study?

      _____

      _____

      _____

      It celebrated Israel's redemption from death and bondage in Egypt.

      I Corinthians 5:7 has meaning for us now _____

      _____

      _____

   (b) THE FEAST OF UNLEAVENED BREAD — Verses 6-8. This followed immediately after Passover and is often counted as a part of the Passover (which lasted one day) while this feast lasted seven days.
      This Feast speaks of communion with Christ in the blessing of our redemption.
      I Corinthians 5:8. I Corinthians 11:23-26.

_____

_____

Also see John 6:51 _____

_____

(c) FEAST OF FIRSTFRUITS — Verses 9-14.
This Feast marked the beginning of the harvest on the "day after the Sabbath."
Christ the "firstfruits" of "them that slept" was raised the "morrow after the Sabbath" which is the first day of the week.
I Corinthians 15:20-23 _____

_____

_____

Also refer to James 1:18 _____

_____

_____

(d) FEAST OF PENTECOST — Verses 15-22.
Note that this Feast occurred *50 days* (the word Pentecost comes from the Greek word meaning fiftieth) after the Feast of Firstfruits.
After Christ's resurrection He was on earth 40 days (Acts 1:3) before he ascended. The disciples waited in the upper room until the Day of Pentecost was fully come — 10 days — and on the anniversary of this Feast, the Holy Spirit came upon them and the Church was born.

See Acts 2:1 _____

_____

I Corinthians 10:16-17 _____

_____

I Corinthians 12:13 and 20 _____

_____

_____

(e) FEAST OF TRUMPETS — Verses 23-25
This was New Year's Day for Israel. It was a special Sabbath in the seventh month. A calling to a holy gathering.
Refers to future for Israel — Isaiah 18:3-7; 27:12-13; 58:1-14.

_____

_____

(f) THE DAY OF ATONEMENT — Verses 26-32
The greatest day for Israel because on this day her sins were confessed. This followed immediately after the blessing of the Trumpets. This was seen in Leviticus 16.

See Hebrews 9:11-14 _____

_____

(g) THE FEAST OF TABERNACLES — Verses 33-44.
This was the completion of the harvest and was the final religious convocation of the year. It is called "booths" in King James. It looked back on their Exodus from Egypt — Verses 42-43 and reminded them of their dependence upon the Lord God. Read Zechariah 14:16-20.

_____

_____

(4) A HOLY LAND — Chapters 25-27.
Thirty times we find a reference to "the Land" in this section.

(a) The key to the 7th year Sabbath is the word "rest" — 25:4.
Rest for the land — Verse 4.
Rest from toil — Verses 5-6.

See Hebrews 4:9 _____

_____

_____

(b) The key to the year of Jubilee — (50th year) is the word "liberty" — 25:10.
The Jubilee year brought liberty to property, the land, and the servant — Chapter 25.

(c) The Law of the Land — Chapter 26.
Conditions of blessing — Verses 1-13.

_____

_____

Warnings from God — Verses 14-31.
Scattering of Israel because of disobedience (predicted) Verses 32-39.

See Galatians 6:7_____

_____

_____

(d) The Land and All Resources Belong to God — Chapter 27.
Here we see the voluntary consecrations and tithing. This is not obligatory, as most of the Book of Leviticus, but is an expression of love toward God.

HOW MUCH DO YOU REMEMBER?

Q. What is the theme or central truth of Leviticus?

Q. Can you explain what "atonement" means in Leviticus? What does it mean to us?

Q. What does "Pentecost" mean?

Q. Can you name five of the "offerings" of Leviticus 22?

YOUR ASSIGNMENT FOR NEXT WEEK
1. Read the Book of Numbers (6 chapters each day) or key chapters 1 through 5, 9, 11, 13, 17, 20, 21, 27 and 35.
2. Review our study of Leviticus from the notes made in class.
3. Mark your Bible from your notes.
4. Be present next Lord's Day with your Bible and notebook.

Remember — this course is "Through The Bible In One Year." You will be tempted to stop and study *a subject* and lose sight of *the object* — the object being — to let the big, broad meaning of each Book get hold of you — that you remember the overall message of each Book.

Lesson 5
"The Book of Numbers"

(Where lines are provided, please look up Scripture and fill in the entire Scripture or the main Truth of the passage.)

1. **Its Name**

   Numbers gets its name from the Greek name "Arithmai" which in Latin is "Numeri" — in English "Numbers." It was so named because in it the children of Israel are twice numbered — once at the beginning and again toward the end.

   The *Old Hebrew* name was "In the Wilderness" — Verse 1. Both names tell the story — "Numbers — In the Wilderness."

2. **Its Nature**

   Numbers takes up where Exodus left off. Just one month between the two Books with Levitical instructions coming in between.

   Compare Exodus 40:17 with Numbers 1:1.

   The census is taken — the people organized — the march begun to Canaan — God leads — Canaan is in sight — Israel disbelieves and rebels — judgment falls — 40 years' wandering set in — old generation dies off — new generation is numbered (counted) — to go into the land of Canaan.

3. **Its Importance**

   Referred to in New Testament again and again.

   Read in detail I Corinthians 10:1-12 and make notes on your readings:

   _____

   _____

   _____

   Also read Hebrews 3:7-19: _____

   _____

   _____

4. **Its Structure**

   It is a Book of Movement by the people. It deals with two different *generations*. Thus the structure is:

   THE OLD GENERATION — Chapters 1 through 14.
   THE WANDERING-TRANSITION ERA — Chapters 15 through 20.
   THE NEW GENERATION — Chapters 21 through 36.

   REMEMBER IN NUMBERS
   Two Generations — Chapters 1-14 and 21-36.
   Two Numberings — Chapters 1-4 and 26-27.
   Two Journeyings — Chapters 10-14 and 21-27.
   Two Instructions — Chapters 5-9 and 28-36.

5. **Its Central Message — Numbers 9:15-23**

   GUIDANCE — Direction by the Lord God.
   See John 14:6 and John 8:12.
   DELIVERANCE — See Numbers 10:29 and Numbers 21:6-9.

6. **The Old Generation — Chapters 1-14 (Sinai to Kadesh)**
   (1) THE NUMBERING — Chapters 1-4.
       Chapter 1 — Numbering of adult males.
       Chapter 2 — Distribution of the tribes.
       Chapter 3 — Numbering of Levite males (priests).
       Chapter 4 — Distribution of Levite duties.

   The numbering (census) was for military purposes. Each of the twelve tribes were numbered and assigned a position around the Tabernacle.

   Chapter 3 gives the census of the tribe of Levi — exempt from the general census. They were priests, set apart to serve God and care for the Tabernacle. Chapter 3:38 tells the position of Moses, Aaron and his sons.

   (2) THE INSTRUCTING — Chapters 5 to 10:10.
   (The first four chapters dealt with the outward formation of the camp.)

   These five chapters deal with the inward condition of the camp.

   Chapter 5 — Deals with purity, honesty and truth (Note Verse 3.)

   _____

   _____

   Chapter 6 — The vows of the Nazarites — meaning totally separated unto the Lord.

   _____

   _____

   Chapter 7 — The free-will offering of leaders of each tribe. The Lord recorded the offering. See Mark 12:41-44.

   _____

   _____

   Chapter 8 — Describes the consecration of Levites.

   _____

   _____

   Chapter 9 — Shows the people keeping the Passover and tells us of *the pillar of cloud by day and fire by night*. This indicated the guidance of the Lord. Don't forget the Passover was a memorial of past deliverance. The Lord's Supper is a memorial for us of deliverance from sin through Christ. See I Corinthians 11:26.

   _____

   _____

   Chapter 10:1-10 — The Lord commands Moses to make two trumpets for calling the assembly. The pillar of cloud gave guidance for the eye while the trumpets gave guidance for the ear. See I Thessalonians 4:13-18.

   _____

   _____

   (3) THE JOURNEYING — Chapter 10:11 through Chapter 14.
       Chapter 10:11 — They had been at Sinai getting ready for the march to Canaan. Now the pillar of cloud lifts, the trumpets sound and the whole camp moves.
       Chapters 11 through 14 find the people moving toward the Promised Land — and after three days they begin to murmur and

complain. Even Aaron and Miriam become jealous of their brother, Moses. At Kadesh-barnea they displayed their sinfulness of unbelief. They send twelve spies to search out the land and ten came back with a negative report. Only *two,* Joshua and Caleb, said, "Let us go up and possess the land." The crowd would not believe them. Judgment falls in the form of 40 years' wandering. See 14:29-33.

7. The Wilderness Wandering — Chapters 15 through 20

In this section is the transition from the old to the new generation with the exception of Joshua and Caleb. *The Lord told the people they would die* (14:29) and that their children would go into the land.

For all those years they wandered and finally came to the same spot where they had been, Kadesh-barnea.

God continued to communicate with them through Moses during this time (15:1, 17, 35). He gave them food and water, clothes and shoes (Deut. 8:2-6).

In Chapters 16-18 comes an attack on the Aaronic priesthood and over 15,000 die in earthquake, fire, and plague. Then God causes the rod of Aaron to blossom — showing His approval of the office. The budding of the rod speaks of Christ, our High Priest, and of His resurrection. See Hebrews 4:14; 5:4-10.

_____

_____

Chapter 20 — We see the death of Miriam and the sin of Moses when he smote the rock *twice* and God told him just to speak to it. Because Moses did not believe the Lord — he would not go into the land (Verse 12).

Aaron dies (Notice Verse 24).

8. The New Generation — Chapters 21 through 36

(From Kadesh-barnea to Moab)

The delay is over. The old generation is gone and a new generation has arisen.

(1) THE NEW JOURNEYING — Chapters 21-25.

The journey was made longer because Edom refused to let them go through their land. (See 20:14-22 and 21:4.)

(a) Note the lesson of despair and murmuring again, and God sends the serpents. God provides a way to be saved in 21:8-9.

See John 3:14-15 _____

_____

See I Corinthians 10:9-10 _____

_____

(b) Chapters 22 to 25 — The Confrontation with Balaam.

See II Peter 2:15. _____

_____

Jude 11 _____

_____

Revelation 2:14 _____

_____

(2) THE NEW NUMBERING — Chapters 26-27.

At the beginning of the 40 years there were about 600,000 men and at the end of the 40 years there were about 600,000. Notice 26:64.

In Chapter 27:12-14 Moses is told of his impending death and then . . . Joshua is appointed in his place.

(3) THE NEW INSTRUCTING — Chapters 28-36.

Chapters 28-29 — Offerings to be given to the Lord.

Chapter 30 — The vows of men and women.

Chapter 31 — "Avenge the children of Israel" against the Midianites. Not one Hebrew life was lost — Verse 49.

Chaptes 32-36 — Request of Reuben, Gad and Manasseh to settle on the east of the Jordan. Their place was inside Canaan, not just outside. The results are found in I Chronicles 5:18-26.

They chose from what they could *see* (32:1) instead of accepting the instructions of the Lord.

The Cities of Refuge — Chapter 35.

Their number — Verses 6-8.
Their purpose — Verses 9-12.
Their distribution — Verses 13-14.
Their regulations — Verses 15-34.

Finally the Book closes dealing with the security of their inheritance which teaches of our eternal security in Christ.

HOW MUCH DO YOU REMEMBER?

Q. Who is the main character in Numbers?

Q. Who holds the office of High Priest?

Q. How many generations are found in the Book?

Q. Why did they wander in the wilderness for 40 years?

Q. What is the central truth of Numbers?

Q. Can you name the three main sections in our outline of Numbers?

YOUR ASSIGNMENT FOR NEXT WEEK
1. Read the Book of Deuteronomy — 6 chapters each. Try to read entire Book.
2. Review the study in Numbers from your own notes made in class.
3. Mark your Bible from these notes.
4. Be present next Lord's Day with your Bible, pen or pencil and notebook.

Lesson 6
"The Book of Deuteronomy"

(Where lines are provided, please look up Scriptures and fill in the entire Scripture or the main Truth of the passage.)

1. **The Final Book of Moses**

    This is the last Book of the Pentateuch — the five Books of Moses.

    In Genesis we have the "beginnings" — the *ruin* of man, the fall.

    In Exodus, the law and a way out — *redemption* by blood and the power of God.

    In Leviticus, the worship of the people — *communion* on the ground of the atonement.

    In Numbers, the wanderings — *direction* by the will of God.

    In Deuteronomy, final preparation to go into Canaan — *destination* through the faithfulness of God.

2. **Its Name**

    Deuteronomy gets its name from the Greek "deuteros" meaning "second" and "nomos" meaning "law." So in this Book we have a second giving of the law — or better, a new expounding of it to the new generation of Israel who had grown up in the wilderness. It is *not* the giving of a new law, but an explication, a giving in detail, that which was already given.

3. **It is a Book of Transition**

    FIRST, a transition to a new generation.

    SECOND, a transition to a new possession

    THIRD, a transition to a new experience

    FOURTH, a transition to a new revelation of God — the revelation of *His love*.

    Getting ready for the new land, from tents to houses and milk and honey of Canaan.

    From Genesis to Numbers the love of God is never spoken of; but here in Deuteronomy we have the wonderful words of His love:

    Look up Deut. 4:37 _____

    _____

    Deut. 7:7-8 _____

    _____

    Deut. 10:15 _____

    _____

    Deut. 23:5 _____

    _____

4. **The Structure of the Book**

        Looking Backward — Chapters 1-11.

                and

        Looking Forward — Chapters 12-34.

5. **The Central Message**

        Obey, obey — Obedience to God.

        4:1, 2, 5, 9, 15, 23, 40

        5:1; 6:1-3; 11:26-27

6. **The Basic Things of Deuteronomy**

Deuteronomy will be best remembered if we clearly point out the truths in it — upon which all the other teachings are built:

(1) THE BASIC FACT

Deut. 6:4-5 _____

Jesus affirmed the Basic Fact in Matthew 22:35-39.

This was the first article of Israel's relationship with God. This was also the basic fact on which Christianity is built. "This is the first and the great Commandment."

(2) THE BASIC TRUTH

Deut. 6:23_____

_____

(a) "He brought us out" — We see the power of God.

(b) "That He might bring us in" — We see the grace of God.

(c) "Which He sware unto our Father . . ." — The faithfulness of God.

This Basic Truth takes on a new meaning when applied to Christian believers today. He has brought us out from a condemnation of sin for "there is now no condemnation to them which are in Christ Jesus," Romans 8:1. He has delivered us from the bondage of sin. Look up Romans 8:2: _____

_____

_____

He has brought us into a Spiritual Canaan which is ours in Christ. Gal. 2:20: _____

_____

_____

Ephesians 1:3-4 _____

_____

Ephesians 2:19 _____

_____

He is faithful to keep His promise — I Thessalonians 5:23-24

_____

_____

(3) THE BASIC REQUIREMENT

Deut. 10:12-13 _____

_____

Obedience is the requirement in one word. The Lord Jesus requires nothing less of believers today: John 14:21-23

_____

(4) THE BASIC PLEDGE

Deut. 4:27-31 (Note the basic, unconditional pledge of God is the one He made to Abraham, note Verse 31.)

_____

_____

Deut. 29:12-13 _____

_____

The Sinai or Mosaic Covenant was broken but God has kept His basic pledge.

(5) THE BASIC DIFFERENCES

The Old and the New Testaments differ basically. A special place is emphasized in the Old. (Deut. 12:10-14)

_____

_____

Jesus changed the old emphasis from *a place* to a person. (John 4:20-26)

_____

_____

Acts 8:27-31 and 35-37 — The eunuch had been to right place, for the right purpose, and read the right Book. Philip preached unto him Jesus and he went away rejoicing. From a place in the Old to a Person in the New.

(6) THE BASIC BLESSING

Deuteronomy was a basic Book for our Lord. He quoted from it frequently:

Matthew 4:4, 7, 10 _____

_____

Compare these three verses with Deut. 8:3_____

_____

Deut. 6:16_____

_____

and Deut. 10:20 _____

_____

7. **Moses, the Man**

Deut. 34:10_____

_____

His life falls into three periods of 40 years each.

First 40 years — Exodus 2:11 (in Egypt) _____

_____

Compare with Acts 7:22-23 _____

_____

Second 40 years. Exodus 2:15 (in Midian)_____

_____

Compare with Acts 7:29-30 _____

_____

Third 40 years, Exodus 7:7 and Deut. 31:2 (Leader of Children of Israel till his death) _____

_____

Moses was 120 years old when he died. Deut. 34:7. He is the only man God buried — 34:6.

He was raised and glorified and he appeared on the Mount of Transfiguration — Luke 9:30-31.

Read Hebrews 11:23-29.

Christ in the Book — Deut. 18:15-18.

HOW MUCH DO YOU REMEMBER

Q. What does "Deuteronomy" mean?

Q. What is the Basic Fact of the Book?

Q. What is the Basic Truth of the Book?

Q. In one word, what is the Basic Requirement of the Book?

Q. There are three periods in the life of Moses. How long was each period?

Q. What happened to him when he died and afterward?

YOUR ASSIGNMENT FOR NEXT WEEK

1. Read the Book of Joshua — 4 chapters each day.
2. Review the study in Deuteronomy from your own notes made in class.
3. Mark your Bible from your notes.
4. Be present next Lord's Day with your Bible, pen or pencil and notebook.

Lesson 7
"The Book of Joshua"

(Where lines are provided, please look up Scriptures and fill in the entire Scripture or the main Truth of the passage.)

1. The Book

The five Books of Moses (Genesis through Deuteronomy) lead the childen of Israel *up to* Canaan — Joshua leads the children of Israel *into* Canaan. The remainder of the historical Books (Joshua through Esther) covers Israel's history inside the land.

2. The Author

The author is Joshua. If he did not pen it by his own hand — he gave the words and substance to a scribe who wrote it.

3. The Structure

Entering the Land — Chapters 1 through 5.

Overcoming the Land —Chapters 6 through 12.

Occupying the Land — Chapters 13 through 24.

4. The Central Message

The Victory of Faith — Joshua 1:5 and 9; 3:17.

Clearly the lesson in Joshua proclaims the New Testament Truth — "This is the victory that overcometh the world, even our faith" — I John 5:4.

(Note — There are many types, symbols in Joshua, and in the Pentateuch, but time does not permit our teaching all of these. Joshua means "Jehovah is salvation." Our salvation came after Moses. See John 1:17.)

(Note — There is a remarkable parallel between Joshua and Ephesians. In Joshua we see Israel entering and possessing the earthly inheritance given to Abraham. In Ephesians we see the church entering and possessing the heavenly inheritance given to us in Christ.)

5. Entering the Land — Chapters 1 through 5

(1) JOSHUA COMMISSIONED FOR LEADERSHIP — Chapter 1.

His authority was based upon the Word of God. Read Verses 5-9. Notice what real "success" is in Verse 8 and name the steps to success in Verse 8:_____

_____

_____

(2) JERICHO SPIED — Chapter 2.

Joshua sends two spies to Jericho because it was a key city. This did not degrade nor do away with Joshua's faith. True faith does not despise the use of means because there is a wide difference between believing and presuming.

Note the acts and rewards of Rahab — Verse 11, Verse 12 and Verse 18.

_____

_____

(3) JORDAN CROSSED — Chapter 3.

This was a critical moment for Israel. They were at the same place as their parents — 40 years earlier. Now they were to move — led by the priests and Levites. God would work miracles *if* they would follow. Note Verse 3 and Verse 5 and Verse 13, and Verse 17. These Verses teach us that it is one thing to be brought out of the "Egypt" of sin but another thing to trust and obey the total Word of God.

(4) MEMORIALS RAISED — Chapter 4.

They must not forget what God had done. There was to be a *memorial* in the river Jordan — Verse 9. And a memorial at Gilgal — Verses 3 and 19. Each memorial was made up of twelve stones. These memorials reminded them of the power of God in holding back the waters and the faithfulness of God in bringing them into the land. Can you name a memorial which we observe speaking of our salvation? _____

_____

(5) THE SEAL OF THE COVENANT — Chapter 5.

Circumcision was the seal of the covenant between God and Israel. The children born during the forty years' wandering had to bear the mark of Israel — which spoke of moral and spiritual separateness. Look up — Deuteronomy 10:16

_____

_____

Deut. 30:6_____

_____

Colossians 2:11-13_____

_____

6. **Overcoming the Land — Chapters 6 through 12**

(1) THE FALL OF JERICHO — Chapter 6.

The Lord would do the conquering if Israel would do *exactly* what God commanded. They did and God did. Rahab was saved — Verses 13 and 17.

(2) THE SIN OF ACHAN — Chapter 7.

One sin affected the whole camp — Verses 11 and Verses 20-21.

(3) THE CONQUEST OF THE LAND — Chapters 8 through 12.

After sin had been confessed and dealt with, God gave Joshua and Israel victories at Ai — and through the central, southern and northern campaigns. Chapter 12 gives a summary of all the kings and cities that fell at the hands of Israel.

Note especially 11:23 _____

_____

7. **Occupying the Land — Chapters 13 through 24**

(1) THE DIVISION of the land among the tribes and Levites was no simple task. God went into detail. Chapter 13.

(2) THE DIVIDING of the land was by "casting lots before the Lord" — 18:6-7. The Lord was to settle the tribes where he wanted them. Note also 14:2. Notice that Gad, Reuben and the half tribe of Manasseh settled on the east of Jordan . . . (Genesis 48:19-22) — the other nine and one-half on the west side.

(3) MARK WELL the *principle* which governed Israel's occupation of the land. Note Chapter 11:23 and compare that with Chapter 13:1. There is no contradiction here but they complement each other. The decisive blow had been struck and it only remained that they should

go on through to the last detail. The same is true in our lives — the blow against Satan has been struck in the acceptance of Christ.

All that He has is ours if we will possess all "blessings in Christ" but we must go on and possess them ourselves.

The key passage in this section is Chapter 21:43-45. Note what "the Lord gave" them: _____

_____

_____

NOTICE THE THREE THINGS GOD GAVE TO ISRAEL:

1. The Lord gave to Israel *all the land*.
2. The Lord gave them *rest*.
3. The Lord gave all *enemies* into their hand.

Note Chapter 14:2-3 the number of tribes in Canaan.

_____

_____

(4) THE CITIES OF REFUGE — Chapter 20.

Here we have the six Cities of Refuge — three on the west of the Jordan and three on the east. They were a merciful provision to protect those who had committed "sins of ignorance," mistakes and unintentional wrongs. Christ, Himself is our "City of Refuge."

(5) JOSHUA'S FAREWELL — Chapters 23 and 24.

Read 23:14.

Read 24:14-16.

What do you learn from these verses?_____

_____

At 110 years of age Joshua died — 24:29.

HOW MUCH DO YOU REMEMBER?

Q. What is the central Truth of Joshua?

Q. Can you recall the three main divisions of the Book?

Q. Who was the woman who hid the spies in Jericho?

Q. How did they cross the Jordan River into Canaan?

Q. What was the memorial the Lord told them to make upon coming into the Land?

YOUR ASSIGNMENT FOR NEXT WEEK

1. Read the Books of Judges and Ruth — four chapters each day.
2. Review the study in Joshua from your notebook.
3. Mark your Bible from your notes.
4. Be present next Lord's Day ready to study Judges and Ruth from your own Bible. Bring your notebook.

Lesson 8
"The Book of Judges" and "The Book of Ruth"

(Where lines are provided, please look up Scriptures and fill in the entire Scripture or the main Truth of the passage.)

1. **The Book of Judges**

   The Book of Judges takes its name from its contents — the people raised up as judges to deliver Israel in a time of declension and disunion after the death of Joshua.

2. **Its Nature**

   The nature of the Book places the emphasis upon the spiritual significance of events recorded and not on chronological continuity.

   The author of the Book is not named, though Jewish tradition attributes it to Samuel. The main thing for us is — it is part of the canon of Scripture and is given "by the inspiration of God."

3. **Its Central Message**

   Failure Through Compromise. Why this tragic landslide? The verse that rings out loud and clear is Judges 17:6 _____

   _____

   Read II Corinthians 6:17-18 _____

   In answering the question — "Why the decline?" we will form the guide for our study.

4. **Its Structure**

FAILURE THROUGH COMPROMISE		
Prologue — Chapters 1 and 2		
MAIN NARRATIVE — CHAPTERS 3-16		
THE SIN OR APOSTASY	SERVITUDE	DELIVERER
Judges 3:5-8	To the King of Mesopotamia — 8 years	Othniel —3:9-11
Judges 3:12-14	To the King of Moab — 18 years	Ehud — 3:15-30 and Shamgar — V-31
Judges 4:1-3	To the King of Canaan — 20 years	Deborah — 4:4 to 5:31 and Barak
Judges 6:1-10	To Midianites — 7 years	Gideon — 6:11 to 8:35
Judges 10:6-18	To Philistines — 18 years	Jephthah — 11:1 to 12:7
Judges 13:1	To Philistines — 40 years	Samson — 13:2 to 16:31
Illustrative Epilogue — Chapters 17-21		

(Note: The old Scofield Bible names *seven* Apostasies. There are only *six* which are introduced by "The children of Israel did evil in the sight of the Lord." The one Scofield mentions that is not introduced like that is in Chapter 8:33.)

The prologue (Chapters 1 and 2) is explanation of how the period came about.

The epilogue (Chapters 17 and 21) is illustration of the conditions themselves.

The body of the Book (Chapters 3 through 16) speaks of *thirteen* judges. Of these, *six* stand out pre-eminently — because the entire story is based upon six successive apostasies and servitudes, (or punishments), of Israel and the six judges or deliverers. All six servitudes, or punishments, are said to have been brought about by Jehovah Himself, i.e. "The anger of the Lord was hot against Israel and He sold them into the hands of the King of Mesopotamia" — 3:8.

5. **The Emphasis of the Main Narrative — Chapters 3-16**

The main body of the Book is easily seen if we diagram the six episodes in parallel columns, in order, under a quadruple emphasis which is seen throughout.

THE SIX EPISODES

	1st 3:7-11	2nd 3:12-30	3rd 4:1-5:31	4th 6:1-8:35	5th 10:6-12:7	6th 13:1-16:31
SIN	V-7 "The children of Israel did evil in the sight of the Lord . . . etc.."	V-12 "The children of Israel did evil . . "	4:1	6:1	10:6	13:1
SUFFER-ING	V-8 "Therefore the anger of the Lord was hot against Israel etc. . ."	V-12-14 "The Lord strength-ened Eglon etc. . ."	4:2	6:1	10:7	13:1
SUPPLI-CATION	V-9 "When the children of Israel cried to the Lord. . ."	V-15 "When the children of Israel cried to the Lord. . ."	4:3	6:6-7	10:10 and 15	No suppli-cation re-corded. See 10:15 "Deliver us only this day. . ."
SAL-VATION	V-9 "The Lord raised up a de-liverer.."	V-15 "The Lord raised up a de-liverer.."	4:4-6 DEBORAH AND BARAK	6:12-14 GIDEON	11:29 and 33 JEPHTHAH	13:3 and 5 and 15:20 SAMSON
	OTHNIEL	EHUD				

The emphasis above is meant to do its own work in the student's mind. Write a part of each verse in the blank areas as shown in the first two episodes.

6. **The Epilogue — Chapters 17-21**

This section illustrates the confusion and the depths to which Israel had sunk. Judges 17:6 gives the reason for it all:

"_____

_____"

First, you will see confusion in the religious life of the nation. Judges 17 and 18.

Second, confusion in the moral life of the nation — Judges 19.

Third, confusion in the political life — Judges 21.

7. **In the entire Book of Judges we see**
   - the sinfulness of man —
   - the constant failure of man —
   - but — we also see the constant mercy of God.

We also see God's delight in using the weak things.
Note: the strength of Gideon and the 300 men (7:6-8).
   —the jaw bone used by Samson (15:15).
   —Deborah, a woman (4:4 and 5:1-2).

Look up I Corinthians 1:26-29 _____

HOW MUCH DO YOU REMEMBER?

Q. Where does Judges get its name?

Q. What is the central message of the Book?

Q. What character stands out in your mind?

Q. How many apostasies or sins are mentioned in our study?

THE BOOK OF RUTH

1. **The Book**
   According to Verse 1, it clearly belongs to the period covered by the Book of Judges and is named for its heroine, Ruth.

2. **Its Features**
   It is one of only two Books in Scriptures which bear the names of women — Ruth and Esther. The Book of Ruth is a love story. It is unique in the fact that Ruth was the great-grandmother of David, placing her in the line of Christ. Ruth is one of the four women named in the Messianic line. The other three — Tamar, Rahab and Bathsheba recall to our mind unworthy conduct; but Ruth is virtuous.

3. **Its Central Message**
   The Kinsman Redeemer — (Christ is our Kinsman Redeemer)
   Godly love.

4. **Its Structure**
   DECISION — Love's Choice — Chapter 1
   SERVICE — Love's Response — Chapter 2
   REST — Love's Security — Chapter 3
   REWARD — Love's Reward — Chapter 4

5. **Truths you should know**
   (The Story of Ruth speaks for itself, therefore, we shall point out some of the Truths of the Book, that you should remember and apply.)
   (1) Ruth was a Moabitess — descendant of Lot — 1:4.
   (2) Ruth's love for Naomi, her mother-in-law — 1:16.
   (3) Boaz is a picture of Christ — our Kinsman-Redeemer. The word "kinsman" in the Hebrew is "goel." The law of the "goel," or next of kin, is found in Lev. 25 and Numbers 35 and Deut. 19 and 25. There were three requirements of the "kinsman."
   (a) He must be willing to redeem — Lev. 25:25: Gal. 4:4-5.

   _____

   _____

   (b) He must be a kinsman — have the *right* to redeem — Lev. 25:48-49; Ruth 3:12-13; *Hebrews 2:11*.

   _____

   _____

(c) He must have the power — the *means* to redeem. Ruth 4:4-6; John 10:11-18.

_____

_____

Christ as our Kinsman-Redeemer has the *right* as our true Kinsman. He has the *power* as the Son of God. He is graciously *willing* to "pay the price" and He has.

Christ is our "Redeemer" — He paid the price. We are the redeemed — the freed ones because He has paid the price for us on the Cross.

(4) In the last verse of the Book we discover the significance of the lesson. "Obed (Ruth's son) begat Jesse, and Jesse begat David." The Lord Jesus is from the line of David.

HOW MUCH DO YOU REMEMBER?

Q. What is the theme of Ruth?

Q. What period does the Book of Ruth belong?

Q. What does Ruth teach us about redemption?

Q. What does "redemption" mean?

YOUR ASSIGNMENT FOR NEXT WEEK

1. Read the Book of I Samuel — less than 5 chapters each day.
2. Review the study of Judges and Ruth from your notes made in class.
3. Mark all Scripture references in your Bible from your own notes.
4. Be present next Lord's Day with your Bible and notebook.

Lesson 9
"The Book of
I Samuel"

(Where lines are provided, please look up Scriptures and fill in the entire Scripture or the main Truth of the passage.)

1. **The Book**

   The Book of First Samuel heads what some call the "three double Books of the Old Testament" — I and II Samuel, I and II Kings, I and II Chronicles. These three double Books form the record of the rise and fall of the Israelite monarchy.

2. **The Manuscripts**

   In the Hebrew manuscripts, I and II Samuel form *one* Book as do I and II Kings and I and II Chronicles. The Book of I Samuel marks off a definite period — from the birth of Samuel, the *last* of the Judges, to the death of Saul, the *first* of the Kings and covers a period of about 115 years.

3. **The Author**

   The author of the Book, of course, is the Holy Spirit — but a part of it was written by Samuel himself, I Samuel 10:25. Other suggestions for co-authors are found in I Chronicles 29:29.

4. **The Structure**

   SAMUEL: The Last of the Judges — Chapters 1-8

   SAUL: The First of the Kings — Chapters 8-15

   DAVID: The Anointed Successor — Chapters 16-31

   (The three personalities overlap but it is obvious that Samuel is the prominent character in the first eight chapters. In the next seven chapters the focus is on Saul and in the remaining chapters we find David the main attraction. Our main study of David will come in next week's lesson on II Samuel.)

5. **The Central Message**

   The people demand a king — choosing less than God's best. (Read Chapter 8.)

6. **Some Distinctive Points of I Samuel**

   This Book contains many unique things that will help you remember this Book:

   (1) Oft quoted words —

   > "Ichabod" — 4:21
   > "Ebenezer" — 7:12
   > "God save the king" — 10:24
   > "the Word of the Lord was *precious*" — 3:1

   (2) The word "prayer" is used 30 times in this Book.

   (3) The first time we find the phrase "Lord of Hosts" is in this Book and is used eleven times in I and II Samuel (Note I Sam 1:3).

7. **Samuel — Chapters 1-8**

   (1) The ministry of Samuel marks the beginning of the prophetic office. There were those before on whom the mantle of prophecy

had fallen, i.e. Moses — Deut. 18:18. But Scripture indicates that the prophetic order was founded by Samuel.

Look up I Samuel 3:20; 10:5; 19:18-24 _____

_____

_____

Now look up Acts 3:24 _____

_____

Acts 13:20 _____

_____

Hebrews 11:32 _____

_____

(2) The silent years of Samuel — 4:1-7:3. In these three chapters Samuel is not mentioned. It was a period of about 20 years — 7:2. The Ark of the Lord is the feature here.

(3) Samuel as the Judge — 7:3 — 8:22. He continued to serve after Chapter 8:22 but then the head of the nation is a king, beginning at Chapter 9.

Note 7:15 _____

_____

(4) The people demand a king from Samuel — 8:5. Note 8:7 — the real meaning of their demand is given "they have not rejected thee, but they have rejected me," said the Lord.

8. Saul, the first of the kings — Chapters 8-15

(1) Israel wanted a king — like the other nations and God granted their request — 8:19-22. Here is a great lesson for us — we can have God's best or His second best — His direct will or permissive will.

(2) Saul was chosen to be king, 9:2 and was anointed by Samuel, 10:1. Look up these verses. _____

_____

_____

_____

(3) Saul's decline is in Chapters 13-26. See 13:12-13. An act of impatience.

_____

_____

See 15:19-23 — An act of rebellion.

See 16:14 — "The spirit of the Lord departed from Saul."

See 18:7-11 — Saul tried to kill David because of jealousy. Note Verse 9 _____

_____

See 26:21 — Saul says, "I have played the fool."

See 28:7-20 — Saul's final downward plunge is "witchcraft" and in Chapter 31, suicide.

Note Verse 28:7 _____

_____

9. **David, the Anointed Successor — Chapters 16-31**
   (1) David was chosen by the Lord, through Samuel, to be the successor to Saul — 16:1-11.
   (2) David is anointed to be king — 16:12-13 _____

   _____

   Note: David was not enthroned until the death of Saul. Even though he was to become king, David took his place as a servant which should remind us of Phil. 2:7 _____

   _____

   _____

   (3) David meets Goliath 17:31-54. Look up Ephesians 6:13-17.

   _____

   _____

   (4) Jonathan, *Saul's son,* loved David — Chapter 18.
   David was hated by Saul (through the rest of I Samuel.) Read David's words in Psalm 59 _____

   _____

   Psalm 59:1 and 16 _____

   _____

   This was a time of testing and preparation for David. He has been threatened by Saul and found refuge among the Philistines. Here he wrote Psalm 56. (Read this.)

HOW MUCH DO YOU REMEMBER?

Q. Name the three "double books" of the Old Testament.

Q. Name the three main personalities of this Book.

Q. Can you state the Central Message of this Book?

Q. What other personality is known for his love for David?

Q. Was David enthroned in I Samuel?

YOUR ASSIGNMENT FOR NEXT WEEK
   1. Read the Book of II Samuel — 4 Chapters each day.
   2. Review the study of I Samuel from your notes made in class.
   3. Mark all Scripture references in your Bible from your notes.
   4. Be present next Lord's Day with your Bible and notebook.
   5. Read the KEY CHAPTERS if you cannot read the whole Book. The Chapters are: 2, 5, 7, 8, 11, 12, 18, 23; less than two Chapters each day.

Lesson 10
"The Book of II Samuel"

(Where lines are provided, please look up Scripture and fill in the entire Scripture or the main Truth of the passage.)

1. **The Book**

    The Book of II Samuel is the "Book of David's Reign." It opens with David reigning in Judah immediately after Saul's death. The Book closes just before David's death when he "was old and stricken in years" (I Kings 1:1 and 2:10-11).

    _____

    _____

2. **Its Period**

    David reigned 40 years and this Book covers that time.

    See II Samuel 5:4-5 _____

    _____

    See I Kings 2:10-11 _____

    _____

3. **The Author**

    The authorship of II Samuel is far from certain, though the likeliest indication is that this is the work of Nathan and Gad. (I Chron. 29:29-30.)

    _____

    _____

    _____

4. **The Structure**

    David's Triumphs — Chapters 1-12
    David's Troubles — Chapters 13-24

    (Note: The Book divides itself right in the middle of the narrative and in the middle of David's 40-year reign. Thus, there are 12 Chapters in each part.)

5. **The Central Message**

    Triumphs turned to troubles through sin.

6. **David's Triumphs — Chapters 1-12**

    (Note: We shall *not* go through this Book Chapter-by-Chapter but we will call attention to key facts and truths. Many of these will be covered and added in the Kings and Chronicles.)

    (1) DAVID AT HEBRON — Chapters 1-4 (Civil War Period)
    David reigned at Hebron 7 years and 6 months, over Judah only, because the other tribes would not accept him as Saul's successor. Israel (all the tribes other than Judah) had decided to have their own king. (See Chapter 2:8-11.)

Note Chapter 3:1 _____

_____

(2) DAVID, KING OF ALL ISRAEL, at Jerusalem — Chapters 5-11 (Conquest Period).

David is declared to be king of all Israel and he transfers the seat of government to Jerusalem. Note the acknowledgement of all the tribes of David's right to be king — 5:1-5:

"We are thy bone and thy flesh"
"Thou leddest out and brought in Israel"
"The Lord said, thou shalt be captain over Israel"

Jerusalem at that time was called Jebus — I Chron. 11:4 after the Jebusites. Now read II Samuel 5:6-10.

(3) THE DAVIDIC COVENANT — Chapters 7:8-16.

This is one of the supremely great passages of the Bible. That the Messiah should be from David's line was affirmed later by the prophets in such passages as:

Isaiah 11:1 _____

_____

Jeremiah 23:5 _____

_____

Ezekiel 37:25 _____

_____

In accord with these prophecies the angel Gabriel announced to Mary concerning Jesus: Luke 1:32-33 _____

_____

_____

There are several significant things we should remember about the Davidic Covenant — (Chapter 7):

FIRST, V-13 — the Divine Confirmation of the throne in Israel.

SECOND, the perpetuation of the Davidic rule — V-11-16 and here three things are made sure to David:
        —"house" or posterity — V-11 and 13
        —"throne" or royal authority — V-13
        —"kingdom" or sphere of rule — V-13 and then in V-16
          all three are secured to him *forever.*

Psalm 89 is a confirmation and exposition of this Davidic Covenant Read there especially V-3, 4, 20 through 37 _____

_____

_____

_____

THIRD, it is unconditional because it shall be fulfilled in the Messiah. Acts 2:29-31 _____

_____

and Acts 15:14-17 _____

_____

FOURTH, It is a sure prophecy of Christ.
    The first such prophecy was made to Adam: Gen. 3:15

_____

The second to Abraham in Gen. 22:18

_____

The third to Jacob in Gen. 49:10

_____

The fourth is now made to David in this Chapter.

Notice the development in these words of Prophecy:

1st to Adam, the promise is to a *race* in general.

2nd to Abraham, to a *nation* in the race, Israel.

3rd to Jacob, to one *tribe* in that nation, Judah.

4th to David, to one *family* in that tribe, that of David.

(4) DAVID'S REIGN AT ITS HIGHEST — Chapters 8-10. He is victorious on every hand.

(5) DAVID'S GREAT SIN — Chapter 11.

His first sin — V-3-4_____

_____

His first sin led to a worse second sin — V-15-17

_____

(6) DAVID'S CONFESSION — Chapter 12:13-18 and V-23 _____

_____

_____

_____

Then Solomon is born to David — V-24_____

_____

7. **David's Troubles — Chapters 13-24**

The rest of the Book is not of triumph but of troubles. The last recorded victory is at the end of Chapter 12 when he conquers the royal city of Ammon. The rest of the Chapters records all of David's troubles in his family and as a nation.

Note especially that Chapters 15 through 18 are concerning Absalom, the son of David, and his rebellion. This was a part of the bitter fruit of David's sin according to Chapter 12:11-12. The only way Absalom could secure the throne was by defeating his father in battle. He tried but Joab, David's captain, showed no mercy and killed Absalom — 18:14. When David heard it he cried the familiar words found in the last part of 18:33 _____

_____

David was restored to the throne in Jerusalem followed by more experiences of retribution from the hand of God. The Book closes with David's purchase of the threshing floor on Mt. Moriah which became the site of the temple. It was here, hundreds of years earlier, where Abraham offered Isaac.

HOW MUCH DO YOU REMEMBER?

Q. What is another name for this Book?

Q. How long did David reign?

Q. What is the Central Message?

Q. How long did David reign in Hebron, over Judah only?

Q. Is the Davidic Covenant a prophecy? If so, what is its fulfillment?

YOUR ASSIGNMENT FOR NEXT WEEK
1. Read as much of I and II Kings as you can; 7 chapters each day. If you can't read all chapters then read the Key Chapters — 1, 3, 4, 8, 9, 11, 12, 17, 19 in I Kings — and 2, 5, 11, 18, 20, 22 in II Kings — 2 chapters each day.
2. Review the study of II Samuel from your notes.
3. Mark the Scripture references in your Bible.
4. Be present next Lord's Day with your notebook and Bible.

Lesson 11
"The Books of I and II Kings"

through the Bible in one year

(Where lines are provided, please look up Scriptures and fill in the entire Scripture or the main Truth of the passage.)

1. The Book

This is the second in the series of three *double Books*. They were originally one Book and we shall study them as such because they tell a continuing story. I Kings records the *division* of the united kingdom of Saul, David and Solomon into *two kingdoms* — known henceforth as *Israel* and *Judah*. II Kings records the collapse or should we say, the *captivity* of both, Judah and Israel.

A word of explanation is due here. The name Israel, comprising ten of the tribes, becomes the northern kingdom with Samaria as capital. The kingdom of Judah, comprising two tribes, Judah and Benjamin, becomes the southern kingdom with Jerusalem as the capital. Now, fix this in your mind because it is necessary if you are to understand the remainder of the Old Testament:

NORTHERN KINGDOM — Israel — 10 tribes — Samaria
SOUTHERN KINGDOM — Judah — 2 tribes — Jerusalem

2. The Author

The author of Kings is unknown. Tradition says Jeremiah wrote them but this is not conclusive.

3. The Central Message of I Kings

The main message is *Division Because of Disobedience*. This is clearly seen in I Kings 11:11 which marks the tragic turning point and becomes the key to the whole story. Read 11:11 and write in the last part of that verse_____

_____

4. The Structure of the Book of I Kings

THE GREAT FORTY-YEAR REIGN OF KING SOLOMON — Chapters 1-11
    (one half of the Book we have one united kingdom)

THE FIRST EIGHTY YEARS OF THE TWO KINGDOMS — Chapters 12-22
    (one half of the Book we follow the two kingdoms and their leaders)

5. The Forty Year Reign of Solomon — Chapters 1-11

(1) Solomon was the last of the kings to reign over a *united* Hebrew kingdom. He was but a child (according to 3:7) when he became king.

(2) Notice Solomon's prayer for wisdom and understanding.

Read 3:5-13. God's promise V-5 _____

_____

_____

Compare this with Matthew 7:7 _____

_____

Solomon's request — V-9 _____

_____

Compare with James 1:5 _____

_____

The answer of the Lord — V-12-13 _____

_____

(This prayer is also recorded in II Chronicles 1:7-13)

    (3) The wisdom of Solomon — 4:29-34 (Read this and note here V-32.)

        _____

        _____

    (4) Solomon begins to build the *first* temple in Chapter 6 and the prayer of dedication is given, Chapter 8. Now read II Chron. 7:1-3. Who filled the temple? _____

        _____

        _____

    (5) The Lord's warning and promise to Solomon — 9:3-9. Note the conditions the Lord gave in V-6 _____

        _____

    (6) His transgression against God — Chapter 11. Some four and a half centuries before, God had written the qualifications for all future kings of Israel. Read Deut. 17:14-17. Solomon had disobeyed God in all these areas.

        He had much gold and silver — I Kings 10:14-27.
        He had thousands of horses — 4:26.
        He had hundreds of wives and concubines — 11:3.

    (7) The result of Solomon's transgression:
        The Lord says the kingdom shall be divided after the death of Solomon — 11:9-13 and 31.

    (8) Solomon's death and the rest of his works — 11:41-43. Look up Gal. 6:7 _____

        _____

        _____

6. **The First Eighty years of the Two Kingdoms — Chapters 12-22**

    (1) Immediately after the death of Solomon the division of the kingdom takes place and ten tribes are led by Jeroboam — two by Rehoboam (the son of Solomon). See 12:16-21.

        (We shall not go into details about all of the kings of each side, but we shall point out only the main thoughts of this part of God's Word.)

    (2) The sin of Israel (the north) 12:25-33. Jeroboam built false centers of worship at Dan and Bethel to keep the people from going to Jerusalem to worship — and he made "priests of the lowest people, not of the sons of Levi."

        And again, we see the judgment of God — 14:14-16.

    (3) There are two lines of Kings and during this 80-year period of I Kings, Judah had four kings and Israel had eight. Everyone of the

NOTES

eight kings of Israel were *evil*. Two kings of Judah (these two reigned 66 years, Asa and Jehoshaphat) were *good* kings.

7. **Enter the Prophet Elijah — Chapters 17 to 22**

   (1) The last six chapters of I Kings gives the ministry of Elijah, the prophet, in the *northern* kingdom of Israel — (the ten tribes). The New Testament speaks of him more than any other prophet. It was Elijah who appeared with Moses at our Lord's transfiguration — Matthew 17:1-5.

   It is at this point in the divided kingdoms that the work of God's prophets is emphasized. Elijah suddenly appears as a crisis-prophet and disappears as suddenly in a chariot of fire (II Kings 2:11). Between these lies a succession of miracles.

   (2) He was a prophet of deeds. He wrote nothing. He pronounced for God:

   > 3 years of drought — 17:1.
   > He was a bone in the throat of King Ahab in Chapter 18:17. Many other miracles are recorded here by Elijah (example 17:21).

   (3) Elijah teaches us that God always has a man to match the hour. After fleeing from a threat on his life (19:2) he is told to go back and find and anoint two kings and find Elisha and begin training him to succeed him — 19:15-16. Elijah pronounced doom on King Ahab — 21:19 and it came to pass — 22:38.

   (4) Elijah proves what God can do through a man when the truth of God is being hurt by a person or a nation. We, like Elijah, should be separated servants of the Lord — II Timothy 2:19.

THE BOOK OF II KINGS

1. **This is the Book of the Captivities**

   In Chapter 17 the ten tribes of the northern kingdom (Israel) goes into the Assyrian captivity from which they have never returned.

   In Chapter 25 the southern kingdom (Judah) goes into the Babylonian captivity (and the temple burned) from which only a remnant returned.

2. **The Central Message**

   Wilful sin brings a dreadful end. Galatians 6:7 _____

   _____

3. **The Structure of the Book**

   Events of Israel, the Northern Kingdom — Chapters 1-10.

   This part contains the ministry of Elisha.

   Alternating Events of Both Kingdoms — Chapters 11-17.

   This part runs to the Assyrian Captivity of Israel. Jonah, Amos, Hosea prophesied at this time to Israel (Northern Kingdom).

   Events of Judah, the Southern Kingdom — Chapters 18-25.

   This part ends with the captivity of Judah in Babylon by which time Obadiah, Joel, Isaiah, Micah, Nahum, Habakkuk, Zephaniah and Jeremiah had prophesied in Judah.

   Now — notice the important names of the prophets we shall meet in our Old Testament. Study and mark them in your mind as prophets to Israel or Judah. The prophets of God *after* the captivity (post exile) were Ezekiel, Daniel, Haggai, Zechariah, Malachi. Now you can place these prophets in your mind.

4. **The Number of Kings**

   There were 19 kings, in all, that reigned over Israel, the 10 tribed kingdom, and the kingdom lasted about 250 years.

   Judah had 20 kings and it lasted some 390 years.

   The 19 kings of Israel came from seven different families while the

20 kings of Judah were of *one and the same family – that of David*.

5. **God's Faithfulness**

One of the ruling purposes of Scripture history is to show the faithfulness of God to the Davidic Covenant (II Samuel 7:8-17) in the preservation of the line of David — II Kings 8:19 and II Chronicles 21:7.

6. **Jesus and Throne of David**

The Lord Jesus Christ will re-establish the throne of David in His Kingdom at His second advent. Luke 1:30-33 _____

_____

See Psalm 89:30-37 _____

_____

See Acts 2:29-31_____

_____

From the "Structure of the Book" read the Book of II Kings and see the different stages of Kings and prophets. You will see the *Divine* and the *human*.

First, the human failure as seen in kings and people.

Second, the Divine, as seen in the prophets and their messages.

"Where there is no vision the people perish" we see the human. But on the Divine side there is to be ultimate triumph when David's greater Son, our Lord, sits on the throne and reigns over all.

HOW MUCH DO YOU REMEMBER?

Q. The kingdom of Saul, David and Solomon was divided into two kingdoms. Name them.

Q. What was the Northern Kingdom? Southern Kingdom? How many tribes in each?

Q. The first half of I Kings covers what period?

Q. What happened when Solomon died?

Q. Who was the prophet of God in I Kings?

Q. What is II Kings known as?

Q. From what family did all the kings of Judah spring? Why?

Q. Who shall occupy the throne of David in the future? Can you name one Scripture concerning this?

YOUR ASSIGNMENT FOR NEXT WEEK
1. Read I and II Chronicles, 10 chapters each day, or key chapters — I Chronicles 10, 11, 15, 16, 17, 28; II Chronicles 6, 7, 28, 29, 32, 36 — less than two chapters each day.
2. Review our study of the Kings from your notes.
3. Mark your Bible from the notes taken in class.
4. Be present next Lord's Day with Bible and notebook.

Lesson 12
"The Books of
I & II Chronicles

(Where lines are provided, please look up Scripture and fill in the entire Scripture or the main Truth of the passage.)

1. **The Books**

Having gone through the Books of Samuel and Kings we shall not need to give more than an overview of Chronicles. They are a "Chronicle" (an account of events arranged in order) which takes us from Adam to Nehemiah, giving us the main genealogies of the nation Israel — and also the main events of the Davidic kingdom to the time of the Babylonian captivity.

2. **The Central Message of Both Chronicles**

THE TEMPLE (HOUSE) OF THE LORD

For example, these Books deal with matters of the Temple, not mentioned in Samuel or Kings. In I Chronicles 11 to the end gives the reign of David and his preparation for the building of the Temple.

II Chronicles 2 through 9 gives the account of the reign of Solomon and the building of the temple.

The Books deal solely with Judah and Jerusalem (often called Zion, Romans 11:26) because that is the kingdom and the city where the temple was built.

The Temple was:

(a) a symbol of the unity of the nation
(b) a reminder of the nation's high calling
(c) a sign that Jehovah was still with His chosen people

3. **Relation to Samuel and Kings**

Samuel and Kings are more biographical — Chronicles more statistical.

Samuel and Kings are more personal — Chronicles more official.

Samuel and Kings give history of both Israel and Judah after the division of the kingdom — Chronicles gives only the history of Judah after the division.

Samuel and Kings emphasize the throne — Chronicles emphasizes the Temple.

Chronicles goes back and reviews a history of a people to apply a vital lesson for them and for us, namely, that a *nation's response to God is the decisive factor in its history.*

4. **Relation to Ezra and Nehemiah**

"These Books, Chronicles, Ezra and Nehemiah, originally were a single great history" (Ellicott). Perhaps this is confirmed by the termination of the Chronicles in an unfinished sentence which is finished in Ezra 1:3. These Books form a group:

CHRONICLES — Retrospection
EZRA — Restoration
NEHEMIAH — Reconstruction

5. **The Structure of the Books**

I CHRONICLES

The People of the Lord — Chapters 1-9

DAVID'S REIGN ⎯
The Anointed of the Lord — Chapters 10-12
The Ark of the Lord — Chapters 13-16
The Covenant of the Lord — Chapters 17-21
The Temple of the Lord — Chapters 22-29

II CHRONICLES

SOLOMON'S FORTY-YEAR REIGN — CHAPTERS 1-9

Solomon's Prayer For Wisdom — Chapter 1
Solomon Builds the Temple — Chapters 2-7
Solomon in All His Glory — Chapters 8-9

JUDAH'S HISTORY TO THE CAPTIVITY — CHAPTERS 10-36

The Division of the Kingdom — Chapter 10
The Twenty Kings of Judah — Chapters 11-36
Deportation of Babylon — Chapter 36:15-21
(Edict of Cyrus — 36:22-23)

6. **A View of the Above Structure**

(1) THE PEOPLE OF THE LORD — Chapters 1-9

This is a geneology for certain but it has more for us to see. We are to see a family tree of a certain *people* — the people of Jehovah. The stock of Adam shoots out three great branches: the sons of Japheth, Ham and Shem. In the great purpose of God the oldest is passed over and Shem, the youngest, is chosen — so is Abram, the youngest son of Terah chosen; so is Isaac over Ishmael; so is Jacob over Esau. All this in Chapter 1. In Chapter 2 the redemptive line goes through Jacob to Judah, to Jesse, to David. In Chapter 3 the Davidic line continues down to the last of Judah's kings. The writer then reviews the genealogy of the tribes of Israel and their allotments in Canaan — Chapters 4-8.

(2) THE ANOINTED OF THE LORD — Chapters 10-11.

Here begins the reign of David, the *Anointed* of the Lord and how he made Jerusalem the capital when he was made King. He was the king of *Divine* choice whereas Saul the king of *human* choice. Read 10:14: _____

_____

(3) THE ARK OF THE LORD — Chapters 13-16.

The first outstanding recorded act of King David — the bringing of the Ark of the Lord to Jerusalem. This would mean the presence of Jehovah. In Chapter 15 the Ark is brought to Jerusalem and God blesses David — Chapter 16:7-36 is a psalm of thanksgiving, he teaches the people the mercy of God in the sacred Ark of Jehovah.

(4) THE COVENANT OF THE LORD — Chapters 17-21.

It pleased God to choose out of the race one nation — Israel — then out of that nation one tribe, Judah — then out of that tribe one family — the house of David, and to make with him a wonderful Covenant — Chapter 17:7-15.

Chapters 18-20 give the Divine implementation of that Covenant. When David later fell to the strategy of Satan (Chapter 21) God overruled and that led to the fixing of the spot where the future temple was to stand. Compare 21:28 with II Chron. 3:1.

(5) THE TEMPLE OF THE LORD — Chapters 22-29.

David was not allowed to build the Temple, but he amply prepared for it:

—Materials — Chapter 22
—Levites — Chapter 23
—Priests — Chapter 24

—Singers, porters etc. — Chapters 25-27

—Charge to Solomon and the nation — Chapters 28-29

Since the central message of both Books of Chronicles is "the House of the Lord" we can see the importance of that theme in I Chronicles 17:10 "The Lord will build *thee* an house."

NOW WE COME TO II CHRONICLES. It has a glorious opening and a terrible ending.

(6) THE FORTY-YEAR REIGN OF SOLOMON — Chapters 1-9.

In these chapters we see the national and moral significance of Solomon's reign. Solomon was promised "wisdom, wealth, and power," and he received them. He was promised "length of days" *if* he would walk with God — I Kings 3:13-14 (read this). This he forfeited and he died at 59 years. See outline on I Kings 1-11. We have already covered the building of the Temple so we need not speak of that. We should point out II Chronicles 7:14 as God's promise to Solomon (and to us). Read and underline this verse.

(7) JUDAH'S HISTORY TO THE CAPTIVITY — Chapters 10-36.

In the preceding chapters of both Chronicles there has risen up a THRONE founded in a Divine Covenant — and a TEMPLE founded by Divine Guidance. The throne and the temple were to uphold and glorify each other — but a condition of great apostasy develops in which the throne becomes the worst enemy of the temple. One must go and it had to be the throne. (There were twenty kings over Judah from Rehoboam to Zedekiah.) Thus the captivity (exile) and the suspension of the throne of David. Then the temple is allowed to be burned. II Chronicles 36:19 and II Kings 25:9. Read the prophecy of Jeremiah concerning this — Jeremiah 25:9-12. _____

_____

_____

In the two Books of Chronicles we have the full historical view of the Davidic monarchy. In it we see *high calling, great blessing, ill doing, bad ending.* When a king and a people honored God there was peace, prosperity — whereas when they were unfaithful to God there was adversity.

The truth for us to learn, once again, from these Books is: Galatians 6:7 _____

_____

Dr. J. H. Moulton said, "There can be no greater exercise in the study of historic Scripture than to compare the two divisions of the Bible — Chronicles with Samuel and Kings — in their treatment of the same incidents."

HOW MUCH DO YOU REMEMBER?

Q. What is a Chronicle?

Q. What is the Central Message of the Chronicles?

Q. Why the genealogies in the first 9 chapters?

Q. Who was the Anointed King of I Chronicles?
Who was the Anointed King of II Chronicles?

Q. Did David build the Temple? (Read I Chronicles 28:2-6) Why?

YOUR ASSIGNMENT FOR NEXT WEEK

1. Read Ezra and Nehemiah (4 Chapters each day). If you cannot read all Chapters then read the Key Chapters: Ezra 1, (2:64-65), 4, 5, 6, 7. Nehemiah 1, 2, (7:66-67), 8, 10, 13.
2. Review our study of the Chronicles from your notes.
3. Mark your Bible from the notes taken in class.
4. Be present next Lord's Day with your Bible and notebook.

Lesson 13
"The Books of Ezra & Nehemiah"

(Where lines are provided, please look up Scriptures and fill in the entire Scripture or the main Truth of the passage.)

1. **The Books**

   Ezra and Nehemiah deal with the return of the "remnant" which returned to Jerusalem. The Book of Esther (the next in our study) deals with those who stayed on in the land of their captivity. In conjunction with the study of these Books we should read the prophetical Books of Haggai, Zechariah and Malachi for these were the three prophets whom God raised up among His people in the period after the captivity (post exile period).

2. **The Central Message**

   This can be best expressed in the words of Jeremiah in Lamentations 3:31-32 _____

   _____

   _____

   God judges as necessary but He is very gracious.

3. **The Structure of the Book of Ezra**

   (1) The Return Under Zerubbabel — Chapters 1-6.

   (2) The Return Under Ezra — Chapters 7-10.
       (See diagram of the Book on next page.)

4. **The Return of the Remnant**

   (1) This is one of the most important subjects in Jewish history, namely, the return of the elect to their own land after the Babylonian captivity.

   This was predicted by the prophet Isaiah 200 years before Cyrus was born. Read Isaiah 44:28 through 45:1-4 and 45:13. Also read Jeremiah 25:11-12 and 29:10-11. Now notice the first three verses of Ezra.

   (2) The second Chapter gives the size of the remnant. They are first broken down into groups:

   —the people 2:1-35
   —the priests 2:36-39
   —the Levites 2:40-54
   —others 2:55-63

   The total is given in V-64-65. A round figure of about 50,000. Such a number out of the national total was small — thus "a remnant." Many of those who had grown up in Babylon did not want to leave the only life they had known. *This was under Zerubbabel –536 B.C.*

   (3) A further return was *under the leadership of Ezra* about 80 years later in 456 B.C. The total in this expedition was about 2,000 (males only numbered) including the Nethinims (8:20).

   (4) Between these two expeditions, the narrative of the Book of Esther took place.

5. Parallelism Between the Two Main Parts of Ezra

THE RETURN UNDER ZERUBBABEL Chapters 1-6	THE RETURN UNDER EZRA Chapters 7-10
• The decree of Cyrus — 1:1-4	• The decree of Artaxerxes — 7:1, 11-26
• The leader Zerubbabel — 1:8; 2:2	• The leader Ezra — 7:1-10
• Names and number of the remnant — 2:3-65	• Names and number of the company — 8:1-20
• Sacred vessels and gifts — 1:6-11 & 2:68-70	• Sacred vessels and gifts — 7:15-22 & 8:24-35
• The coming to Jerusalem — 3:1	• The coming to Jerusalem — 8:32
• Prophet Ministry: Haggai & Zechariah — 5:1-6:14	• Intercessory Ministry of Ezra — 9:1-15
• Main outcome — Temple is rebuilt — 6:15-22	• Main outcome — separation of the people — 10:1-44

6. **The Two Leaders**

"Zerubbabel" means "descended of Babylon" which indicates that he was born in Babylonia. His going to Jerusalem was undoubtedly a *"first"* for him for there is nothing to suggest that he had ever seen the land of promise before. His full lineage is given in Matthew 1:12-17. Matthew carries the lineage on to Christ.

Ezra was a great figure in Jewish history. Jewish tradition (the Talmud) has made him one of the great leaders of his day. He is attributed to be the founder of the "Great Synogogue," a group of Jewish scholars who recognized the Canon of Scripture and settled it as the "Word of God." He was a descendant of Israel's high priest, Aaron, and this is in Chapter 7:1-5. He was also a Scribe — 7:6 which means he was an expert instructor in Scripture.

7. **What about the Ten Tribes?**

Were only the tribes of Judah and Benjamin in the return to Jerusalem? Ezra gives some interesting verses for us to study:

• In Ezra 1:3-5 "among *all* his people." Undoubtedly the chiefs of Judah and Benjamin led the way but with "*all* them whose spirit God had raised."

• In 2:70 not only was Jerusalem reoccupied but so were "*all* Israel in their cities in Judea."

• In 6:17, "Twelve he goats (were offered) according to the number of the tribes of Israel."

• In 8:29 — "the chief of the *fathers of Israel.*"

• It must be remembered that Assyria (which took the ten-tribed kingdom into captivity) had become absorbed in the Babylonian empire which in turn had become a part of Cyrus' dominion.

8. **The Main Spiritual Applications of the Book for Us**

(1) Return to the Land, Chapters 1 & 2 — *back to a right relationship with Christ.*

(2) Altar re-erected — 3:1-6 — *Our dedication renewed.*

(3) New Temple begun — 3:8-13 — *We are to daily renew our service and witness.*

(4) "Adversaries" obstruct — Chapter 4 — *Our faith under testing.*

(5) Prophets exhort — 5:1-6 — 6:14 — *Know what God says and tell it.*

(6) Temple finished — 6:15-22 — *Faith always wins.*

(7) Ezra "prepared his heart to seek, do, teach" — 7:10 — *So should we.*

(8) Ezra depended on God 8:21 — "To seek a right way" — *So should we.*

(9) No compromise — 9:5 — "spread out my hands to Lord." — *Pray instead of yielding.*

(10) Confession and Separation 10:11 — *Exactly what we are to do.*

THE BOOK OF NEHEMIAH

1. This gem of Scripture gives us a man, Nehemiah, who was a spiritual leader with keen conviction and complete dependence on God. He is a good example for all of us to study.

2. Nehemiah is certainly the composer of the Book. Some scholars say he either wrote or compiled all the Book. It was written about 432 B.C. Chapter 13:6 "in the 32nd year of Artaxerxes" which was thirteen years after Chapter 2:1.

3. **Subject and Structure of the Book**

   Nehemiah's special object was to rebuild the city walls of Jerusalem. In this Book the first part deals with this construction (Chapters 1-6). In the second part we see the reinstructing of the people (Chapters 7-13). This is the Book of Reconstruction. Look now at the structure:

   THE RECONSTRUCTION OF THE WALL — CHAPTERS 1-6

   - Nehemiah, the Cupbearer — 1:1 to 2:10
   - Nehemiah, the Wall-builder — 2:11 to 6:19

   THE REINSTRUCTING OF THE PEOPLE — CHAPTERS 7-13

   - Nehemiah, the Governor — Security and Population — Chapter 7
   - Back to the Word of God Movement — Chapters 8-10
   - A new census and dedication of the wall — Chapters 11-12
   - Nehemiah's zeal endures — Chapter 13

4. **The Central Message**

   There is no opportunity without opposition. There is no "open door" before us without there being many "adversaries" to obstruct our entering. The Scripture says it in I Corinthians 16:9:

   _____

   _____

5. **The Reconstruction of the Wall — Chapters 1-6**

   (1) NEHEMIAH, THE CUPBEARER — 1:1 to 2:10

   Nehemiah was apparently of the tribe of Judah — 2:3. He was raised in exile and became prominent in the Persian Court. He was the royal cupbearer (1:11) a position of high honor and great influence.

   His brother told him of the condition in Jerusalem and Judea. The walls were in ruins and gates were as they were left by the Babylonians 140 years earlier. Walls and gates were the only way to protect a city.

   Nehemiah gave himself to fasting and prayer (1:4-11) and he was convicted to undertake the task. For four months (1:1 compare with 2:1) he knew this grief and burden and his appearance changed to the point that the king asked what was wrong (2:2). He responded (2:5) and the king granted the request and he is commissioned to do what God led him to undertake.

   (2) NEHEMIAH, THE WALL-BUILDER — 2:11 to 6:19.

   Nehemiah reaches Jerusalem and makes a secret survey of the ruins and then he encourages the people to build — 2:11-20.

   His plan was to section off the wall (Chapter 3) to different groups, all working at the same time. It was so successful, that in spite of opposition, the wall was rebuilt in just over seven weeks (6:15) after which the gates were finished (7:1). All was completed within six months of the mandate from the king of Persia. Here we see the blending of practical organization and spirit led leadership. In 4:9 we see this, "we made our *prayer* unto God and set a *watch* against them day and night."

We should blend the practical with the spiritual.

The obstructions and setbacks were many and Nehemiah had to overcome them. There were three forms of opposition from *without:*

SCORN — 4:1-6
FORCE — 4:7-23 (note especially V-9 and 17)
CRAFT — 6:1-19 (pretense V-1-4; bluff V-5-9 and treachery V-10-14)

Note now, the hindrances from *within:*

DEBRIS — 4:10
FEAR — 4:11-14 (Note V-14)
GREED— 5:1-13

6. **The Reinstructing of the People — Chapters 7-13**

(1) SECURITY AND THE POPULATION PROBLEM — Chapter 7.

Nehemiah was governor (7:65 — "Tirshatha" means governor) and he appointed his brother and the ruler of the palace to have charge of all security.

There were too many people living outside the city so he took a census and by lot every 10th man moved into the city — Chapter 11.

(2) BACK TO THE WORD OF GOD MOVEMENT — Chapters 8-10.

The people themselves asked for the Scriptures to be expounded to them (8:1). Ezra explains afresh the law and the Feast of Tabernacles is revived (a memorial of the redemption out of Israel). A day of humiliation is observed and confession is made of sin and failure (Chapter 9). Then they enter into a self-imposed covenant according to the will of God in Scripture (Chapter 10).

(3) A NEW CENSUS AND DEDICATION OF THE WALL — Chapters 11-12.

The census was taken (as indicated earlier) and the people "blessed all that willingly offered themselves to dwell in Jerusalem" — (V-2).

The dedication of the walls (12:27-47) was with great pomp and ceremony. There were singers, the reading by the Levites and thanksgiving by all.

(4) NEHEMIAH'S ZEAL ENDURES — Chapter 13.

There are touches of humor in this Chapter by this man who sometimes did the unusual in his zeal for God. We can but smile as we see him throwing Tobiah's furniture out of doors — (V-8), or plucking off the hair of those who had married wives outside of Israel (V-25), or "chasing" the young Jew who had become the son-in-law to Sanballat (V-28). He just kept on praying (V-14, V-22, V-29).

Lord make us Nehemiahs in our day.

HOW MUCH DO YOU REMEMBER?

Q. What prophets coincide with Ezra and Nehemiah?

Q. Who led the returns back to Jerusalem?

Q. Who gave permission for the first return? Why?

Q. What was Nehemiah's object in going to Jerusalem?

Q. Can you recall the Central Message of Nehemiah?

Q. Can you apply the same truth to our lives?

Q. What stands out in your mind about Nehemiah and the building of the walls?

Q. Does Nehemiah 8:5 remind you of something which we practice?

YOUR ASSIGNMENT FOR NEXT WEEK

1. Read the Book of Esther. Less than two Chapters each day.
2. Review our study in Ezra and Nehemiah from your notes.
3. Mark your Bible and insert the "gems" you have learned in the margin of your Bible.
4. Be in class next Lord's Day with your Bible and notebook.

Lesson 14
"The Book of Esther"

NOTES

(Where lines are provided, please look up Scriptures and fill in the entire Scripture or the main Truth of the passage.)

1. **The Book**

    We have studied the fact that Ezra and Nehemiah deal with the "remnant" which returned to Jerusalem and Judah. Now we see that the Book of Esther has to do with those who stayed in the land of captivity. The story takes place in "Shushan" the palace, (Esther 1:2 and Nehemiah 1:1) which is Susa, the ancient capital of Persia. The number who stayed in the land was far greater than the number who returned to Jerusalem.

2. **The Central Message of Esther**

    The Book of Esther teaches the *providence of God*. Providence means — *pro* — "before" — *video* — "I see." God saw beforehand what the people would do and even though they were out of the will of God by not going back to their homeland, they were not beyond His care.

    Providence then, is God providing, directing, leading people who sometimes do not want to be led.

3. **The Author**

    The Author of Esther is unknown. The name of God is *never* mentioned in this Book but Matthew Henry says, "If the name of God is not here, His finger is." Esther is never quoted in the New Testament. Could Deut. 31:18 give the reason why God is not directly mentioned? (Look up) _____

    _____

    _____

4. **The Structure of the Book**

    ### THE BOOK OF PROVIDENTIAL CARE

    (1) THE ANTI-SEMITIC CRISIS — CHAPTERS 1 THROUGH 5.
    - The wife — Vashti — Chapter 1
    - Esther becomes queen — Chapter 2
    - Haman contrives to kill the Jews — Chapter 3
    - "For such a time as this" — Chapter 4
    - The nobility of Esther — Chapter 5

    (2) PROVIDENTIAL OVERRULING OF THE CRISIS — CHAPTERS 6 THROUGH 10.
    - A Jew is exalted — Chapter 6
    - A woman gets her way — Chapter 7
    - The Jews are avenged — Chapter 8
    - The Feast of Purim is instituted — Chapter 9
    - Mordecai becomes prime minister — Chapter 10

5. **The Personalities of the Book**

    The structure gives a bird's eye view of the contents by chapters. We shall study the Book mainly by looking at the people in the story.

    (1) KING AHASUERUS

    He was a real historical figure. He is known to us in secular history as Xerxes, which is the Greek form of his Persian name. He reigned over the Persian Empire from 485 B.C. to 465 B.C. According to the first verse in Esther, he reigned over a province from India to Ethiopia with 127 provinces under his rule.

(2) VASHTI

The name means "beautiful woman." In Chapter 1 she is queen. The king orders her to come and show her beauty to a host of drinking men. She refused (V-12) and in their drunken stupor the king and his "leaders" wrote a decree concerning women honoring their husbands. Vashti is set aside because of her courageous act.

(3) ESTHER

While Ruth was a Gentile girl who married a Jew — Esther was a Jewess who married a Gentile. Ruth became the ancestress of the Deliverer (Christ) and Esther saved the people of Israel so that the Deliverer might come as promised.

Esther, the cousin of Mordecai, was an orphan and was adopted by Mordecai — 2:7. She was a beautiful girl and was entered into the "beauty contest" in Shushan, the palace. She was made the queen 2:17 but Mordecai instructed her not to tell that she was a Jew.

(4) MORDECAI

Mordecai was in the royal service of the palace, 2:5; 2:19-21 (at the king's gate); 3:2 (he was among the king's servants); 6:10 (the king knew him as "Mordecai the Jew").

Mordecai refused to bow before Haman. He was a Jew and he knew the law of God — See Deut. 5:7-10 _____

_____

_____

Because of this, Haman launched an anti-Semitic campaign to kill Jews. King Ahasuerus gave permission and sent a letter to all the provinces — 3:13.

Mordecai sent for help from Esther. She was to plead with the king and she took a great risk. She had not been asked to his quarters for thirty days (cool relationship) 4:11. Mordecai sent another message of great importance (to us) in 4:14 — *who knoweth whether thou art come to the kingdom for such an hour as this.* Esther responds that she would appeal to the king even *if I perish, I perish* — 4:16.

Because of Mordecai's cry for help, Esther gained freedom for the Jews from the king. Mordecai became premier, or prime minister and was exalted to the highest honor.

We learn from Mordecai the way God deals with nations and peoples to preserve His people. There is much typical meaning in Esther.

(5) HAMAN

Haman was an "Agagite" (A-gag-ite) which was from Amalek (I Samuel 15:8). He was a "big wheel" under the king and a man of pride. He hated the Jews because Mordecai would not bow before him, so he appealed to the king to kill all of the Jews (3:8). Also see 3:10; 8:1; 9:10; 9:24.

The whole meaning of the Book of Esther is found here. God's people were about to be destroyed but God used a person, Esther, at the right time. Refer again to 4:14.

The slaughter would have been similar to what Hitler did in the '40's.

Haman prepared a gallows for Mordecai (5:14). Mordecai had saved the king from harm and the king heard about it — (6:1-2). He decides to honor Mordecai — thus the gallows for Mordecai became the death trap for Haman.

The entire story is one of God's providence in the preservation of His people.

The Book of Esther closes with the establishment of the "Feast of Purim" and Mordecai becoming the one just under the king. The Feast celebrates the deliverance of the Jews. It was a Thanksgiving Day, for although they had forsaken God, He had spared them. The name "Purim" comes from Haman casting lots (Pur) against them. Esther — 9:24-26.

Now, in reference to the story in Esther, look up the following Scriptures and see if you understand more completely God's dealings:

Proverbs 21:1 _____

_____

(Compare with Esther 5:2).

Phil. 4:19 _____

_____

(Compare with Esther 5:3).

Isa. 54:7 _____

_____

(Compare with Esther 7:9-10).

Proverbs 16:33 _____

_____

(Compare with Esther 9:24-26).

Remember — the Old Testament history *closes* after the account of Ezra, Nehemiah and the events of Esther. The rest of the Old Testament Canon of Scripture is in the main, *prophecy* concerning Israel before, during and after the captivity. All of the prophets shed light on God's message and His leading of His children, Israel. When you comprehend this fact, the Old Testament becomes easier to understand.

There is much type teaching that could be applied in this Book. Time does not permit this during this course of study. If you would like to study this on your own it will reward you greatly. (For the new student, we give two or three examples.)

HAMAN — prefigures "the man of sin" —
    — in his name (7:6)
    — in his power (3:1-3)
    — in his pride (5:11)
    — in his hate (3:10, 8:1; 9:10-24)
    — in his doom (7:9-10)

ESTHER — prefigures the church
    — in her beauty
    — in her exaltation
    — in her intercession

MORDECAI — prefigures the Jewish remnant through the tribulation.

HOW MUCH DO YOU REMEMBER?

Q. What is the message of Esther?

Q. The Book of Esther deals with which group of Israelites?

Q. Is the mention of God to be found in the Book? Why?

Q. Who are the main characters of the Book? Name four.

Q. What lesson have you learned from your study of Esther?

YOUR ASSIGNMENT FOR NEXT WEEK

1. Read the Book of Job or Key Chapters: 1 through 6, 8, 11, 12, 13, 14, 16, 19, 23, 38 through 42. (Less than three chapters each day.)
2. Review our study of Esther from your notes.
3. Mark Scripture references in your Bible from your notes.
4. Be present next Lord's Day with your Bible and notebook.

Lesson 15
"The Book of Job"

(Where lines are provided, please look up Scriptures and fill in the entire Scripture or the main Truth of the passage.)

1. **The Book**

   The seventeen Books we have covered are all historical. The five we take up now are poetical Books — Job, Psalms, Proverbs, Ecclesiastes and the Song of Solomon. These five are experiential. The past seventeen Books concerned a *nation* — these five concern *individuals*. The seventeen deal with the Hebrew race — these five deal with the human heart. (There is much to learn about Hebrew poetry but time does not permit our dealing with this now. Just remember that these five are poetry.)

2. **An Explanation**

   A brief explanation of the Book of Job is necessary to understanding it. Chapters 1 and 2 are not poetry, but a historical *prologue* to the poem. The poem begins at Chapter 3 and it ends at Chapter 42:6. The final eleven verses are not poetry but a historical *epilogue* to the poem.

   The simple fact that gives the whole Book meaning is that Job did not know the divine counsel of God. Between the prologue, which shows how Job's trials originated in the Counsels of heaven, and the epilogue, which shows how Job's trials and afflictions served as enrichment and blessing, we have a group of older men giving advice on *"why"* these things happened to Job. They knew nothing of God's reasoning and they were theorizing in the dark. We are to see that when affliction comes, God has a reason. If Job had known the reasons for his afflictions there would have been no faith involved on his part. The Scriptures are as wise in their reservations as in their revelations. Job was not meant to know the reasons — and in this lies the message of the Book.

3. **The Central Message**

   The central message is "Blessing Through Suffering" or, why do the godly suffer? The solution is found in the explanation of the prologue and in the blessing of God upon Job in the epilogue.

   The Book is a grand illustration of Romans 8:28 _____

   _____

   _____

   and of Hebrews 12:11 _____

   _____

   _____

4. **The Structure of the Book**

PROLOGUE — Chapters 1 & 2	DIALOGUE — Chapters 3 — 42:6	EPILOGUE — Chapter 42:7-17
	Job — Opening Lamentation — C-3	
	FIRST TRIAD	
Job — devotion in prosperity 1:1-5	Eliphaz vs. Job — Chapters 4-7 Bildad vs. Job — Chapters 8-10 Zophar vs. Job — Chapters 11-14	Job — his proven integrity — 42:7
Satan — his lie and malignity 1:6-19	**SECOND TRIAD** Eliphaz vs. Job — Chapters 15-17 Bildad vs. Job — Chapters 18-19	Friends — their rebuke — 42:8
Job — his devotion in adversity — 1:20-22	Zophar vs. Job — Chapters 20-21 **THIRD TRIAD**	Job — his trial ended — 42:10
Satan — his further malignity — 2:1-8	Eliphaz vs. Job — Chapters 22-24 Bildad vs. Job — Chapters 25-31 *Elihu* speaks — Chapters 32-37	Family — restored 42:11
Job — his devotion in extremity — 2:9-13	*God: Closing Intervention:* Chapters 38-41	Job — his prosperity — 42:12-17

5. **Job is Factual**

   Some have suggested that this Book is fiction. The Scriptures state that it is factual.

   Ezekiel 14:14 _____

   _____

   Note also in the same Chapter, Verses 16, 18 and 20. Since Noah and Daniel were real people would God use as an example two men who were real and a third who was fiction?

   Then James refers to Job in James 5:11. "Ye have heard of the patience of Job, etc."

6. **The Prologue — Chapters 1 and 2**

   You can see the conversation in these Chapters between God and Satan. This is a divine revelation of what happened just as we find elsewhere in Scripture. In Revelation 12:10 Satan has access to God as "the accuser of the brethren." Then in Zechariah 3:1-2 Satan is standing in the Lord's presence to accuse Joshua. The most striking proof is in Luke 22:31 _____

   _____

   There are some things you should remember about Satan:
   — Satan is accountable to God.
   — Satan is neither omnipresent nor omniscient. Only God has that power of knowing all and is always present.
   — Satan can do nothing without God's permission — Job 38:11.
   — In every permission there is limitation — Job 1:12; 2:6.

7. **The Dialogue**

   The main body of the Book is in dramatic form in three successive rounds or triads. There are six speakers — Job, Eliphaz, Bildad, Zophar, Elihu and God.

   The central theme in the discussion is: "Why does Job suffer?" The first three friends try to interpret Job's case by analysis. It becomes a deadlock and the voice of Elihu enters but darkness still remains. Finally God speaks and brings to a climax what man could not and cannot solve.

   (1) ELIPHAZ — the first to come from afar to "console" Job. He delivers three speeches (see structure) and he is the oldest and wisest. He bases his argument on *Experience*. Notice: Chapter 4:8

and 5:17-27. Note also Chapter 22:5-9 that Job must be suffering because of sin. (See 22:13)

(2) BILDAD — This "friend" is more severe than Eliphaz. He bases his argument on *Tradition* — Chapter 8:8; 18:5-20. His theory is focused in Chapter 8:20 — "God will not cast away a perfect man; neither will He uphold evil doers." In Chapter 8:6 he infers that Job is a hypocrite.

(3) ZOPHAR — He speaks only twice in the debate. In the third round he is replaced by Elihu. He bases his theory and argument on *Assumption*. He just assumes and pronounces as a dogmatist — and he was dogmatic — notice Chapter 11:6 and 20:4. His narrow dogmatic opinion is in 20:5, "The triumphing of the wicked is short."

His theory is found in Chapter 11:6, "Know that God exacteth of thee less than thine iniquity deserveth."

(4) JOB'S RESPONSE

Job refutes the theory of the three in the first round, that God always prospers the upright and punishes the sinner. Job is upright, yet he is afflicted. (6:22-28; 12:3; 13:2-5, 15, 16)

In the second triad, all three insist that the wicked always suffer and only the wicked. Job's response is that the righteous suffer also. (19:25-26; 21:7)

In the third round the same theory is restated and Job declares his innocence of being wicked. He declares that the wicked often prosper in this world (24:6).

> Job was broken — Job 16:12-14
> Job was melted — Job 23:10
> Job was softened — Job 19:21 and 23:16

(5) ELIHU — The approach is different and he tries to convince Job that he must become humble and teachable and more patient. He says Job is sinning because of suffering and not visa versa — Chapter 33:8-11 and 35:15-16. But Job needed more than a human voice and it came!

(6) GOD — The Voice of the Whirlwind!

In Chapters 38 through 41 God speaks.

The Lord God speaks to Job about the power of God as compared to the littleness of man:

> — in relation to the earth — Chapter 38:1-18
> — in relation to the heavens — Chapter 38:19-38
> — in relation to living beings — Chapter 38:39 through Chapter 39
> — in relation to special cases — Chapter 40 through 42:6

Clearly, the purpose of God is to bring Job to the end of himself. Read 40:1-5 _____

_____

Now read 42:5-6 _____

_____

8. The Epilogue — 42:7-17

God spoke wrath upon the three "friends" because they had done as much damage to Job's soul as Satan had done.

God transforms, vindicates and restores Job:

- *Transformation* — "him will I accept" — V-8.
- *Vindication* — "my servant" — V-8.
- *Restoration* — "the Lord gave Job twice as much" — V-10.

Let every godly sufferer "rest in the Lord and patiently wait for Him." Psalm 37:7

Some of the most quoted passages in Job are:

1:21	16:21
5:17	19:23-27
13:15	23:10
14:14	42:1-6

What does 19:25 say?

HOW MUCH DO YOU REMEMBER?

Q. What are the three main divisions of the Book?

Q. Is Satan limited by God?

Q. Was the conversation between God and Satan real or fictional?

Q. Name the three "friends" of Job who gave him advice.

Q. What is the message of Job to you?

YOUR ASSIGNMENT FOR NEXT WEEK
1. Read 4 Messianic Psalms each day — They are 2, 8, 16, 20, 21, 22, 23, 24, 31, 35, 40, 41, 45, 50, 55, 61, 68, 69, 72, 89, 96, 97, 98, 102, 109, 110, 118, 132.
2. Review the Book of Job from your outline and your study in class.
3. Mark your Bible from your notes.
4. Be present next Lord's Day with your Bible and notebook.

Lesson 16
"The Book of Psalms"

(Where lines are provided, please look up Scriptures and fill in the entire Scripture or the main Truth of the passage.)

1. The Book ·

This Book is like all the others in Scripture — "all Scripture is profitable for instruction, etc." — II Timothy 3:16, and the end product is indefectable — "Scripture cannot be broken," John 10:35. The Psalms have their original setting in the arena of human experience. Remember that the five poetic Books are experiential.

When the collection of Psalms was brought together as one — the Hebrew title for the collection was Tehillim, meaning "praise songs." The Greek translators gave it the title "Psalmoi," meaning "songs to the accompaniment of a stringed instrument," and this was the title used in the days of Jesus (see Acts 1:20). Jesus authenticated the Psalms in that familiar verse, Luke 24:44.

This collection of Psalms was the inspired prayer and praise Book of the nation Israel in their temple worship; the Jews today use them in the synogogue; the Christians of the New Testament times sang them (Col. 3:16 and James 5:13); and all denominations of Christendom use them today. They are loved because they speak to what all of us feel during this life.

2. The Authors

This Book is commonly called "the Book of David" because he wrote a large number of them. The following is a classification of the Psalms by authors as designated by the superscription:

DAVID — 73 — (3 thru 9; 11 thru 32; 34 thru 41; 51 thru 65; 68 thru 70; 86; 101; 103; 108 thru 110; 122; 124; 131; 133; 138 thru 145).

ASAPH (David's choir leader at Jerusalem) 12 — (50; 73 thru 83).

DESCENDANTS OF KORAH — 10 (42; 44 thru 49; 84-85; 87).

SOLOMON — 2 (72; 127).

ETHAN — 1 — (89).

HEMAN — 1 — (88).

MOSES — 1 — (90).

ANONYMOUS — 50 — There is reason to think that David wrote some of these; example Psalm 2 is ascribed to David in Acts 4:25.

3. The Central Message

The central message can be summed up in:

"Praise Ye the Lord"

— or if you prefer — "Praise Through Prayer."

4. The Structure

The 150 Psalms were divided into five divisions from the time of Ezra. The "Midrashim" meaning "interpretation" was the "commentary" of that day, explaining the Scriptures. The Midrash, or Jewish Comment, on the first Psalm states, "Moses gave to the Israelites the five Books of the Law, and as a counterpart to these, David gave the Psalms which consists of five Books." It is the "fivefold *Book of the Congregation to Jehovah,* as the Pentateuch is the fivefold *Book of Jehovah to the Congregation."*

Now, in the structure of the Book we shall show the *facts* you should remember:

	BOOK 1 **41 PSALMS** Begins at Chapter 1	BOOK 2 **31 PSALMS** Begins at Chapter 42	BOOK 3 **17 PSALMS** Begins at Chapter 73	BOOK 4 **17 PSALMS** Begins at Chapter 90	BOOK 5 **44 PSALMS** Begins at Chapter 107
DOXOLOGY AT	41:13	72:18-19	89:52	106:48	150:6
WORSHIP THEME	ADORING WORSHIP	WON- DROUS WORSHIP	CEASE- LESS WORSHIP	SUB- MISSIVE WORSHIP	PER- FECTED WORSHIP
LIKENESS TO THE PENTA- TEUCH	GENESIS —ISRAEL— —MAN—	EXODUS —ISRAEL— DELIVER- ANCE	LEVITI- CUS —SANC- TUARY—	NUMBERS —MOSES & WILDER- NESS—	DEUTER- ONOMY —LAW AND LAND—
AUTHORS	MAINLY DAVID'S	MAINLY DAVID'S & KORAH'S	MAINLY ASAPH'S	MAINLY ANONY- MOUS	MAINLY DAVID'S

Note that the Doxology appears at the end of each Book. Your own Bible will probably have the 5 divisions indicated at the top of each section.

5. Classification of the Psalms

Many subjects are covered in the Psalms. These are the major types:

(1) INSTRUCTION OR DIDACTIC — Psalms 1, 5, 7, 15, 50, 73, 94, 101.

(2) HISTORY — (in reference to Israel) — Psalms 78, 105, 106, 136.

(3) PRAISE — Psalms 106, 111, 112, 113, 115, 116, 117, 135, and 146 through 150.

(4) CONFESSION — Psalms 6, 32, 38, 51, 102, 130, 143.

(5) SUPPLICATION — Psalms 86.

(6) THANKSGIVING — Psalms 16 and 18.

(7) MESSIANIC — Prophesies concerning Christ, and this is the major thrust of this lesson so we will deal with it as a major section of our study —

6. Messianic Psalm

The Psalms are full of Christ — in His two advents — His first advent in humiliation, and His second advent in glory.

(1) In these Psalms Christ is not only referred to, but He actually speaks and we get a wonderful glimpse into the inner heart life of Jesus. In these Psalms we find some of our Lord's prayers, *pre-written,* which is basic testimony to the divine inspiration of the Scriptures.

(2) Take Psalm 22 for instance. This is an amazing pre-written account of our Lord's death on the cross and through the human writer, the pre-incarnate Christ Himself actually speaks as though He were already on the cross.

Read Matthew 27:35-36: _____

_____

This Scripture gives us part of the happenings surrounding the cross but Psalm 22 tells us what Jesus thought and said as He hung on the cross. This, then, is prophecy in detail that actually came to pass even to the words spoken. Compare Psalm 22:1 to Matthew 27:46

_____

_____

When you read Psalm 22 and compare it to Matthew 27 you would think they were written at the same time, but remember that hundreds of years separated the writers and that death by crucifixion was a thing unknown, being introduced later by the Romans — Another proof that the inspiration of the Scriptures is a fact.

(3) The messianic Psalms are a rich study of their witness to Christ.
The witness to His *person,* the Son of God — Psalm 2:6-7

_____

_____

They witness to Christ as the *Son* of man — Psalm 8:4-6

_____

_____

As the Son of David — Psalm 89:3-4 and V-27_____

_____

The Psalms witness to His *offices,* as *Prophet* — Psalm 22:22; as *Priest* — 110:4; as *King* — Psalm 2.

(4) The Principal Messianic Psalms are:
Psalms 2, 8, 16, 20, 21, 22, 23, 24, 31, 35, 40, 41, 45, 50, 55, 61, 68, 69, 72, 89, 96, 97, 98, 102, 109, 110, 118, 132.
In these Psalms we have Christ's birth, betrayal, agony, death, resurrection, ascension, coming again in glory and His reign — all pictured with inspired vividness.

(5) There are groups of Psalms that go together. For example, the group you are most likely to remember would be Psalms 22, 23, 24. These should be remembered as follows:

PSALM 22	PSALM 23	PSALM 24
Suffering Savior	Living Savior	Exalted King
The Good Shepherd	The Great Shepherd	The Chief Shepherd
John 10:11	Hebrews 13:20	I Peter 5:4
Past	Present	Future
Cross	Crook	Crown

7. **Imprecatory Psalms (Cursing):**
There are some Psalms which express anger against enemies and evil doers. They are looked upon with a great deal of perplexity. This can be solved when you realize that a faithful Hebrew, to the Lord God, considered God's enemies as his own and he would pray to God to honor His own righteousness by inflicting punishment upon those who denied the sovereignty of God.

Some of the "Cursing" Psalms are: Psalms 35, 52, 58, 69, 83, 109, 137, 140.

These Psalms are crystallized in 139:21-23 _____

_____

_____

8. **The Word of God**
All of the teaching in the 119th Psalm is around the Word of God. This is the longest chapter of the Bible and it reveals the heart of God. Every verse speaks of the Word of God, or law, or precepts, or statutes of God.

In this chapter there are 22 sections of 8 verses each — one section for each of the 22 letters of the Hebrew alphabet, in order.

Memorize 119:11 _____

_____

Also 119:105 _____

_____

9. Conclusion

Don't forget, the Psalms are the expression of human experience written through Divine inspiration. They will meet a need in every life if they are read for enrichment and for meditation. What a storehouse of precious Truths!

HOW MUCH DO YOU REMEMBER?

Q. What is the meaning of the title "Psalms"?

Q. How many Psalms were written by David?

Q. How do the Psalms relate to the Pentateuch?

Q. Can you list at least one thing under Psalms 22, 23, and 24?

Q. What is an "imprecatory" Psalm?

Q. What Psalm is altogether about the Word of God?

YOUR ASSIGNMENT FOR NEXT WEEK

1. Read the Books of Proverbs, Ecclesiastes and Song of Solomon; or Key Chapters — Proverbs 1, 2, 3, 6, 8, 9, 14, 20, 25, 31; Ecclesiastes 1, 5, 11, 12; Song of Solomon 1, 2.
2. Review your notes on the Psalms.
3. Mark your Bible from the notes taken in class.
4. Be present next Lord's Day with your own Bible and notebook.

Lesson 17
"The Books of Proverbs, Ecclesiastes, Song of Solomon"

(Where lines are provided, please look up Scriptures and fill in the entire Scripture or the main Truth of the passage.)

1. **Proverbs**

   We turn now from the devotional reading of the Psalms to the practical wisdom of the Proverbs. This Book is meant to be to our practical life what the Psalms are to our devotional life. This is a Book of Divine wisdom applied to earthly conditions.

   A proverb (in our English) means a brief saying instead of many words. *Proverbs are short statements drawn from long experiences.* A proverb does not argue — it assumes.

2. **The Author**

   Solomon is the writer of the next three Books: Proverbs, Ecclesiastes, Song of Solomon. Solomon probably gathered together wise sayings along with his own — but Solomon is generally credited with the authorship since he wrote 3,000 proverbs.

   1 Kings 4:32 _____

   _____

   We have only 917 Proverbs in this Book.

3. **The Central Message**

   The message of the Book is "The Wisdom of God," Christ is our wisdom.

   I Cor. 1:30_____

   _____

4. **The Structure of the Book**

   (1) WISDOM AND FOLLY — Chapters 1-9.

   (2) PROVERBS OF SOLOMON — Written and compiled by him — Chapters 10-24.

   (3) PROVERBS OF SOLOMON — Compiled by men of Hezekiah — Chapters 25-29.

   (4) WORDS OF AGUR — Chapter 30.

   (5) WORDS OF A MOTHER — Chapter 31.

5. **The Form of the Proverbs**

   The Book of Proverbs says things, as you have noticed, in short repeat or back up statements. This is called "parallelism." Three kinds of parallelism are pointed out:

(1) SYNONYMOUS PARALLELISM. Here the second clause restates what is given in the first clause. Example: Proverbs 19:29.

_____

_____

(2) CONTRAST PARALLELISM. A truth stated in the first clause is made stronger in the second clause by contrast with an opposite truth. Example: Proverbs 13:9.

_____

_____

(3) SYNTHETIC (OR COMPLETIVE) PARALLELISM. The second clause develops the thought of the first. Example: Proverbs 20:2.

_____

_____

6. **The Spiritual Value**

Proverbs are inspired and placed in the Scripture by the Holy Spirit of God. The spiritual value comes in the reading of these proverbs as compared to modern man's so-called proverbs. Man says such things as — "He who hesitates is lost" — "Look before you leap" — "The best things in life are free," etc.

The Word of God says: "In all thy ways acknowledge Him and He shall direct thy paths" — Proverbs 3:6, Proverbs 9:10 — "The fear of the Lord is the beginning of wisdom etc."

Notice seven things which God hates: 6:16-19.

(1)_____ (5)_____

(2)_____ (6)_____

(3)_____ (7)_____

(4)_____

Notice also Proverbs 8:22-26 and see the Eternal Son of God.

_____

_____

_____

THE BOOK OF ECCLESIASTES

1. The Book of Ecclesiastes is God's record of man's argument about life — his experience and reflection about life while out of fellowship with God. "Ecclesiastes" comes from the Latin form of the Greek word meaning "Preacher."

2. **The Author**

The author of Ecclesiastes was Solomon. He calls himself "the Preacher" but his description is given in Chapter 1:1 and Verse 12 and Verse 16; Chapter 2:9; Chapter 12:9.

3. **The Central Message**

This Book teaches, above all else, the emptiness of everything apart from God.

The "key word" is *"vanity"* (37 times) and does not mean only foolish pride but the emptiness of everything apart from God.

This Book should say to us, "Love not the world neither the things that are in the world: for all that is in the world, the lust of the flesh, the lust of the eyes, and the pride of life, is not of the Father, but is of the world" — I John 2:15-16.

Ecclesiastes also teaches us Matthew 6:19-21 _____

_____

_____

4. **The Structure of the Book**
   (1) THE THEME — "All is vanity" (Empty) — 1:1-3.
   (2) SEEKING SATISFACTION IN LIFE — 1:4 — 12:12.
      — through nature and science — 1:4-11.
      — through wisdom and philosophy — 1:12-18.
      — through pleasure — 2:1-11.
      — through materialism — 2:12-26.
      — through fatalism and self-centeredness — 3:1-4:16.
      — through religion — 5:1-8.
      — through wealth — 5:9-6:12.
      — through morality — 7:1-12:12.
   (3) A SPIRITUAL ADMONITION — 12:13-14.

5. **The Ten Vanities of Ecclesiastes**
   (1) Chapter 2:15-16 — *Vanity of human wisdom* — Wise and foolish die alike.
   (2) Chapter 2:19-21 — *Vanity of human labor* — Laborer and the wise die alike.
   (3) Chapter 2:26 — *Vanity of human purpose* – Man proposes, God disposes.
   (4) Chapter 4:4 — *Vanity of envy* — Success brings envy, not joy.
   (5) Chapter 4:7 — *Vanity of greed* — Get more and remain empty.
   (6) Chapter 4:16 — *Vanity of fame* — One day popular and then forgotten.
   (7) Chapter 5:10 — *Vanity of wealth* — Money does not satisfy.
   (8) Chapter 6:9 — *Vanity of coveting* — Wanting begats more wanting.
   (9) Chapter 7:6 — *Vanity of frivolity* — Time wasted brings sad end.
   (10) Chapter 8:10 & 14 — *Vanity of recognition* — Bad are often honored by men.

6. **Conclusion**
   The one lesson we should learn from this Book is — that a life lived for self and this world, and without God, is vanity, and that nothing "under the sun" can ever satisfy the human heart except the Lord Jesus, the Son of God. Read Psalm 90:12.

THE BOOK OF THE SONG OF SOLOMON

1. **The Book**
   The Song of Solomon is a love poem. The Jews called it the Holy of Holies of Scripture. Jerome tells us that the Jews would not permit their young men to read it until they were thirty years old. It is a part of inspired Scripture and thus, it has a profound lesson for us.

2. **The Author**
   Solomon is the author as stated in Chapter 1:1. Solomon was the author of 1,005 songs, I Kings 4:32 but we have only the one, the Song of Solomon.

3. **The Central Message**
   Chapter 2:16 expresses the central message — and such is the union between Christ and His redeemed people which can best be expressed to us in the form of a marriage union.

4. **The Structure of the Book**

    (1) Initial Love — 1:2 — 2:7.

    (2) Faltering Love — 2:8 — 3:5.

    (3) Growing Love — 3:6 — 5:1.

    (4) Transforming Love — 5:2 — 7:13.

    (5) Mature Love — 8:1-14.

(The brevity of time will not allow the teaching of the structure of the Book — but, mark these *"loves"* in your Bible.)

5. **Teaching Scripture with Scripture**

The key to the Song of Solomon is found in Psalm 45. It is titled a "Song of Loves" and it is a "royal marriage hymn" and it refers to Solomon. While the primary reference is to Solomon, the ultimate reference is to Christ as taught in Hebrews 1:7-8.

This 45th Psalm goes with the Song of Solomon. In it we see (1) in Vs. 2-9 an address to the royal bridegroom, and (2) in Vs. 10-17 an address to the royal bride.

6. **What It Teaches**

This Book, with the 45th Psalm, teaches us what Paul teaches in II Corinthians 11:1-2 _____

_____

and also in Ephesians 5:25-27 _____

_____

The Song of Solomon speaks then of *our* (the church) relationship to the heavenly Bridegroom, Our Lord Jesus.

(This Book is written in parabolic form — one of the Master's unique ways of teaching.)

HOW MUCH DO YOU REMEMBER?

Q. What is a Proverb?

Q. How many proverbs did Solomon write?

Q. What does Ecclesiastes mean?

Q. Who wrote the three Books of this lesson?

Q. What is the key word of Ecclesiastes?

Q. What does the Song of Solomon teach us as believers today?

YOUR ASSIGNMENT FOR NEXT WEEK:

    1. Read the Book of Isaiah or Key Chapters 1, 2, 4, 6, 7, 9, 11, 14, 35, 38, 39, 40, 41, 44, 45, 53, 55, 59, 61, 63, 66; 3 chapters each day.

    2. Review your notes on the three Books taught in this lesson.

    3. Mark your Bible from the notes you have made.

    4. Be present for the beginning of the prophetic Books, Isaiah, next Lord's Day.

Lesson 18
"The Book of Isaiah"

(Where lines are provided, please look up Scriptures and fill in the entire Scripture or the main Truth of the passage.)

1. **The Final Section of the Old Testament**

   We have now reached the final group of writings in the Old Testament. We have finished twenty-two Books and now the last seventeen, the Books of the prophets, are before us.

   Reviewing for a moment, to recall to your memory, we shall set forth a part of the first lesson:

   The first section of the old Testament are seventeen in number, falling into a subdivision of:

   > FIVE BOOKS — **PENTATEUCH** — LAW REDEMPTIVE, HISTORICAL
   >
   > TWELVE BOOKS — **JOSHUA THROUGH ESTHER** — HISTORICAL

   The middle five Books:

   > These are **JOB, PSALMS, PROVERBS, ECCLE-SIASTES, SONG OF SOLOMON.** These five are personal and deal with human problems of the heart. These are poetry.

   The last seventeen Books are prophecy and fall into a like sub-division of twelve and five (as the first seventeen Books).

   > FIVE — MAJOR PROPHETS
   >
   > TWELVE — MINOR PROPHETS

2. **What "Prophet" Means** (Read I Samuel 9:9)

   The word "pro" in "prophet" does not mean "beforehand" as it does in the word "provide" but it does mean "in place of." The remainder of the word "prophet" is from the Greek "phemi," which means "to speak." So then a prophet is *"one who speaks in place of another."*

   We see an example of this with Moses and Aaron in Exodus 7:1 when God said to Moses: "I have made thee a god unto Pharoah; and Aaron thy brother shall be thy *prophet.*" Aaron was to speak in place of Moses and for him.

   Prophecy is not merely prediction. The common idea today is that prophecy is a matter of foretelling. Prophecy, in the nonpredictive sense, is declaring a truth by the inspiration of God. Prophecy, in the predictive sense, is a declaring of the future which can only be by the direct inspiration of God. (See Isaiah 2:1, "The Word that Isaiah *saw.")*

3. **Qualifications of a Prophet**

   The supreme example is the Messiah-Prophet as described by the Lord God in Deut. 18:15 and 18. _____

   _____

   _____

   Also Acts 3:22-23_____

   _____

through the Bible in one year

NOTES

The test of a prophet is found in Deut. 18:22.

The prophet was to deal with the moral and religious life of his own people. A prophet was always a Hebrew.

4. **The Central Message of Isaiah**

"A throne" (6:1) — "A lamb" — (53:7).

"A Lamb — in the midst of the throne" — Rev. 7:17 and Rev. 4:2.

5. **The Structure of the Book**

(1) THE JUDGMENT OF GOD — GOD'S GOVERNMENT — Chapters 1-39

a. Judgment on Judah and Jerusalem — Chapters 1-12

b. Judgment on nations — Chapters 13-27

c. Warnings and promises — Chapters 28-35

d. Historical — Chapters 36-39 — (See II Kings 18-20)

(2) THE COMFORT OF GOD — GOD'S GRACE — Chapters 40-66

a. Jehovah and idols — Chapters 40-48

b. The Coming Messiah — Chapters 49-57

c. Final restoration and promised glory — Chapters 58-66

6. **Isaiah's Prophetic Perspective**

Isaiah was given a divine revelation concerning prophetic points:

(1) UNDER THE JUDGMENT SECTION (1-39)

a. Isaiah saw things to come to pass in his own time

b. He saw the coming captivity by Babylon (39:6)

(2) UNDER THE COMFORT SECTION (40-66)

a. He saw the coming of Christ — both first (Chapter 7) and second (Chapter 11) advents (Chapter 61).

b. He saw and proclaimed finally — the millenium and the new heavens and new earth (Chapter 66).

7. **How to Remember the 66 Chapters**

(1) Isaiah has 66 Chapters — The Bible has 66 Books.

(2) ISAIAH HAS TWO MAIN DIVISIONS — the first of 39 Chapters . . . the second of 27 Chapters.

So, the Bible has two main parts — the Old Testament of 39 Books and the New Testament of 27 Books.

(3) The prevailing note in the *first division of Isaiah* is *judgment*.

The prevailing note in the *Old Testament* is *Law*.

The prevailing note in the *second division* of Isaiah is *comfort*.

The prevailing note in the *New Testament* is *grace*.

8. **Isaiah's call to the Prophetic Office**

In the 6th Chapter we have a vivid description of God's call in the life of Isaiah:

Note: He got a vision of God — 6:1-4 (See John 12:41)

   — That produced conviction and confession — V-5

   — He was forgiven and cleansed — V-6-7

   — He heard God's call — V-8

   — He offered Himself for service — V-8

   — He was commissioned to serve — V-9-13

These are the steps which God might apply to your life.

9. **Isaiah saw the Birth of Christ**

Look up Isaiah 7:14 and Matthew 1:23 _____

_____

_____

Look up Isaiah 9:6-7 and Luke 2:11_____

_____

_____

Isaiah saw His death on the cross — Isaiah 53 (we will look at this chapter next).

Isaiah saw His second coming and Jesus reigning over His Kingdom. Isaiah 11:1, 6, 8, and Isaiah 59:20-21.

Look up Romans 11:26-27_____

_____

10. **Isaiah, the Evangelical Prophet (Isaiah 53)**

Of the many Messianic passages in Isaiah, we only have time for a quick glance at the preeminent one — the 53rd Chapter. The Chapter written about 700 B.C. proves the miracle of the inspiration of the Word of God.

The Chapter suits only one figure in human history — *The Man of Calvary!*

THE 12 POINTS BELOW CONFIRM THIS:

(1) He came in lowliness — "A root out of a dry ground" — V-2. Look up Romans 15:12 and Isaiah 11:1 _____

_____

_____

(2) He was "despised and rejected of men" — V-3. Look up Matthew 27:30-31 _____

_____

(3) He suffered for us — "He was wounded for our transgressions" V-5. Look up I Peter 2:24_____

_____

(4) God placed on Him the vicarious (substitute — to suffer for another) suffering for us —. "The Lord hath laid on Him the inquity (sin) of us all" — V-6. Look up Matthew 8:17_____

_____

_____

(5) "He was afflicted, yet He opened not His mouth" — V-7. See Acts 8:32-33_____

_____

_____

(6) He died as a felon — "He was taken from prison and judgment" — V-8. See Acts 4:27-28 _____

_____

(7) He was guiltless. "He had done no violence" — V-9. See I Peter 2:22 _____

_____

(8) "My servant shall justify many" — V-11. See Romans 5:15 _

_____

_____

(9) "He poured out His soul into death" — V-12. See Romans 3:25

_____

_____

(10) "He was numbered with the transgressors" — V-12. See Matt. 27:38 _____

_____

_____

(11) "He bare the sin of many" — V-12. See I Peter 2:24_____

_____

_____

(12) "Made intercession for the transgressors" — V-12. See Luke 23:34 _____

_____

_____

11. **Isaiah and the New Testament**

The Book of Isaiah is quoted over 66 times in the New Testament. Read some of the New Testament passages — (in the Greek his name is *ESAIAS* and mark the passages in your Bible).

QUOTED BY	PASSAGES
Matthew	Matt. 4:14-16; 8:17
John the Baptist	John 1:23
Jesus	Luke 4:16-21
Apostle John	John 12:38-41
Ethiopian	Acts 8:28
Paul	Acts 28:25-27; Rom. 9:27,29
	Romans 10:16, 20 and 15:12

Isaiah has been called the fifth evangelist and his Book has been called the fifth Gospel.

HOW MUCH DO YOU REMEMBER?

Q. What does the word "prophet" mean?

Q. What is the central message of Isaiah?

Q. Name the two great sections of Isaiah?

Q. How does the Book parallel the Bible?

YOUR ASSIGNMENT FOR NEXT WEEK

1. Read the Books of Jeremiah and Lamentations or Key Chapters: Jeremiah 1, 7, 11, 14, 15, 21, 23, 24, 25, 30, 31, 33, 39, 52. Lamentations — all 5 chapters — about 3 chapters each day.
2. Review your notes from the study of Isaiah.
3. Mark your Bible from the notes in Isaiah.
4. Be present next Lord's Day for another prophetic study.

Lesson 19
"The Books of Jeremiah and Lamentations"

(Where lines are provided, please look up Scriptures and fill in the entire Scripture or the main Truth of the passage.)

1. **Jeremiah**

   The Book of Jeremiah does not follow a topical or chronological order. In reading the Book one should disregard the time element except as it is definitely stated, and concentrate on the matters Jeremiah deals with in each chapter.

2. **The Man**

   Jeremiah lived in a time very much like our day. Isaiah had told Judah in his prophecy that judgment was coming unless they turned to God. Jeremiah's message was to notify the people of Judah that their judgment was now at hand and that nothing could save them from punishment.

   Jeremiah is known as the "weeping prophet" and "the prophet of a broken heart" — (9:1; 13:17).

   The historical setting of Jeremiah's time is found in II Kings 22 through 25.

3. **Who He Was**

   Jeremiah is partly autobiographical since he gave us so much of his personal history:

   (1) Born a priest — (1:1)

   (2) Chosen to be a prophet before he was born — (1:5)

   (3) Called to the prophetic office — (1:6)

   (4) Forbidden to marry because of the terrible times — (16:1-4)

   (5) Rejected by his people (11:18-21); hated and beaten (20:1-3); imprisoned (37:11-16)

   (6) Wanted to resign but couldn't (20:9)

4. **The Central Message**

   "Thou shalt go — I have set thee over nations and kingdoms to root out, to pull down, to destroy — to build and to plant" — 1:7 and 10, or 26:12-13.

   If men accept God's Word, it will give life; if they reject it, it will bring condemnation — John 3:36.

5. **The Structure of the Book**

   (1) The Prophet's Call — Chapter 1.

   (2) Sermon delivered before the fall of Judah — Chapters 2-38.

   (3) The Fall of Jerusalem and Judah — Chapter 39.

   (4) Messages to Jewish Remnant — Chapters 40-44.

   (5) Prophecies Against Gentile Nations — Chapters 45-51.

   (6) Appendix — Looking Back to Fall of Judah — Chapter 51.

6. **A Brief Look at Parts of the Structure of the Book**
   (1) Chapters 1 to 39 are all before the fall of Jerusalem.

   First, the prophet's call in Chapter 1. Then all the Chapters from 2 to 20 are general prophecies and are not necessarily given a time of delivery.

   Next, the prophecies from Chapters 21 to 39 are specific and they do give a time of their delivery in the first words of each chapter.

   (2) Chapter 39 gives the fall of Jerusalem to Babylonia.

   (3) Chapters 40 to 44, Jeremiah's prophecies on the nine Gentile nations.

7. **The Messianic Prophecies in Jeremiah**
   (1) The ministry of Jeremiah includes some wonderful prophecies concerning Christ and the future. Note Jeremiah 23:3-6 _____

   _____

   _____

   Notice, a righteous "Branch," "A King." "The Lord our Right-eousness." All these names mean Christ. Look up Luke 1:30-33

   _____

   _____

   (2) Now in Jeremiah 30:1-10 we see a Gospel — a good news. Notice — *"I will bring again the captivity of my people"* – *"I will cause them to return to the land and possess it"* – *"I will raise up unto them David, their King."* This is a scene of millennial blessing. The people are to be regathered. The land is to be possessed and the Messiah-King is to reign. (Compare with Romans 11:26-27)

   (3) Look up Jeremiah 33:15 _____

   _____

   _____

   (The Branch, is Christ. See Romans 1:3)
   Look back to God's Covenant with David — II Samuel 7:8-16. These prophecies look on to the second coming of the Lord Jesus Christ and His reign as King.

8. **The New Covenant — Jeremiah 31:31-34**
   Jeremiah saw that if there was to be any hope for his people, it could not be by a return to the old covenant made through Moses. The Lord told him of this *new covenant;* a covenant of grace, not law: not an outward command demanding obedience — but an inward renewal causing them to have a holy desire and motive. This new covenant was to be centered in the Son of David.

   The Son of David came and the new convenant has been sealed by His own blood.

   Look up Hebrews 8:6-7 _____

   _____

   In Hebrews 8:8-12 — Jeremiah's words are quoted.

   Now look up Hebrews 9:14-15 _____

   _____

   Jeremiah could not see this present church age but he clearly saw the glories of the Kingdom of Christ beyond this age. His people, the Jews, (few exceptions) await the time when they shall "look on Him whom they have pierced" as Messiah and Savior.

9. **Jeremiah teaches us some divine truths**
    (1) That God calls men to speak for Him — 1:5-9
    (2) That God rules in the affairs of men — 18:6-10.
    (3) That sin does not go unnoticed — 17:5-6.
    (4) That God will faithfully keep His promise to Israel — 31:1-9.
    (5) That God would send Messiah and set up His reign — 23:5-6; 30:7-9; 33:15-16.
    (*Note: The message against faithless shepherds – 23:1-2. The 70 year captivity prophecied – 25:9-13. The Word destroyed – but never dies – 36:18-28*).

THE BOOK OF LAMENTATIONS

1. **The Book**

    This Book, written by Jeremiah, looks *back* to the same event which Jeremiah anticipated in the Book of Jeremiah, namely, the fall of Jerusalem. This Book of Lamentations is a Book of Mourning. His soul was caused to grieve as he saw his people taken and the holy city destroyed.

2. **Its Title**

    The Book gets its title from the Hebrew "*QINOTH*" and Greek "*THRENOI*" meaning "lamentations" or "to cry aloud."

3. **Its Place in the Bible**

    It appears in the Jewish grouping of the Old Testament in the "Writings" (Law, Prophets, Writings) and is a part of the "*Megilloth*" or "*Rolls*." The "*Rolls*" are made up of five Books which the Jews read publicly at Jewish festivals:

    THE SONG OF SOLOMON — at the Passover
    RUTH — at the Feast of Pentecost
    ECCLESIASTES — at the Feast of Tabernacles
    ESTHER — at the Feast of Purim
    LAMENTATIONS — at the anniversary of the destruction of Jerusalem

4. **Characteristics and style**

    Lamentations is a set of five poems or elegies. The Chapters, except the middle one (Chapter 3) have the same number of verses, that is, *twenty-two,* and the third Chapter has *three times* the number of the others, that is, *sixty-six verses.* This is because there are *twenty-two* letters in the Hebrew alphabet. In Chapters 1, 2, 3, 4 — each verse begins with each letter of the Hebrew alphabet. The third Chapter has *sixty-six verses* and it runs triplets of verses (the first three verses beginning with the first letter, etc.) *thus the sixty-six verses correspond to the twenty-two letters.* The fifth Chapter contains twenty-two verses, but does not follow the same pattern.

5. **The Structure of the Book**
    (1) The Plight of Jerusalem — Chapter 1
    (2) The Anger of Jehovah — Chapter 2
    (3) The Grief of Jeremiah — Chapter 3
    (4) Again, the Anger of Jehovah — Chapter 4
    (5) The Prayer of Jerusalem — Chapter 5

6. **The Message of the Book**
    (1) The mourning over Jerusalem because of her sin — 1:18-21. Compare this thought with Luke 13:34-35 and 19:41-44.

(2) Confession of sin — 3:59; 5:16. See Matthew 10:32

_____

_____

See Romans 10:9 _____

_____

(3) A ray of hope — 3:21-32; 5:21.
Babylon was the conqueror and Jerusalem the conquered. In the future — it would be glory for Jerusalem and doom for Babylon. See Col. 1:4-5 _____

_____

_____

Also Col. 1:27 _____

_____

(4) The mercy and goodness of God — 3:21-32 and we can say with Jeremiah "great is thy faithfulness" — 3:23. See I Thess. 5:24 and II Thess. 3:3_____

_____

_____

HOW MUCH DO YOU REMEMBER?
Q. Jeremiah is known as _____.
Q. When was Jeremiah chosen to be a prophet?
Q. What covenant did Jeremiah see and record?
Q. What was Jeremiah lamenting over?

YOUR ASSIGNMENT FOR NEXT WEEK
1. Read the Book of Ezekiel — 7 chapters each day. If you can't read the entire Book . . . read the Key Chapters: 1, 2, 3, 8, 11, 20, 26, 28, 34, 36, 37. Less than two chapters each day.
2. Review your Bible from your notes.
3. Mark your Bible from your notes.
4. Be present next Lord's Day for another major prophet — Ezekiel.

Lesson 20
The Book of Ezekiel

(Where lines are provided, please look up Scriptures and fill in the entire Scripture or the main Truth of the passage.)

1. The Book

Among the Jews taken captive by Nebuchadnezzar of Babylon in his second invasion of Judah (597 B.C.) was a man named Ezekiel. Daniel had been taken captive in an earlier invasion (606 B.C.). Ezekiel was to be the *prophet to the Jews in exile,* while Daniel served as God's ambassador to the court of the king.

Ezekiel, like Jeremiah, was a priest as well as a prophet (1:3). He was thirty years of age when he began his prophetic ministry to the Jews gathered there in Babylon (1:1). He had been captive in Babylon five years when he began prophesying (1:2). For six years he told of the coming fall of Jerusalem, and this takes up one-half of the Book — 24 Chapters.

His name means *"God strengthens."*

2. The Author

The author can be none other than Ezekiel who recorded all that God showed him.

3. The Central Message

Seventy times we read the central message of the Lord God in this Book and it is:

> "They shall know that I am the Lord."
> (Examples: 6:7, 10, 13, 14; 7:4, 9, 27; 11:10; 12:16 etc.)

4. The Structure of the Book

(1) The Call and Commission of Ezekiel — Chapters 1-3

(2) The Judgments On Jerusalem — Chapters 4-24

Chapters 4-7 — Prophecies of Judgment

Chapters 8-11 — Reasons For Judgment

Chapters 12-24 — Symbols and Messages of Judgment

(3) Judgment On the Foes of Judah — Chapters 25-32

(4) Israel's Resurrection — Chapters 33-39

(5) Israel in the Land During the Kingdom Age — Chapters 40-48
(Note, we shall study the Structure of the Book in part.)

5. The Call and Commission of Ezekiel — Chapters 1-3

(1) The call and commission from God came in the form of a vision. "I saw, I fell, I heard" (1:28), "stand, heard, send, say" — 2:1-4.

Compare 1:28 with Rev. 1:17 _____

_____

_____

(2) Ezekiel saw the signs of judgment in the whirlwind and fire followed by the four cherubims with four faces — the same living beings were at the Garden of Eden in Genesis 3:24 and who appear at the throne of God in Rev. 4:6-8. Each had four faces — *a lion, an ox, a man, an eagle.*

When the Son of God became flesh He is pictured in Matthew as the lion; Mark, the ox; Luke, the man; John, the eagle.

(3) The Commission is given to Ezekiel beginning at 2:3.

6. **The Judgments On Jerusalem — Chapters 4-24**

(1) Ezekiel preached to the Jews in Babylon that Jerusalem would be destroyed. He received this message through a vision (Chapters 8-11). He saw in Chapter 8 — Judah profaning the temple:

- Verse 3 — Image of Jealousy
- Verses 7-12 — Seventy Jewish elders offer incense to beasts.
- Verses 13-15 — Women weeping for Tammuz (Greek god).
- Verse 16 — Twenty-five men worshipping the sun.
- Verses 17-18 — The Lord says, "I will deal in fury."

Chapter 9 — A picture of judgment.

Chapter 10 — Departure of the presence of God from the temple.

Chapter 11 — The departure of the glory of the Lord from Jerusalem. The doom of the city was sealed. Ezekiel saw this coming.

(2) Ezekiel also preached and prophesied through symbolic actions (visual aids). They were done to impress the people and cause them to remember the message.

Some of these symbolic actions were:

- God caused him to be dumb — 3:26-27; 24:27
- His posture in public (on side for days) 4:4-8
- Sign of the brick (with drawing of Jerusalem) 4:1-3
- Shaving of his hair — 5:1-17
- Removal of household goods — 12:1-17
- The death of his wife (no mourning) 24:15-27

Name some signs Jesus used to teach during His ministry:

_____

_____

7. **Judgments on Foes of Israel — Chapters 28-32**

We shall pick out only one direct prophecy concerning these nations.

(1) The prophecy of Tyre — Chapters 26-28

Read 26:7-11 –

This took place when Nebuchadnezzar overcame the city.

A further prophecy is in Verses 14-21.

This was fulfilled exactly, by Alexander the Great some 250 years later.

(2) The Evil Force Behind Tyre — *Satan* — Chapter 28

In V-1-10 we see the reason behind the judgment of God upon Tyre. The *pride* of the king of Tyre which is used by the Lord God to speak of the real sinister force, Satan himself. God often spoke to Satan through another indirect source:

Genesis 3:14-15 — He spoke to Satan through the serpent.

Matthew 16:23 — He spake to the devil through Simon Peter.

Note in Ezek. 28:12-19 God speaks through Ezekiel to Satan through the king of Tyre. Here God describes the unfallen state of Satan:

- "wisdom and beauty" — V-12
- "you were in Eden" — V-13
- "anointed cherub that covers" — V-14
- "perfect — till iniquity was found in thee" — V-15
- "sinned — therefore I cast thee — out of mountain of God" — V-16 (See Luke 10:17-18)

● "thy heart was lifted up because of thy beauty" — V-17 (Pride)

Now read Isaiah 14:12-14.

Both of these Scriptures (Ezekiel 28 and Isaiah 14) give the fall of Satan and his original state.

8. **Israel's Resurrection — Chapters 33-39** (We take only two of these prophecies) —

(1) The True Shepherd — Chapter 34

The false shepherds are described in 34:1-10.

The *One True Shepherd* — Jesus, is described in detail — V-11-31.

Read John 10:1-14 and pick out the verses with "sheep" or "shepherd."

_____

_____

_____

Read Psalms 23.

Look up Hebrews 13:20; I Peter 5:4 _____

_____

_____

(2) The Vision of the Valley and dry bones — Chapter 37.

The one vision of Israel's resurrection, remembered by most people is this one.

The vision is symbolic of national restoration in their own land — (37:11-14). This does not speak of individual but national resurrection. *Note that the vision is explained in Verses 11-14.*

The two kingdoms of Israel and Judah shall be one again, as symbolized by the two sticks which became one (V-22) and the Messiah — King, David shall be over them (V-24-25).

This yet awaits fulfillment. Paul does give clear New Testament teaching in:

Romans 11:1_____

_____

Romans 11:26-27_____

_____

9. **Israel in the Land During the Kingdom Age — Chapters 40-48**

(1) The Millennial Temple — Chapters 40-42.

(2) Its Purpose — For the reign of Christ and the glory of God — 43:1-17.

(3) The East Gate closed — 44:2.

(4) The Sacrifices — 40:39-43; 42:13; 43:19-27. (We shall leave lines here for added Scripture and comments.)

_____

_____

_____

(5) For additional Scripture on Millennial Kingdom — See Zech. 14; Rev. 19:11 through Rev. 20:1-6.

(6) Jerusalem will be called "Jehovah-Shammah" meaning "The Lord Is There" — 48:35.

HOW MUCH DO YOU REMEMBER?

Q. Ezekiel was a prophet to _____.

Q. What is the Central Message of Ezekiel?

Q. Ezekiel used unique methods of making his message remain in the minds of listeners. What do we call these methods today?

Q. God judged the enemies of Israel. Name one such enemy.

Q. Who was described as the evil force behind the King of Tyre?

YOUR ASSIGNMENT FOR NEXT WEEK

1. Read the twelve chapters of Daniel — less than two chapters each day.
2. Review your notes on Ezekiel.
3. Mark your Bible from your notes.
4. Be present next Lord's Day for a great study — Daniel.

Lesson 21
"The Book of Daniel"

(Where lines are provided, please look up Scriptures and fill in the entire Scripture or the main Truth of the passage.)

1. The Man

About eight years *before* Ezekiel was taken captive by Nebuchadnezzar — the young man, Daniel, was taken from Jerusalem to Babylon by Nebuchadnezzar, the king. He was young, intelligent and skillful in wisdom (See 1:4). Daniel is one of the few men about whom God says only good. Three times he is referred to as "the greatly beloved" one (9:23; 10:11 and 19). Taken into captivity with Daniel were three other young men whom you know by their Babylonian names — Shadrach, Meshach, Abed-nego. The name "Daniel" means — "God is Judge."

2. The Book

Daniel is the Old Testament "Apocalypse" while Revelation is the New Testament "Apocalypse." The word "Apocalypse" means — "an unveiling of the secret purposes of God." The secret purposes of God can never be known until they are revealed. The manner in which the events are unveiled in Daniel is mainly by visions. In the Book of Daniel the word "vision" or "visions" appears thirty-two times.

We shall see that the themes of Daniel are the themes of New Testament prophecy — namely, the manifestation of the man of sin, the great tribulation, the return of the Lord, the resurrections and the judgments.

Daniel is distinctly the prophet of "the times of the Gentiles" — Luke 21:24. His vision sweeps the entire course of Gentile world rule to its end and on to the Messianic kingdom of our Lord.

3. The Central Truth

"That the most High ruleth in the kingdom of men and giveth it to whomsoever He will." See Chapter 4:17, 25, 32.

This theme is essentially the same as that of Ezekiel, the other Book of the captivity. Ezekiel's theme is . . . *"They shall know that I am Jehovah."*

4. The Structure of the Book

HISTORY — Chapters 1-6
PROPHECY — Chapters 7-12

(Let me explain. The historical section reveals God's plan to Daniel and all of that plan speaks of the immediate future and actually took place. Yet the six chapters are not only history but they look to a distant fulfillment. Example: Chapter three recounts the story of the three Hebrew children in the fiery furnace but it is also a picture of Israel in the furnace of tribulation. Chapter two is Nebuchadnezzar's dream and most of that is history yet it looks to the end of the times of the Gentiles.

The prophetic section — Chapters 7-12 — deal with the events of this age and the events of the end time.)

5. The Books of Daniel and Revelation

The Book of Daniel cannot be fully understood without the Book of Revelation and visa versa. Both men were loved of the Lord and saw the visions God gave them while in exile; Daniel, a captive in Babylon, and John on the isle of Patmos. Five times in Revelation we read that it is a prophecy — Rev. 1:3; 22:7, 10, 18, 19. Daniel is a prophet — Jesus referred to him as such in Matthew 24:15.

_____

_____

_____

So much that was sealed in Daniel is unsealed in Revelation. Compare Daniel 12:8-9 to Rev. 5:1-5.

_____

_____

_____

What was hidden from the eyes of Daniel is open to view in Revelation.

6. **Nebuchadnezzar's Dream and Daniel's Vision — Chapters 2 and 7**

God gave Nebuchadnezzar a dream — a prophetic outline of the future history of world powers (Chapter 2).

Sixty years later Daniel had a vision, also called a dream (7:1) concerning the same world powers (Chapter 7).

WE SHALL STUDY CHAPTERS 2 AND 7 TOGETHER

NEBUCHADNEZZAR'S DREAM		DANIEL'S DREAM	
The Setting	2:1-30	The Setting	7:1
The Dream	2:31-35	The Dream	7:2-14 & 21-22
The Interpretation	2:36-45	The Interpretation	7:15-26
The Results	2:46-49	The Results	7:27-28

The two prophetic dreams should be compared so you will always remember their meaning.

NEBUCHADNEZZAR		DANIEL
Nebuchadnezzar's Dream — IMAGE	FULFILLMENT	Daniel's Vision 4 Beasts
Daniel 2:31-35 (Note V-29 — "What shall come to pass hereafter")	WORLD POWERS	Daniel 7:1-27 (Note V-18 — "The saints shall take the kingdom forever")
Head — (V-38) Gold	BABYLON	Lion (V-4)
Breasts & Arms — (39-a and 32) Silver	MEDO-PERSIA	Bear (V-5)
Belly & Thighs — (39-b) Brass	GREECE	Leopard (V-6)
Legs & Feet — (V-40) Iron	ROME	Diverse Beast — (V-7 & 19)
10 Toes — (V-41-42)	OLD ROMAN EMPIRE	10 Horns — (V-7 & 20)
	ANTI-CHRIST	Little Horn (V-8 & 21)
The Stone — (V-34-35 & 45)	CHRIST	Ancient of Days — (V-22)
The Mountain — (V-35)	KINGDOM (MILLENNIAL)	Everlasting Kingdom — (V-27)

The four kingdoms symbolized by the great image and the beasts were literal kingdoms. It follows then that the *Stone* kingdom which is to take place is also a literal kingdom — the Millennial Kingdom of our Lord — Jesus the King.

Look up Psalms 118:22-23 _____

_____

Compare with Luke 20:17-18 _____

_____

7. The King Nebuchadnezzar erects a gold image to perpetuate himself (Chapter 3). He demanded the people to worship the image and the three Hebrew children refused to obey and were cast into the fiery furnace but God made the flames harmless. See V-25 — The fourth person is —

_____

See Hebrews 11:33-34 — "Through faith." We are saved by faith.

Then in Chapter 4, Nebuchadnezzar has a dream of a great tree. Daniel again interprets the dream and it came to pass exactly as God revealed it to Daniel — V-19-28.

The king was stricken with madness for seven years representing the tribulation. The stump was spared and after seven years sprouted — (V-15 & 23) — representing the Gentile nations whose "knee shall bow" and they shall seek out the Lord — Acts 15:14-18.

In Chapter 5 is the account of the handwriting on the wall. (Time does not permit a study of this.)

In Chapter 6 — Daniel in the lions den and the delivering God. Note the *promotion* of Daniel — V-26-28.

In Chapter 8 — We have the details of the second and third kingdoms — Medo-Persia and Greece.

8. **Daniel's Seventy Weeks — Chapter 9**

This is one of the towering chapters in the Bible. The angel Gabriel (V-21) gave the divine revelation. Now, at V-24 through 27 we have the revelation.

70 weeks or 70 — 7's = 490 years.

(See Jeremiah 25:11-12 and Lev. 26:33-34 and you will see the significance.)

Scripture divides these 70 weeks into *three* divisions with a parenthesis — the church age — in between. In V-25 — "7 weeks" — 49 years began at the *"Commandment to restore and rebuild Jerusalem."* (Ezra 1; Ezra 6; Nehemiah 2) and that actually happened as we saw in Ezra and Nehemiah.

Next, 62 — 7's or 434 years (from 396 B.C. to 38 A.D.) Messiah was cut off — crucified (V-26).

The 70th week is set apart. Between the 69th and 70th weeks there is the interlude, the parenthesis of the church age. Note in V-27 "in the middle of the week," the covenant is broken by the Anti-Christ with Israel. This last 7-year period is the tribulation — divided into two 3½ year periods, known in Scripture as 3½ years, 42 months, 1,260 days.

At the end of all of the 70 weeks (after the tribulation) Christ will literally return.

The 70th week, the tribulation, has not yet begun. It is coming soon! I Thessalonians 4:13-18.

HERE IS A VISUAL HELP ABOUT THIS

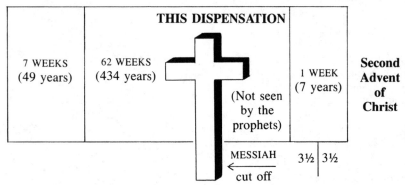

Climax of Jewish History

9. The Vision of the Glory of God — the final vision and the final mysteries are seen in the last three chapters of prophecy.

HOW MUCH DO YOU REMEMBER?

Q. Revelation and Daniel are alike in what way?

Q. Daniel is the prophet of "_____."

Q. How do Chapters 2 and 7 relate to each other?

Q. What does 70 weeks mean, in years?

YOUR ASSIGNMENT FOR NEXT WEEK

    1. Read these chapters: Hosea 1, 2, 3, 4, 6, 13, 14
                               Joel 1, 2, 3
                               Amos 2, 3, 5, 8, 9
    (These are 14 Key Chapters — 2 each day)
    2. Review your notes from your outline.
    3. Mark your Bible from your notes on Daniel.
    4. Be present next Lord's Day for a study of three Books — Hosea, Joel, Amos.

Lesson 22
"The Books of Hosea, Joel, and Amos"

(Where lines are provided, please look up Scriptures and fill in the entire Scripture or the main Truth of the passage.)

1. **Hosea**

   Hosea was a contemporary of Amos — both prophesying to the Northern Kingdom of Israel. Hosea is often called "the prophet of Israel's zero hour." Israel had degenerated into such spiritual depravity that God's judgment could no longer be delayed. II Kings 15-17 covers the period of Hosea and records the terrible sins of idol worship and unbridled sex in that time.

2. **The Central Message**

   "Return unto the Lord" — Hosea 6:1
   (The word *"return"* occurs 15 times in Hosea.)

3. **The Structure of the Book**

   Hosea — His Marriage — Compared to God and Israel —
   Chapters 1-3 (An analogy)

   Sin, Judgment and *Ultimate Blessing* of Israel — Chapters 4-14

4. **Hosea — His Marriage — Compared to God and Israel — Chapters 1-3**

   (1) Through the heartbreak of Hosea's own marriage, he had come to see Israel's sin against God. Gomer, Hosea's wife, typified the nation Israel (1:1-4).

   The children were named to symbolize judgment:

   > JEZREEL (1:4-5) means *"God scatters"*
   > LO-RUHAMAH (1:6-7) means *"not obtained mercy"*
   > LO-AMMI — (1:8-9) means *"not my people"*

   Hosea's patience, compassion and his final acts of redeeming, chastening and restoring Gomer are the same qualities God will, and does, have for sinning Israel.

   (2) The chastisement of Israel is described in Chapter 2 and the symbolism and prophecy was fulfilled. (See II Kings 15:19-20; 17:5-23).

   New names are given to the children to tell of the future restoration of Israel — Jezreel (scattered in 1:5) now becomes "gathered together" in 1:11.

   "Lo-Ammi" *(not my people)* to "Ammi" — *(My people)*
   "Lo-Ruhamah" *(not obtained mercy)* to "Ruhamah" *(have obtained mercy)*

   (3) The latter days for Israel are described in Chapter 3.

   Thus we have the whole story of Israel, past, present, future in these first three chapters.

   In V. 3:2 — we see "redemption"

5. **Sin, Judgment and Ultimate Blessing of Israel — Chapter 4-14**

   (1) THERE WAS A LACK OF KNOWLEDGE OF GOD in Israel

accounting for the adulterous nation:

NOTE: Hosea 4:1 — "There is no knowledge of God in the land"

Hosea 4:6 — "My people are destroyed for lack of knowledge, etc."

(2) THERE WERE FALSE PRIESTS AND PROPHETS.

NOTE: Hosea 4:5 — "The prophet shall stumble."

Hosea 4:9 — "Like people — like priest."

(3) THERE WAS IMMORALITY.

NOTE: Hosea 4:13-14, 16 & 17

Hosea 7:4

Hosea 8:9

(4) JUDGMENT AND PUNISHMENT OF ISRAEL.

NOTE: "They shall sow the wind and shall reap the whirlwind" — Hosea 8:7.

"He will remember their iniquity" — 9:9.

"Samaria shall become desolate — they shall fall by the sword" — 13:16.

(Ephraim is used as a name for Israel in connection with sin or backsliding. It is used 37 times in this Book.)

(5) ULTIMATE BLESSING OF ISRAEL.

The day is coming when Israel will return to God and He will receive them.

Hosea 3:5 _____

_____

and 14:4 _____

_____

APPLICATION FOR US TO REMEMBER: Israel is the adulterous wife of Jehovah, to be restored in grace (Hosea 2:16-23). The Church is a virgin espoused to one husband (II Cor. 11:1-2). Israel then, is Jehovah's earthly wife (Hosea 2:23); the Church is the Lamb's heavenly bride (Rev. 19:7).

THE BOOK OF JOEL

1. **The Man**

Joel was a prophet to Judah. Nothing is known of him except what is written in V-1. His name means "Jehovah is God."

2. **The Central Message**

"The Day of the Lord" — (Joel 1:15; 2:1, 2, 10, 11, 30, 31; 3:14-16).

Note: To remember in a general way the meaning of "The Day of the Lord" — it is that period of time which is in contrast to man's day or Satan's day. It begins with the Great Tribulation and extends through the Millennial Kingdom.

3. **The Structure of the Book**

GOD'S JUDGMENT — 1:1 — 2:27

THE PROMISE OF THE SPIRIT — 2:28 — 3:1

GOD'S JUDGMENT OF NATIONS — 3:1-17

THE RESTORATION OF JUDAH — 3:18-21

4. **God's Judgment On Judah — 1:1 — 2:27**

(1) This was a literal plague of locusts and it is used to speak of a fact but also to symbolize the destruction of "the Day of the Lord." This was a foreshadowing of an ultimate and future event. Nothing escapes because all are affected — drunkards (1:5) — priests (1:13-16) — the whole earth (1:17) — the cattle (1:18-20).

(2) The judgment points to that period of tribulation. Compare 2:2 with

Matthew 24:21 and Daniel 12:1.

(3) Deliverance only if there is repentance — 2:18-27.

5. **The Promise of the Spirit — 2:28 — 3:1**

(1) This is one of the prophecies which had *a part* of its fulfillment at Pentecost. Peter quotes the words of Joel 2:28-29 in Acts 2:16-18. The events prophesied in Joel 2:30-31 and Acts 2:19-20 have not yet been fulfilled. Compare these 2 Scriptures.

_____

_____

_____

(2) Jesus told His disciples that the Holy Spirit dwelled *with* them but that He would be *in* them — John 14:17 — Acts 1:8. Look up John 14:17 _____

_____

(3) Peter used the prophecy of Joel to describe the power of the coming of the Holy Spirit at Pentecost for all who believe. The entire prophecy of Joel was not fulfilled then (only a part) but was a *guarantee* that God would ultimately fulfill all Joel said in the day when Israel returns to the Lord (Joel 2:31-32).

6. **God's Judgment of Nations — 3:1-17**

(1) This occurs at the end time in the Valley of Jehoshaphat (Judgment) at Christ's actual return — V-2 & 14.

Look up Matthew 25:31-32 _____

_____

7. **The Restoration of Judah — 3:18-21**

(1) Look up Zechariah 14:4, 8.

(2) The Lord Jesus shall reign in person and the land will be a land of milk and honey.

THE BOOK OF AMOS

1. **The Man**
Amos, the author of this Book, was a layman. He was a herdsman — (1:1 and 7:14-15). The Lord called him to prophesy to the Northern Kingdom of Israel chiefly and to the whole house of Jacob (3:1, 13). He ministered during the reign of Uzziah, King of Judah, and Jeroboam, King of Israel.

2. **The Central Message**
"Can two walk together, except they be agreed?" — (3:3).

3. **The Structure of the Book**
(1) JUDGMENT of Surrounding Nations — 1:1 — 2:3.
(2) JUDGMENT of Judah and Israel — 2:4 — 6:14.
(3) VISIONS of the Future — Chapters 7-9.

4. **Judgment of Surrounding Nations — 1:1 — 2:3**
(1) JUDGMENT against Syria for cruelty — 1:3-5.
(2) JUDGMENT against Philistia for selling Israelites into slavery in Edom — 1:6-8.
(3) JUDGMENT against Phoenicia for breaking their covenant with Israel — 1:9-10.
(4) JUDGMENT against Edom for causing Israel to suffer — 1:11-12.
(5) JUDGMENT against Ammon for violence against Israel — 1:13-15.
(6) JUDGMENT against Moab for injustice — 2:1-3.

5. **Judgment of Judah and Israel — 2:4 — 6:14**

    (1) JUDGMENT against Judah for despising the law — 2:4-5.

    (2) JUDGMENT against Israel for immorality — 2:6-16.

    (3) GOD'S CHARGE against the whole house of Israel — the 12 tribes — 3:1 — 6:14.

6. **Visions of the Future — Chapters 7-9**

    (1) VISION of the grasshoppers — 7:1-3.

    (2) VISION of the fire — 7:4-6.

    (3) VISION of the plumbline — 7:7-17.

_____

_____

    (4) VISION of basket of summer fruit — Chapter 8.

_____

_____

_____

    (5) VISION of the Lord at the Altar — 9:1-10.

_____

_____

_____

    (6) FUTURE Kingdom and David's Tabernacle — 9:11-15.

_____

_____

_____

HOW MUCH DO YOU REMEMBER?

Q. Hosea preached a modern day truth to Israel because of his own marriage. Can you name that truth?

_Q. The people lacked of the knowledge of _____in Israel._

Q. What is another name for Israel?

Q. What is the central theme or truth of Joel?

Q. Was Amos trained to be a prophet?

YOUR ASSIGNMENT FOR NEXT WEEK

    1. Read Obadiah, Jonah and Micah — only 12 chapters in all (2 chapters a day).

    2. Review your notes taken in class.

    3. Mark your Bibles from your notes made in class.

    4. Be present next Lord's Day for three of the minor prophets.

Lesson 23
"The Books of Obadiah, Jonah, Micah"

(Where lines are provided, please look up Scriptures and fill in the entire Scripture or the main Truth of the passage.)

1. **Obadiah**

   Obadiah means "Servant of Jehovah." The name appears *twenty* times in the Bible representing *thirteen* different people but the only reference to this writing Prophet is in Verse 1 of his Book. He was God's messenger to Edom. This Book is the *shortest* Book of the Old Testament.

2. **The Central Message**

   Pride deceives a person or a nation (V-3) and "As thou hast done, it shall be done unto thee" — V-15.

3. **The Structure of the Book**

   The DESTRUCTION of Edom — V-1-16

   The RESTORATION of Israel — V-17-21

4. **The Destruction of Edom — V-1-16**

   The name Edom means "red." It is the name given to Jacob's brother, Esau, because he sold his birthright for red pottage — Gen. 25:30

   _____

   _____

   The Edomites, therefore, came from Esau (Gen. 36:1) and they lived in Mount Seir — a mountainous region south of the Dead Sea. It is in what we know as Jordan today. Seir means "hairy, rugged" and Esau was a hairy man — Gen. 27:11.

   The antagonism originating with the twin brothers, Jacob and Esau (Gen. 27), persisted through the centuries and is seen throughout the history of Edom.

   The Edomites rejected the request of Israel to travel through Edom on their journey from Egypt (Num. 20:14-21).

   Edom lost its identity as a nation before the time of Christ and disappeared from history in 70 A.D.

   In Obadiah's day the capital of Edom was Sela or Petra, the rose red city. The ancient capital, before Obadiah, was Bozrah (Isa. 63:1).

   The Edomites had a bitter, persistent spite for Israel. They *hated everyone from the family of Jacob and this was her great sin* — See V-10-14.

   Because of her great sin against Israel, divine judgment is pronounced upon Edom and it is summed up in V-15 — "As thou hast done, it shall be done unto thee."

   It happened just as God pronounced and Edom as a nation perished — Israel remains.

5. **The Restoration of Israel — V-17-21**

These verses teach God's protective mercy for His people. No one who fought God's covenant people ever prospered but paid dearly.

These verses stress the bright hope of Israel in the Messianic Kingdom. Edom has perished but Israel flourishes.

THIS CHART WILL HELP YOU REMEMBER THE BOOK OF OBADIAH

BROTHERS	**Esau**	**Jacob**
NATIONS	**Edom**	**Israel**
CITIZENSHIP	**Earthly**	**Heavenly**
CHARACTER	**Proud/Rebellious**	**Chosen/Set Apart**

History tells us that Edom fell to the Babylonians five years after they had helped Babylon destroy Jerusalem, as indicated in V-13. Thereafter the Nabatheans, an Arabian tribe, occupied Edom's capital, Petra. By the third century even the language of Edom had ceased.

See Dan. 11:41 for an amazing prophecy concerning Edom.

THE BOOK OF JONAH

1. **The Book**

Jonah means "dove." His hometown, according to II Kings 14:25, was Gath-hepher, a village just three miles from Nazareth, the hometown of Jesus. He was a good example of God working through a man who was like most of us — wanted his own way, disobedient, pouted, etc.

If the Book of Jonah is really a narrative of actual fact, *as I believe it to be,* it brings to us one of the most striking revelations of God. On the other hand, if it is only fictional, it contains no authentic significance at all. The lessons of Jonah and the literal interpretation of the Book are imperative because the integrity of the Scripture and the Word of the Lord Jesus is at stake here.

Jonah, then, was a *real* person — II Kings 14:25 and Jonah 1:1.

The narrative of the Book *is actual* and there is nothing in Scripture to suggest otherwise. (Those who say the Book of Jonah is a fantasy, are the so-called "modern critics" who would look upon anything supernatural as incredible.)

2. **The Central Message**

"Arise — go — preach." (1:2 and 3:2)

3. **The Structure of the Book**
   • Jonah Flees — Chapter 1
   • Jonah Prays — Chapter 2
   • Jonah Preaches — Chapter 3
   • Jonah Learns — Chapter 4

4. **Jonah Flees — Chapter 1**

Jonah was a Hebrew and he had been called by the Lord God to go to the Gentile capital city of Assyria, Nineveh, and preach in *person,* face to face. Instead he flees, not that he could escape God, but from his calling as a prophet. He did not want Nineveh spared as we shall see. So, he took a ship the opposite direction (V-3). God brought about a storm — in order to get Jonah where He wanted him to be. (V-12-17)

5. **Jonah Prays — Chapter 2**

Jonah was in a "prepared fish" as an act of preservation, not punishment. There is not one word of petition in Jonah's prayer. It is a prayer of thanksgiving and praise and rededication. Jonah had a change of heart in V-9 — "I will pay that that I have vowed." Jonah was *then* vomited out on dry land — safe and sound.

6. **Jonah Preaches — Chapter 3**

   This lone prophet preached to the "great city" of Ninevah. The city was turned upside-down for God because a servant of God had been given a second chance and he preached.

   The *Lord Jesus* gives us a clue to Jonah's power in preaching. Luke 11:29-30 — ". . . for as Jonah was a sign unto the Ninevites." Jonah then was a *sign* by his miraculous experience in the great fish. How did they know about the "fish" story? Remember the sailors of Chapter 1? At any rate, Jesus said he was a sign just as "the Son of Man be to this generation."

   The city repented and God changed His heart toward them.

7. **Jonah Learns — Chapter 4**

   Here in this chapter is a dialogue between Jonah and the Lord.

   In V-1-3 Jonah is angry and displeased over Israel's dark future now that Ninevah had been spared and he even prays that his life will be taken. Jonah went outside the city, "till he might see what would become of the city."

   God prepared three things for Jonah while he was waiting:

   - Verse 6 — *a gourd*
   - Verse 7 — *a worm*
   - Verse 8 — *an east wind*

   — causing Jonah to wish for death — V-8, followed by the Divine utterance closing the Book — Read V-10-11.

   This statement is the *revelation of the heart of God*. Jonah is not the important factor here — it is God. We should see God's tender patience with a resentful prophet — also, that the election of the one nation did not mean the rejection of others.

8. **Jonah As a Type**

   FIRST — *he foreshadows the history of Israel, his nation*. Israel, out of her own land, finding refuge with Gentiles, crying out to Jehovah, displeased with some nations — all of these were seen in Jonah.

   SECOND — *Jonah signifies the death, burial, resurrection of our Lord*. Jesus confirmed this in His own words in Matthew 12:38-41. Read and write in V-40. _____

   _____

   _____

   HERE WE SEE OLD TESTAMENT TYPOLOGY AS AN IMPRESSIVE CREDENTIAL OF DIVINE INSPIRATION.

   THIRD — *Jonah is a type of Christ Himself as a "sign."* See Luke 11:29-30 and write in V-30 _____

   _____

   Just as Jonah was a sign to Ninevites so shall the Son of Man be: Jonah came out of the fish, after three days and three nights, just as Christ came out of the tomb. The Gospel was *then* taken to the Gentiles (just as Jonah was instructed). Jesus therefore has attested the Book of Jonah and all Scripture.

THE BOOK OF MICAH

1. **The Book**

   Micah is the prophet usually quoted at Christmas for prophesying the actual city of the birth of Christ. (Micah and Isaiah might have been close to each other.) It is interesting to observe that even today we associate Micah with the prophecy of Jesus' birth while Isaiah is remembered for the prophecy of the death of Jesus (Isa. 53). Isaiah was a well-educated man while Micah was a man of the fields.

   "Micah" means "Who is like Jehovah." He was a prophet to Judah, though he often included Israel (the 10 tribes) and Samaria, its capital. He prophesied during the reigns of Jotham, Ahaz and Hezekiah (1:1) as is indicated in Jeremiah 26:18.

2. **The Central Message**

Present judgment — future blessing.

3. **The Structure of the Book**
   - Judgment Declared — Chapters 1-3
   - Blessing Promised — Chapters 4-5
   - Exhortations to Repentance — Chapters 6-7

4. **Judgment Declared — Chapters 1-3**

Jehovah's rod to inflict judgment was Assyria (1:9). The verse says, "It (the wound, Assyria) is come unto Judah; *it* (not 'he') is come unto the gate of my people, even to Jerusalem." The names of the places in V-10-16 were all in a small area where Micah was reared.

Chapters 2 and 3 give the details of the coming judgment against "the house of Israel." Note 2:7 and 3:1.

5. **Blessing Promised — Chapters 4-5**

In Chapter 4 we have the *future* kingdom.

In Chapter 5 we have the *future* king.

It is thrilling to know that these Hebrew preachers of twenty-five centuries ago could be telling us — today — of things which are still to happen. Chapters 4 and 5 show that these things are still future and await the Millennial era.

In Chapter 4:1 note "in the last days." In V-2 the nations, other than Israel, are to be a part of the Messianic Kingdom.

But in 4:9 note the change from future tense to *"now* dost thou cry" and V-10 *"Now* shalt thou go" and V-11 *"Now* many nations are against thee" and 5:1 *"Now* . . . he laid siege against us."

In 5:3 "He gives them up *until"* — the coming of Christ.

In 5:2 is the remarkable prediction of the place of Christ's birth. Micah says this so plainly that when the Magi asked Herod where the king of the Jews should be born, the scribes gave a definite answer based on Micah 5:2. Look up Matthew 2:5 _____

_____

Between the first half of 5:3 and the second half, this present age intervenes, which Micah could not foresee. The remainder of the chapter looks to the Kingdom Age yet future.

6. **Exhortations to Repentance — Chapters 6-7**

These chapters are in the form of a conversation (a colloquy) between Jehovah and His people. The high mark of these pleadings is in 6:8, "He hath shown thee, O man, what is good; and what doth the Lord require of thee, but to do justly, and to love mercy, and to walk humbly with thy God?"

God pardons and forgets — 7:18-19.

7. **Points of Interest in Micah**

Six specific prophecies of Micah have become history.

They are: (1) FALL of Samaria in 722 B.C. (1:6-7)

(2) INVASION of Judah in 702 B.C. (1:9-16)

(3) FALL of Jerusalem in 586 B.C. (3:12 and 7:13)

(4) CAPTIVITY in Babylon in 586 B.C. (4:10)

(5) RETURN from captivity (4:1-8; 7:11, 14-17)

(6) BIRTH of Jesus in Bethlehem (5:2)

HOW MUCH DO YOU REMEMBER?

Q. The Edomites came from_____.

Q. Did Edom perish as a nation?

Q What names were given to Edom's capital?

Q. Is the Book of Jonah literal–?

Q. Why did Jonah flee?

Q. What does Jonah signify according to the words of Jesus?

Q. Micah is remembered best for what prophecy?

YOUR ASSIGNMENT FOR NEXT WEEK

1. Read Nahum, Habakkuk, Zephaniah, only 9 chapters in all three Books.
2. Review your notes of this weeks lesson. Mark your Bible.
3. Be present next Lord's Day for three more Prophets of God.

Lesson 24
"The Books of Nahum, Habakkuk, Zephaniah"

(Where lines are provided, please look up Scriptures and fill in the entire Scripture or the main Truth of the passage.)

1. **Nahum**

   Nahum prophesied about one hundred and fifty years after Jonah. He has the same subject as Jonah — *"the destruction of Ninevah."* There is little known about the prophet Nahum. It is only surmised that he was from the Galilee area and from the area of Capernaum, the name (Kapher-Nahum) means Village of Nahum. Nahum addressed Judah (1:15).

2. **The Central Message**

   "The Lord is slow to anger — great in power — and will not at all acquit the wicked" (1:3).

3. **The Structure of the Book**
   * The Certainty of Ninevah's Doom — Chapter 1
   * The Siege and Capture of Ninevah — Chapter 2
   * The Reasons For Judgment — Chapter 3

4. **The Certainty of Ninevah's Doom — Chapter 1**

   Ninevah, the capital of Assyria, was the world's greatest city in Nahum's day. It is interesting to note that two of the Minor Prophets are devoted to this city, Jonah and Nahum. A century before, Jonah had preached to them, and now they had gone into deeper sin. In reading the two Books we see the goodness of God in Jonah and His severity in Nahum.

   Note especially Chapter 1:2-3 — also 1:6-8.

   Note 1:15 and compare with Isaiah 52:7. Now look at Romans 10:15.

5. **The Siege and Capture of Ninevah — Chapter 2**

   Ninevah is pictured as making preparation (2:1) for the attack from an alliance of the Medes, Babylonians, Scythians, and others. The battle is vividly described — the river gates opened and the palace dissolved (2:6).

6. **The Reasons For Judgment — Chapter 3**

   The chapter shows that Ninevah's *sins* (V-4-6) are the *causes* of her judgment. Ninevah fell in 608 B.C. according to the prophecy of Nahum. So completely was Ninevah destroyed that in the 2nd Century A.D. — even the site of it had become uncertain.

   There is some comfort here (and the name Nahum means "comfort"). As we think of how the ungodly flourish and beat down the innocent we know that God has pledged Himself to avenge in a day to come. Look up Luke 18:7-8 and Romans 12:19.

THE BOOK OF HABAKKUK

1. **The Book**

   The focus of Habakkuk's prophecy is Babylon. Obadiah spoke of the *fate of Edom* — Nahum the *fate of Assyria* — and Habakkuk the *fate of Babylon*.

   Habakkuk speaks to *God alone* about a problem that bothered him relating to Jehovah's government of the nations. The first part of the Book could be called a *colloquy* (a dialogue or discussion) between Habakkuk and Jehovah. The last part is a beautiful description of a "theophany" (a visible appearance of God).

   Habakkuk wrote shortly after the fall of Ninevah in 608 B.C. The Chaldeans (Babylonians) were rising to power (1:6). He wrote concerning Judah.

2. **The Central Message**

   "The just shall live by faith" — (2:4b).

3. **The Structure of the Book**

   - THE BURDEN — Chapter 1
   - THE VISION — Chapter 2
   - A PRAYER — Chapter 3

4. **"The Burden" — Chapter 1**

   The structure comes from the first thoughts of each chapter.

   In Chapter 1, Habakkuk was concerned and perplexed with the silence of God. Sin was abounding — and he cries out to God (1:2-4), and God answers in V-5-11. The prophet is wise to wait and "see what He will say — and what I shall answer" (2:1).

5. **"The Vision" — Chapter 2**

   God gave to Habakkuk a wonderful vision in Chapter 2 (Note V-2). Herein we find *two great pledges* which God gives in V-4 and 14. Verse 4 says: "Behold his soul (the Babylonian's) is puffed up; it is not upright in him; *but the just shall live by his faith.*" Verse 14 says: *"For the earth shall be filled with the knowledge of the glory of the Lord."*

   V-4 is so significant that it is quoted three times in the New Testament — Romans 1:17 _____

   _____

   Galatians 3:11 _____

   _____

   Hebrews 10:38 _____

   _____

   V-14 must be read in the light of the New Testament — Matthew 24:30; 25:31; II Thessalonians 1:7.

   Notice in 2:3 what the Lord says to Habakkuk — "the vision is for an appointed time — wait for it — it will surely come."

6. **"A Prayer" — Chapter 3**

   The prayer of Habakkuk begins with an appeal for revival. Read and underline 3:2.

   From V-3 to V-15 there is an expression of praise in Jehovah's works of the past.

   In the last part, V-16 through 19 we have *the joy of salvation* — the hilarity of faith. In circumstances at their worst we have here rejoicing at its best.

   Learn the lesson of placing your burden before the Lord and then *waiting*. God will answer. We can and should rejoice in spite of circumstances because "the earth shall be filled with the knowledge of the glory of the Lord."

THE BOOK OF ZEPHANIAH

1. **The Book**

   Zephaniah gives more of his background than do the other prophets. In V-1 he says he is the great-great-grandson of King Hezekiah. He prophesied in the days of Josiah and he was therefore a contemporary with Jeremiah (see Jer. 1:2). He was a prophet of Judah. Joel and Zephaniah are the prophets of judgment against Judah — yet both tell of a glorious deliverance.

2. **The Central Message**

   From desolation to deliverance.

3. **The Structure of the Book**

   > WRATH Coming On Judah — Chapters 1:1 to 2:3
   > WRATH On Nations — Chapters 2:4 to 3:8
   > WRATH to Healing — Chapter 3:9-20

4. **Wrath Coming On Judah — 1:1 to 2:3**

   Everything in this section refers to judgment that is coming on Judah in the form of the captivity by Babylon. Why all the wrath described in these verses? V-17 gives the answer — *"Because they have sinned against the Lord."* This section closes with an appeal for repentance and a word of encouragement to the small remnant.

5. **Wrath On Nations — 2:4 to 3:8**

   The prophet looks away from Judah and Jerusalem to the surrounding nations. First to the west, to Philistia and the Philistines (2:4-7). Then he turns east to Moab and Ammon (2:8-11). Then south to Ethiopia (2:12). Then north to Ninevah and Assyria (2:13-15). He concludes by turning to Jerusalem again to indicate that if God so smites the surrounding nations with judgment, then certainly He will smite the people of Judah who have had privileges above all others (note 3:6-8).

6. **From Wrath to Healing — 3:9-20**

   Here the prophet is not looking *within* at Jerusalem and Judah — nor looking *around* at the surrounding nations — he is looking *beyond* to a time of healing and blessing. The coming Messianic Kingdom is to embrace all nations and the covenant people are to be the center of that kingdom. Zephaniah says this in the concluding verses (3:11-20). All afflictions are to be over and Israel is to be made "a praise among all the people of the earth" — V-20.

HOW MUCH DO YOU REMEMBER?

Q. What is the main subject of Nahum?

Q. What other prophet had the same subject?

Q. What is the Central Truth of Habakkuk?

Q. What did Habakkuk pray for?

Q. Why did Zephaniah predict the wrath that was to come on Judah?

Q. What did he see in the future for Israel?

YOUR ASSIGNMENT FOR NEXT WEEK:

1. Read all of Haggai, Zechariah and Malachi. This is about 2½ or 3 short Chapters each day.
2. Review your notes about today's lesson.
3. Mark your Bibles in Nahum, Habakkuk and Zephaniah.
4. Be present next Lord's Day for the last of the Old Testament.

Lesson 25
"The Books of Haggai, Zechariah and Malachi"

NOTES

(Where lines are provided, please look up Scriptures and fill in the entire Scripture or the main Truth of the passage.)

1. **The Books**

   Haggai, Zechariah and Malachi are known as the *Post-Captivity prophets*. They were God's messengers during this period of restoration of Jerusalem and the temple. The main appeal of Haggai and Zechariah was to inspire the Jews to finish building the temple which had been discontinued, while the message of Malachi was the tragic sin and apostasy of God's people. The spiritual revival of the return to the Holy City had turned to spiritual coldness and it seems significant that the last word of the Old Testament is the word "curse."

2. **Haggai**

   Haggai deals with a real situation in the lives of people. Not long after the Jewish "remnant" returned to Jerusalem and Judea, they began to neglect the things of the Lord and spend their time on building their own houses and forsook the rebuilding of the temple. For fourteen years they had been in this backslidden condition; and to this kind of a situation, the prophet Haggai was sent with God's message.

   He was among the first group to go to Jerusalem with Zerubbabel, Ezra 2:2. He was probably born in Babylon during the Captivity.

3. **The Central Message**

   "Consider your ways — build the house" (1:7-8).

4. **The Structure of the Book**
   - FIRST SERMON — Reproof — Chapter 1 (Sept. 1 to Sept. 24)
   - SECOND SERMON — Encouragement — Chapter 2:1-9 (Oct. 21)
   - THIRD SERMON — Blessing — Chapter 2:10-19 (Dec. 24)
   - FOURTH SERMON — Promise — Chapter 2:20-23 (Dec. 24)

   (Note that each message is dated in Scripture as indicated above.)

5. **First Sermon — Reproof — Chapter 1**

   Haggai's first sermon is to reprove the people for their neglect in building the Lord's house. They were postponing what they had gone to Jerusalem to accomplish. Note V-2 — *"These people say,* the time is *not* come — that the Lord's house should be rebuilt." Haggai says, "Consider your ways — build the house." The people were satisfied to sit in their homes and *"wait"* until the time came and they "felt" like doing it. This speaks to us today — we just wait and do not work. We must do both — *wait and work*.

6. **Second Sermon — Encouragement — 2:1-9**

   This is a word of encouragement by Haggai.

   He declares three great facts:

FIRST, Jehovah's covenant with Israel and His faithfulness to that covenant — V-5.

SECOND, the Spirit of God remains with them and they should have no fear — V-5.

THIRD, God says there shall be a great shaking of nations (the tribulation) and that one who is the Desire (Christ) of all nations shall come — and, "the glory of this latter House shall be greater than the former" — V-6-9.

These are the things which should inspire us — a convenant, the Spirit's presence and the promised return of our Lord.

7. Third Sermon — Blessing — 2:10-19

The people were to ask the priests concerning things of the law of Moses — V-11. The holy cannot make the unholy holy by *contact* but unholiness is *communicated by contact* — V-12-13. Haggai applies this to the Jews. Though they had returned to the land and rebuilt the temple, their hearts were far from God — V-14. God judged them because their hearts were not changed toward Him — V-15-17.

Then God says, "consider." God would bless them now because they had obeyed. He would bless because of His grace.

8. Fourth Sermon — Promise — 2:20-23

The message is directed to Zerubbabel, Governor of Judah. The message is the same as in V-6 and 7. It speaks of the final purpose of God. Gentile power will come to an end. "In that day" the Lord will make Zerubbabel a "signet" — a sign of authority, a guarantee of the greater David. It points to the Messiah. Zerubbabel was honored by a place in both genealogies of Christ — Matthew 1:12-17 and Luke 3:27. Christ is truly the Son of Zerubbabel as well as the Son of David. Zerubbabel was and is, a "signet" — prefiguring Christ. Christ the greater Son and the Antitype of David and Zerubbabel shall be the signet of Jehovah whereby He shall imprint His will, His perfect ideal upon all nations.

From the moment of obedience, God blesses each of us. Are you building the spiritual house of the Lord, His Church, made of living stones?

THE BOOK OF ZECHARIAH

1. The Book

Zechariah was contemporary with Haggai — Ezra 5:1; Haggai 1:1 and Zechariah 1:1. Zechariah supplemented the message of Haggai. He was both priest and prophet. He was the son of Berechiah, the son of Iddo, a prophet, (Neh. 12:4) — so this means that Zechariah was of the family of Aaron.

From the time of Zechariah and Haggai, the priesthood takes the lead in the nation. The history of God's people falls into three main periods:

From Moses to Samuel — Israel under Judges

From Saul to Zedekiah — Israel under Kings

From Jeshua to 70 A.D. — Israel under Priests

2. Its Prophecies

There are *more prophecies* of Christ in Zechariah than in any other prophetic Book *except Isaiah*. We shall list only some of the prophecies and at least one Scripture about the fulfillment:

PROPHECY OF CHRIST	FULFILLMENT
• SERVANT — Zech. 3:8	Matt. 12:18
• BRANCH — Zech. 3:8, 6:12	Luke 1:78
• KING-PRIEST — Zech. 6:13	Heb. 6:20-7:1
• LOWLY KING — Zech. 9:9-10	Matt. 21:4-5
• BETRAYED — Zech. 11:12-13	Matt. 27:9
• HANDS PIERCED — Zech. 12:10	John 19:37

- SMITTEN SHEPHERD — Zech. 13:7-9 . . . . Matt. 26:31
- SECOND COMING — Zech. 14:4, 9 . . . . Yet to be.

3. **The Central Truth**

"I am jealous for Jerusalem" — 1:14; 8:1.

4. **The Structure of the Book**

The Night Visions — Chapters 1-6
Four Messages — Chapters 7 and 8.
The Prophetic Burdens — Chapters 9-14.

5. **The Night Visions — Chapters 1-6**

Some students say there are seven visions, some say eight and others ten. I think one can remember them best if we separate the visions and when we do, there are ten. We shall have time to briefly look at each vision.

(1) THE RIDER ON THE RED HORSE — 1:8-17.

The meaning is — God is jealous for Jerusalem and Judgment is to fall upon the nations for abuse of His covenant people.

(2) THE FOUR HORNS — 1:18.

The four horns are the four nations that had scattered Israel — namely, Babylon, Medo-Persia, Greece and Rome.

(3) THE FOUR CARPENTERS — 1:20-21.

These are the instruments of judgment upon the four nations (above).

(4) THE MAN WITH THE MEASURING LINE — 2:1-13.

Jerusalem is not to be measured as man would measure — but the Lord Himself shall be a wall around the glorious city.

(5) JOSHUA THE HIGH PRIEST — 3:1-10.

This vision pictures the removing of iniquity and future glory for Israel. (Filthy garments removed and a mitre placed on the head and clean clothes.)

(6) THE GOLDEN CANDLESTICK AND TWO OLIVE TREES — 4:1-14.

God shall rebuild His temple and shall witness in the power — (4:6).

(7) THE FLYING SCROLL — 5:1-4.

When God builds His temple (as in last vision), His Word goes forth to judge. The scroll is the Word of God.

(8) THE EPHAH — 5:5-11.

The woman in the ephah, a measuring container and a symbol of trade, teaches that all corruption, all against God, should go to Babylon, the city of sin.

(9) THE FOUR CHARIOTS — 6:1-8.

These picture the judgments of the Lord upon the nations.

(10) THE SYMBOLIC CROWNING OF JOSHUA — 6:9-15.

This is a vision of the second coming of Christ.

The unifying idea in all of these visions is that which is expressed in the Central Message — *"I am jealous for Jerusalem – I am returned to Jerusalem"* — 1:14-16.

6. **Four Messages — Chapters 7 and 8**

These four messages found in 7:1-7, 7:8-14, 8:1-7 and 8:18-23 support the Central Message of Zechariah. God's purpose for Jerusalem is unchanged by any ritual or form. He was and is "a jealous God with great jealousy" for His people. These are messages which teach that *worship is a matter of the heart.*

7. **The Prophetic Burdens — Chapters 9-14**

(1) The FIRST burden is in Chapters 9-11.

Here we see the *first* coming of Christ 9:9 and the *second* coming in 9:10-17.

Chapter 10 is a picture of the covenant people scattered and finally restored in their land.

Chapter 11 depicts the first coming of Christ and the rejection of Him as Messiah — Note especially 11:13 and then compare with Matthew 27:9 _____

_____

_____

(2) The SECOND burden is in Chapters 12-14.

These Chapters form one prophecy. The theme is the return of Christ and the establishment of the kingdom on earth.

The order of events are:

- The siege of Jerusalem — 12:1-3
- The battle of Armageddon — V-4-9
- The grace of God and revelation of Christ to House of David — V-10
- Godly sorrow for rejecting Messiah at 1st advent — V-11-14
- The "cleansing fountain" opened to Israel — 13:1
- The summary of these events in Chapters 13-14 (Note 14:4)

Notice that the first and second advents are spoken of in these last chapters (9-14) with no reference to this age of the Church. Jehovah shall again take up and complete His grand purposes with and for and through Israel.

THE BOOK OF MALACHI

1. The Book

We come now to the last Book of the Old Testament. Malachi means "my messenger." He prophesied after the days of Nehemiah and the condition of the Jews had become deplorable. He is "the bridge" between the Old and New Testaments (3:1). Four hundred years of silence is between the voice of Malachi and the "voice of one crying in the wilderness" — (John 1:23).

2. The Central Message

"Behold, He shall come" — 3:1 (last line).

3. The Structure of the Book

- THE LOVE OF GOD STATED — 1:1-5
- THE LOVE OF GOD SCORNED — 1:6 — 2:17; 3:7-15
- THE LOVE OF GOD SHOWN — 3:1-6; 3:16 — 4:6

4. The Love of God Stated — 1:1-5

"I have loved you, saith the Lord," yet on every hand the Israelites asked the flippant questions of Jehovah. These questions came from irritated people who said God had failed to prove His love. Note the seven questions:

(1) Wherein hast thou loved us? 1:2

(2) Wherein have we despised thy name? 1:6

(3) Wherein have we polluted thee? 1:7

(4) Wherein have we wearied Him? 2:17

(5) Wherein shall we return? 3:7

(6) Wherein have we robbed thee? 3:8

(7) Wherein have we spoken against thee? 3:13

5. The Love of God Scorned — 1:6 — 2:17; 3:7-15

The love of God was scorned by the Prophets 1:6 — 2:9. They had cheated the Lord through lame and sick offerings. They gave less than the best. (Notice 1:12-13 especially)

The love of God was scorned by the people. First, by cheating their brother (2:10); then through intermarriage (2:11); by their immorality (2:14); by their insincerity (2:17); by their robbing God (3:8-10); by their speaking against the Lord (3:13-15).

6. **The Love of God Shown — 3:1-6; 3:16 to 4:6**

FIRST, by sending His Son — 3:1-6.

This was announced by John the Baptist. Compare 3:1 with Matt. 11:10

_____

_____

His second coming will be introduced by Elijah, the prophet — 4:5-6. Look up:

- Luke 1:11-17
- Matthew 11:10-14
- John 1:21

SECOND, by remembering His own — 3:16-17.

How precious to God are His own. A "Book of Remembrance" is written containing the "jewels" of the Lord.

The Old Testament closes with the paramount thought — *He is coming.* "Unto you that fear my name, shall the Sun of righteousness arise with healing in His wings" — 4:2.

"Even so, come, Lord Jesus!"

HOW MUCH DO YOU REMEMBER?

Q. Who are the three post-captivity prophets?

Q. What is the main message of Haggai?

Q. The prophecies of Isaiah and Zechariah give us more than any other prophets on the subject of _____?

Q. What is the theme or message of Zechariah?

Q. When did Malachi write his prophecy?

YOUR ASSIGNMENT FOR NEXT WEEK

1. Most Bibles will have a page or two between Malachi and Matthew about the period "from Malachi to Matthew" known as the 400 silent years. Read this in detail.
2. Review your notes on the lesson in this outline.
3. Mark your Bible.
4. Be present this Lord's Day for a study on the "Inter-Testament" period.

Lesson 26
"The Inter-Testament Period"
or
"The Four Hundred Silent Years"

(Where lines are provided, please look up Scriptures and fill in the entire Scripture or the main Truth of the passage.)

1. **The Four Hundred Years**

   The period between Malachi and Matthew covers about 400 years. We do not say that a knowledge of the period is necessary to understand the Gospels, but it is advantageous if we are to understand some of the sayings of our Lord and some of the groups He had to face.

   The Old Testament canon of Scripture closed with Malachi about 397 B.C.

2. **The Beginning**

   The condition of the Jews at the *beginning* of this four hundred year period should be remembered. Two hundred years earlier Jerusalem had been destroyed and the people carried into Babylonian Captivity (587 B.C.). (The Assyrians destroyed the Northern Kingdom of Israel 135 years earlier in 722 B.C.)

   Babylon was overthrown by the Medo-Persian empire, as had been predicted by Daniel (Chapters 2 and 7) and Cyrus issued the order for the Jews to return and build the temple. Under Zerubbabel a "remnant" returned and twenty-one years later the temple was completed (515 B.C.). Ezra then took a small group to Jerusalem and restored the worship in the temple — followed by Nehemiah twelve years later to rebuild the city walls.

   Such is the picture at the beginning of this period between Malachi and Matthew — the Jewish remnant back in Judah, temple and Jerusalem rebuilt, worship restored — but the great masses of the Jews remained in the land of their captivity.

   It is in the remnant that we find Jewish history preserved between the Old and New Testaments.

3. **The Political Background**

   The four hundred year history of the Jews between Malachi and Matthew runs in six periods:

        (1) THE PERSIAN — 538 B.C.
        (2) THE GREEK — 333 B.C.
        (3) THE EGYPTIAN — 323 B.C.
        (4) THE SYRIAN — 204 B.C.
        (5) THE MACCABEAN — 165 B.C.
        (6) THE ROMAN — 63 B.C. to Christ.

4. **The Persian Rule**

   The Persian rule over Palestine continued until Alexander the Great and his Greek empire in 333 B.C. This was the second empire mentioned by Daniel. This means that the Jews were under the Persian rule at the end of Malachi and remained under them for the *first sixty years of the Inter-Testament Period.*

through the Bible in one year

NOTES

During this same period, the *rival worship* of the Samaritans became established. Back in 721 B.C. the Northern Kingdom of Israel, the ten tribes, were scattered by Assyria to "the cities of the Medes." The Assyrian emperor repeopled the cities of Israel with a mixed people known as the Samaritans. It was from this people that Nehemiah faced opposition on his way to Jerusalem. (Neh. 2:10 and 4:1-3) The rivalry persisted through the New Testament times.

5. **The Greek Rule**

Alexander the Great, at twenty years of age, transformed the face of the world in ten years. He is spoken of by Daniel in his prophecy in Daniel 7:6; Daniel 8:1-7 and 21-23.

6. **The Egyptian Rule**

This was the *longest of the six periods* in the Inter-Testament Period. The death of Alexander the Great resulted in Judea falling into the hands of the *first Ptolemaic ruler,* (i.e. Ptolemies were the line of Greek kings over Egypt), Ptolemy Soter. The second Ptolemy (Philadelphus) founded the Alexandrian library and the famous *Septuagint translation of the Old Testament was made from the Hebrew to the Greek during this reign.*

Palestine was becoming the battle ground between Egypt and Syria (Seleucidae were the line of Syrian kings.)

7. **The Syrian Rule**

This was the *most tragic part of the Inter-Testament Period* for the Jews. With the coming to power of Antiochus Epiphanes in 175 B.C., a reign of terror fell on all Jews. He wrecked Jerusalem, tore down the walls and killed the people. He desecrated the temple in every way — culminating in the offering of a pig on the altar of sacrifice and then erecting statues of false gods on the altar. (Dan. 8:13)

8. **The Maccabean Period**

This was one of the most heroic periods in all history. The excesses of Antiochus Epiphanes provoked the movement by the aged priest Mattathias, and carried on by his son, Judas Maccabeus. Judas Maccabeus restored the temple and orthodox services were reinstituted (following the desecration by Antiochus). Judas Maccabeus was killed in one of the battles with the Syrians. His brother, Jonathan, became leader and high priest, uniting the civil and priestly authority in one person, thus commencing the Hasmonean line of high priests (from Hashman, great grandfather of the Maccabee brothers). Jonathan was killed and Simon, his brother, was made leader. Simon was killed and his able son John Hyrcanus reigned twenty-nine years. After changes among the Hasmonean leaders, the Herod family appears on the scene, leading to the Roman period.

9. **The Roman Rule**

Judea became a province of the Roman Empire. When the Maccabean line ended, Antipater was appointed over Judea by Julius Caesar in 47 B.C. Antipater appointed Herod, his son, governor of Galilee. He was appointed king of the Jews by Rome in 40 B.C. He murdered almost all of his own family including his wife and sons. *This was the "Herod the Great" who was king when our Lord was born.*

This is the political background of the Jews during the 400 year period.

10. **The Religious Background During the Four Hundred Years**

The political background changed the Jews but no more than the changes in their Jewish religious customs. There were new groups such as the Scribes, Pharisees, Sadducees and new institutions such as the Synogogue and Sanhedrin.

Because of these changes in Jewry, the period between Malachi and Matthew is important.

The *Oral Law,* after being given orally for generations was committed to writing about the end of the *second century A.D.* into the TALMUD and it remains the authority for Jews to this day. In our Lord's day the Oral Law was still mainly oral. He contradicted its obstacles in Matthew 15:1-9 and in the Sermon on the Mount He said six times, "Ye have heard that it was *said* — but I say unto you." His way of referring to the Scriptures was, *"It is written."*

11. The Pharisees and Sadducees

The Pharisees held that the Oral Law was given orally to Moses, to Joshua, to the elders, to the prophets and then to the men of the Great Synogogue. *The Pharisees were the interpreters of the Oral Law.*

The Sadducees rejected all this, holding to only "the law," meaning the *Pentateuch*. They denied the spirit world of angels, immortality, resurrection from the dead (Acts 23:8) while the Pharisees affirmed all of these doctrines. They always opposed each other.

The name *"Pharisee"* means *"separatists." "Sadducees"* means *"righteous ones."*

You will find references to the Pharisees in Luke 7:39; Luke 15:2 and Matthew 9:11 and many other places.

The Sadducees are mentioned in Matthew 16:11; Matthew 16:1 and 22:23. Also in Acts 23:6.

12. The Scribes

From the time of the Babylonian Captivity, there developed a new line of scribes who were not just transcribers or secretaries, but a new body of men who became the expounders, guardians and teachers of the Scriptures. They became *a distinguished order* in the nation.

They must be distinguished from the priests and the Pharisees. They are mentioned in Scripture along with the Pharisees, i.e., Matthew 5:20, 12:38; 15:1; Mark 2:16; Luke 5:21 but this does not mean that they were alike or even together in function.

Our Lord denounced the scribes because of their corruption and outward piousness — Matthew 23:13-18.

13. The Synagogue

There is not a word about synagogues in the Old Testament, but as soon as we start the New Testament we find them everywhere. The synagogue did not exist before the captivity but it seems to have originated during that time — when the Jews totally turned away from idolatry. There was no longer a Jewish temple and they needed and longed for the reading of the Scriptures. This is believed to be the way the synagogue came into being.

Synagogue discourses were common in our Lord's time — Matthew 4:23; 9:35; Luke 4:15, 44; Acts 13:5; 14:1; 17:10; 18:19.

The synagogue was *congregational* and not priestly. The great institution of preaching had its *beginning* in the synagogue. It was from this background that the early Christian church, as organized by the apostles, took its main form of worship. The titles given to the New Testament church leaders: Elders, Bishops, Deacons are all carried over from the synagogue.

14. The Sanhedrin

There is another Jewish institution called the Sanhedrin, which in New Testament times was the *supreme civil and religious tribunal* of the Jewish nation. WITH THAT BODY MUST LIE THE REAL RESPONSIBILITY FOR THE CRUCIFYING OF THE LORD JESUS. Pontius Pilate was merely a "rubber stamp" of imperial Rome.

The Sanhedrin is referred to in all of the following verses, even though the Greek word "sunedrion" is translated "council:"

- Matthew 16:59
- Mark 14:55
- Mark 15:1
- Acts 4:15
- Acts 5:21, 27, 34, 41
- Acts 6:12, 15

- Luke 22:66
- John 11:47

- Acts 22:30
- Acts 23:1, 6, 15, 20, 28
- Acts 24:20

The Sanhedrin was made up of the high priest: twenty-four "chief priests" who represented the twenty-four orders of the priesthood; twenty-four "elders" called "elders of the people" (Matt. 21:23); twenty-two "scribes" who interpreted the law in both religious and civil matters. This made a total of seventy-one members of the Sanhedrin.

Is there a more tragic verse in the history of Israel than Matt. 26:59?

_____

_____

They had to have the sanction of Pilate for the penalty they imposed on the Lord. The met *illegally* in the high priest's palace (John 18:15) instead of in its own council hall. All surrounding their actions in reference to the death of Christ was illegal and wrong.

With this brief and incomplete background, we can see some of the institutions that were established during this 400 year period between Malachi and Matthew.

For more material on this period read Books 11, 12 and 13 of Josephus and 1 and 2 Maccabees.

We shall study the introduction to the New Testament and the four Gospels collectively next week in Lesson 27. Then we shall devote the next study, Lesson 28, to the Book of Matthew, etc.

YOUR ASSIGNMENT FOR NEXT WEEK
1. In your Bible (most translations) there is an introduction to "The Four Gospels" giving in detail their purpose and the presentation by the four writers of our Lord. Read this in detail at least twice.
2. Review the lesson on the period between Malachi and Matthew.
3. Mark the Scriptures in your Bible.
4. Be present next Lord's Day for the beginning of the New Testament Study.

Lesson 27
"Introduction to the New Testament and the Four Gospels Collectively"

(Where lines are provided, please look up Scriptures and fill in the entire Scripture or the main Truth of the passage.)

1. **Right Idea About the New Testament**

   We have often heard advice given that in coming to the New Testament we should have no preconceived ideas, but just have an open mind. This advice is not really sound because an open mind is not necessarily a blank mind. We may miss a great deal in the New Testament if we come to it without certain right ideas.

   The one right idea you should remember about the New Testament is this:

   > DOMINATING ALL THE NEW TESTAMENT IS THE CHARACTERISTIC THOUGHT AND CONCEPT OF FULFILLMENT.

2. **Fulfillment — the keynote of the New Testament**

   Matthew, from the beginning, sets out with the keynote *twelve times:*
   - Matthew 1:22 — "That it might be fulfilled"
   - Matthew 2:15, 17, 23 — "That it might be fulfilled"
   - Matthew 4:14 — "That it might be fulfilled"
   - Matthew 8:17 — "That it might be fulfilled"
   - Matthew 12:17 — "That it might be fulfilled"
   - Matthew 13:35 — "That it might be fulfilled"
   - Matthew 21:4 — "That it might be fulfilled
   - Matthew 26:56 — "That it might be fulfilled"
   - Matthew 27:9 and 35 — "That it might be fulfilled"

   Our Lord's first word as He began His ministry was "Thus it becomes us to *fulfill*" — Matthew 3:15.

   "I came to *fulfill*" — Matthew 5:17.

   Mark records, "The time is *fulfilled,* the kingdom of God is at hand" (recording the words of Jesus) — Mark 1:15.

   Luke recorded the words of Jesus, "This day is the Scripture *fulfilled* in your ears" — Luke 4:21.

   John, instead of giving the Lord's first declaration gives the reaction of those who received Him — John 1:41, "We have found" and again in 1:45. Then John emphasizes the same as the other Gospel writers — "That it might be *fulfilled*" seven times:

   John 12:38; 13:18; 15:25; 17:12; 19:24; 19:28 and 36.

3. **The New Testament is the answer to the Old**

   More precisely, *Christ is the fulfillment* of all that the prophets saw, the psalmists sang and hearts hoped for.

   Let us illustrate:

   You have read through the Old Testament and the thing that probably made a lasting impression is the prevalence of animal sacrifice.

   From Genesis 4 on you have read of these sacrifices and ceremonies. The impression clings in your mind that these point to realities outside themselves, yet this is not clearly explained.

through the Bible in one year

NOTES

You also read of God's covenant with Noah, with Abraham, renewed with Isaac and Jacob. You saw the twelve tribes freed from bondage in Egypt, given a Law at Sinai, invade and occupy Canaan. Then comes the Judges with decline and punishment of Israel — followed by the Books of Samuel with the change from a theocracy to a monarchy.

The Kings bring the division of the kingdom and both kingdoms taken into captivity. The Chronicles review the tragic story. In Ezra, Nehemiah and Esther, only a remnant returns to Judea. The temple and walls rebuilt but the throne of David no more. You read on through the personal Books but there is nothing to shine light on the remnant or the ones scattered abroad — neither in the prophets until Haggai, Zechariah and Malachi where we find things far from being well with the remnant and you feel *again* — a purpose unfulfilled.

You also read the unique Old Testament prophecy. It spoke to you, and does now, as no other about the future. It all focuses on the idea that SOMEONE IS COMING. Malachi says, "The Lord whom ye seek, shall come" (3:1). But the Old Testament closes with that unfulfilled.

4. But Now — The New Testament completes and fulfills the Old

The sacrifices of the Old point to our Lord — the *One* sacrifice. The unfulfilled purpose of God with His people now is fulfilled in their Messiah and our Messiah. The prophecies of the Old Testament find their fulfillment in our blessed Lord.

In the Old Testament He *is* coming — in the Gospels He *has* come — in the Epistles He has come *in* by the blessed Holy Spirit — in the Revelation He is coming *again*. The fulfillments at His first coming prove Old Testament prophecy to be Divine — and equally guarantees that the unfulfilled remainder in both Old and New shall surely come to pass.

5. The Four Gospels

Why are there four Gospels? The fact is that with perfect naturalness Matthew, Mark, Luke and John have given us four unique presentations of the Lord Jesus, each having its own emphasis — with all four going together to make a full portrayal of the God-Man — Jesus, our Lord.

There is a significant parallel between the four Gospels and the "four living creatures" of Ezekiel. Ezekiel 1:10 says, "As for the likeness of their faces, they four had the face of a *man,* and the face of a *lion,* on the right side; and they four had the face of an *ox* on the left side; they four also had the face of an *eagle.*" The lion speaks of strength and kingship — the man, highest intelligence — the ox of lowly service — the eagle speaks of heavenliness, Divinity.

Thus, in the four Gospels we see:

> In Matthew, the *Messiah-King* (the lion).
>
> In Mark, *Jehovah's Servant* (the ox).
>
> In Luke, the *Son of Man* (the man).
>
> In John, the *Son of God* (the eagle).

As *Sovereign,* He comes to reign and rule. As *Servant,* He comes to serve and suffer. As the *Son of Man,* He comes to share and to sympathize. As the *Son of God,* He comes to redeem. In the four Gospels we see — sovereignty, humility, humanity and deity.

6. The Emphasis of the Four Writers

If we follow the parallel of the four writers to the four emblems of Ezekiel — we see that they are one likeness of the same wonderful Person — the Lord Jesus:

(1) MATTHEW — The lion was the emblem of the tribe of Judah, the royal tribe of David. In Matthew our Lord is uniquely *"the Lion of the tribe of Judah,"* "the Root of David" (Rev. 5:5 and Isa. 11:1 and 10). He is "the King — the Lord our Righteousness" (Jeremiah 23:5). The opening sentence of Matthew gives the key; "The Book

of the generation of Jesus Christ, the Son of David, the Son of Abraham." (Note 1:17) Mark has no such genealogy while Luke goes right back to *Adam* and John back to *eternity*.

Matthew is the Gospel in which our Lord offers Himself to the Jews as their Messiah-King.

(2) MARK — The ox is the emblem of lowly service. The Gospel of Mark is the "Gospel of Action." No genealogy is given. The emphasis is on the *activity of Christ* — the lowly Servant. The characteristic word is "straightway."

(3) LUKE — There is "the face of man." There is no obscuring of His kingship or His Deity, nor His humanity. His lovely manhood is lifted up as Luke tells of His parents and His birth and even then He is called *"King"* and *"Saviour."* Luke tells of His boyhood. Luke 2:41-52.

(4) JOHN — The aspect corresponding to the eagle finishes the pattern of Ezekiel. John goes back to eternity. "In the beginning was the Word (Jesus); and the Word (Jesus) was with God; and the Word (Jesus) was God — All things were made by Him; and without Him was not anything made that was made. In Him was life; and the life was the light of men." (John 1:1-4).

John presents Him as the "Son of God" (1:18 & 34). He is the *"Word,"* the *"Light,"* the *"Life,"* the *"Son."* He is God manifest in the flesh. He is the God-Man.

7. **The Unique Differences of the Four Gospel Writers**

Matthew writes with reference to the *Hebrew mind,* as you will note from his references to the Old Testament.

Mark, the traveling companion of Peter, writes primarily to the *Roman mind,* presenting our Lord pronouncedly as the miracle worker.

Luke, the travel companion of Paul, and a doctor, writes to the *Greek mind* with emphasis upon the matchless manhood of the Lord.

John, the writer of the Divine nature of our Lord could be called the author to the *Church* but there is more than just a message to the Church. He reveals Jesus to the whole world, without racial distinction, as the revelation of Divine "grace and truth" through the "Word that became flesh and dwelt among us, and we beheld His glory, the glory as of the only begotten of the Father."

8. **The Characteristic Endings of the Four Gospels**

Matthew ends with our LORD'S RESURRECTION (Matthew 28).
Mark ends his Book with the LORD'S ASCENSION (Mark 16:19-20).
Luke ends with the blessed promise of the HOLY SPIRIT (Luke 24:49).
John ends the four with the promise of our Lord's SECOND COMING (John 21:20-23).

Thus we see that Matthew, the *Gospel of the Messiah-King* should end with the resurrection — the crowning proof of His Messiahship.

Mark, the *Gospel of the Lowly Servant,* ends with the lowly One exalted in place of Glory and Honor.

Luke, the *Gospel of Ideal Man,* ends with the promise of a Comforter to man.

John, the *Gospel of the Divine Son,* ends with the Lord's own promise of His return.

Thus, the four Gospels, are distinctly the work of the Holy Spirit through the writers to give us a complete portrait of our Blessed Lord.

HOW MUCH DO YOU REMEMBER?

Q. What is the prominent thought in the New Testament as you leave the Old?

Q. What does the New Testament do to the Old in your opinion?

Q. Why are there four Gospel writers?

Q. How is Christ presented by the four Gospel writers?

Q. What are the unique differences of the four writers?

YOUR ASSIGNMENT FOR NEXT WEEK

1. There are 28 chapters in Matthew. This means only 4 chapters each day. Try to read the entire Book. To leave out any part would hinder your understanding of Christ as King.
2. Review our introduction to the New Testament and the Gospels.
3. Mark your Bible.
4. Be ready to begin Matthew next Lord's Day — starting the New Testament.

Lesson 28
"The Book of Matthew"

NOTES

(Where lines are provided, please look up Scriptures and fill in the entire Scripture or the main Truth of the passage.)

1. **The Four Gospels**

   As we enter the New Testament, remember that the four Gospels, Matthew, Mark, Luke and John present four unique presentations of the Lord Jesus:

   - MATTHEW — the Messiah-King
   - MARK — Jehovah's Servant
   - LUKE — the Son of Man
   - JOHN — the Son of God

   The first three Gospels are often called *Synoptic Gospels,* (meaning "affording a general — same or collective view") while the Book of John is separated both in time and character.

   The Synoptists present the *outer, human* and *public* aspects of our Lord's life.

   John reveals the *inner, Divine* and *private* aspects of His life.

   Matthew, then deals with the Lord Jesus and presents Him as King, the Son of David, the Son of Abraham, Solomon and Joseph (the legal descent of Jesus) Matthew 1:1-16, Luke 3:23-38 records His descent through Mary.

2. **Matthew**

   Matthew is the author of the Book. He was a "publican" (10:3), a Jew who had become a tax collector for the hated Romans and is thus classified with "publicans and sinners," which indicated the low moral level. He is also known as Levi in Luke 5:27 and Mark 2:14.

   He became a disciple of Jesus (9:9) then an apostle (one sent forth) in Chapter 10:2-3.

3. **The Central Message**

   > *"That it might be fulfilled."*

   (Matthew speaks to the Old Testament in presenting the promised Messiah, as King, in the statement *twelve* times — "That it might be fulfilled.")

4. **The Structure of the Book**

   (1) INTRODUCTION — Chapter 1 through 4:1-11.

   GENEALOGY — Birth of Christ, His Baptism and Temptation.

   (2) HIS MINISTRY IN GALILEE — 4:12 through Chapter 18.

   HIS TEACHINGS — Chapters 5 through 7.
   HIS WORK Chapters 8 through 10.
   THE REACTION of the people — Chapters 11 through 18.

   (3) HIS MINISTRY IN JUDEA — Chapters 19 through 28.

   PRESENTATION AS KING — Chapters 19 through 25.
   THE EVENTS OF HIS CRUCIFIXION — Chapters 26 through 27.
   THE GLORIOUS RESURRECTION — Chapter 28.

5. **The Introduction — Chapters 1 through 4:1-11**

   (1) Why the genealogy at the first? Matthew wrote primarily for the Jews, who according to their Scripture, the Old Testament, believed their Messiah to come through a certain family. Matthew had only to begin with Abraham, the father of the Hebrew nation — then show the descent through David and the covenant promise of the Messiah. Note in 1:17 there are 42 generations (male line) from Abraham to Christ. This is a miracle. Luke 3:23-38 records His genealogy through Mary conceived by the Holy Spirit.

   (2) The Birth of Christ and events surrounding His coming.

   The Old Testament prophecies and their fulfillment are listed. Look these up and mark your Bible:

PROPHECY	NEW TESTAMENT FULFILLMENT
• Isaiah 7:14	• Matthew 1:22-23
• Isaiah 11:1	• Matthew 2:23
• Jeremiah 31:15	• Matthew 2:17-18
• Hosea 11:1	• Matthew 2:15
• Micah 5:2	• Matthew 2:5-6

   (3) Immediately after His baptism (Matthew 3), He was tempted (Matthew 4). It is vital to realize that our Lord was tempted as a MAN. He was tempted in all ways — *body,* "command these stones to be made bread;" *soul,* "cast thyself down;" *spirit,* "fall down and worship me." That is Satan's technique, physical, mental, and spiritual.

6. **His Ministry in Galilee — 4:12 through 18**

   In Chapter 4:12 we read, "Now when Jesus heard that John was cast in prison, *He departed to Galilee.*"

   (1) HIS TEACHINGS — In Chapters 5 through 7 we have our Lord's *teachings,* commonly called the *Sermon On the Mount.* This famous teaching concerns:

   - VIRTUES, MORALS, MOTIVES — Chapters 5 through 6:18
   - MATERIAL, TEMPORAL, SOCIAL — 6:19 to 7:6
   - ENCOURAGEMENT, SUMMARY, EXHORTATION — 7:7 to 7:27

   The Sermon On the Mount is the law of the Kingdom of our Lord. Fourteen times Jesus says, "I say unto you," as He deals with the law of Moses (mark these in your Bible). There is much to be found in this sermon for practical living today. Read and note —

   - the two WAYS — 7:13
   - the two GATES — 7:14
   - the two DESTINATIONS — 7:21-23
   - the two FOUNDATIONS — 7:24-27

   (2) HIS WORKS — Chapters 8 through 10.

   In these three chapters are recorded *ten* miracles. Name the miracle after each Scripture listed:

   8:1-4 _____

   8:5-13 _____

   8:14-15 _____

   8:23-27 _____

   8:28-34 _____

   9:1-8 _____

   9:18-22 _____

   9:23-26 _____

9:27-31 _____

9:32-34 _____

Only these ten are mentioned in detail even though 9:35 says He went about "healing every sickness and disease." Note the remarkable things said and questions asked as Jesus performed these miracles — Read Matthew 8:18-22; 9:9-13; 9:14-17.

In Chapter 10, Jesus chose the twelve to be His witnesses after He returned to His Father. They, in turn, must train others. Matthew records more of Jesus' instructions to the twelve than do the other Gospels. The Jews were to hear the Gospel first (10:5) then to the Gentiles, Matthew 28:19.

(3) THE REACTIONS OF THE PEOPLE — Chapters 11 through 18.

The "*kingdom*" — a word used *55 times* in this Book sets forth the Gospel of the King. The Jews well understood the term. At Sinai, God said to Israel, "Ye shall be unto me a kingdom of priests and an holy nation" — (Ex. 19:6). The prophets had referred to it over and over again.

After the teachings of Christ in reference to the Kingdom the results of His Galilean ministry are evident:

(a) QUESTIONING — JOHN THE BAPTIST — 11:2-15

(b) UNREPENTING CITIES — 11:20-30

(c) UNREASONABLE PHARISEES — 12:10, 14, 24

(d) UNBELIEVING MULTITUDES — 13:13-15

(e) TRADITIONAL SCRIBES — 15:1-2

(f) "PROOF" DESIRED BY PHARISEES AND SADDUCEES — 16:1

The 13th Chapter gives the "Parables of the Kingdom of Heaven" (13:11) and this would require one entire lesson.

We cannot leave this section without looking at Chapter 16:17-18. When the kingdom was rejected, Jesus and His disciples went to Caesarea Philippi and there He disclosed the great truth of "the Church." The word "Church" means "called out ones" from "ecclesia." He began to build a new edifice, a new body of both Jew and Gentile (Ephesians 2:14-18 — read this). Read Acts 10:34-48.

7. **His Ministry in Judaea — Chapters 19 through 28**

Chapter 19 begins with "And it came to pass when Jesus had finished these sayings, He departed from Galilee and came to the coasts of Judaea." From this point His ministry is in Jerusalem and Judaea.

(1) HIS PRESENTATION AS KING — Chapters 19 through 25.

By this we mean our Lord's public presentation of Himself at Jerusalem as Israel's Messiah-King.

The journey to the city is in Chapters 19 and 20. Our Lord knew the outcome of His appearance — 20:17-19 and 28.

Our Lord's triumphal entry in 21:1-17 we see that He did offer Himself as Israel's Messiah-King and thereby fulfilled Zechariah 9:9.

_____

_____

In Chapter 21:18 through Chapter 23 conflict is noted — they rejected Him and He rejected them (the scoffers and sects). He who had announced eight "Blesseds" in Galilee now pronounced eight "woes" in Jerusalem.

The Olivet Discourse of things to come is found in Chapters 24 and 25. It was uttered *outside* the city. This is sure prophecy spoken by the true Prophet. The triumphal entry of Jesus ends with His words of ultimate triumph.

You may ask — "If Jesus foreknew of His rejection, why did He offer Himself to Jerusalem at all?" Our Lord never once mentions His crucifixion apart from the resurrection. Look up:

Matthew 16:21 _____

_____

Matthew 17:22-23 _____

_____

Matthew 20:17-20 _____

_____

Matthew 26:28-32 _____

_____

We are now in a period when we can see the prophecies of the Olivet Discourse unfolding before our eyes each day.

(2) THE EVENTS OF HIS CRUCIFIXION — Chapters 26 through 27.

FIRST, we see the Lord is withdrawn with the twelve (26:1-56). Christ foresaw all that was to happen —.

Note 26:12_____:

then at supper He reveals betrayal by Judas,

26:25 _____:

then He states "His blood is the blood of the new covenant" —

26:28 _____.

SECOND, Jesus is before the governing body of the Sanhedrin, (26:57-75) and was condemned for claiming to be Israel's Messiah. *He remained silent!* Then He said, "Thou hast said" — V-64. Charged with blasphemy, He was sentenced to die — V-66.

THIRDLY, He is before a Roman governor (27:1-26).

FOURTH, the Crucifixion (27:27-66). Matthew describes more vividly than Mark, Luke or John the miraculous happenings surrounding His death — the darkness at mid-day, the earthquake, the cleaving rocks, the graves disturbed — the rending of the veil of the temple from top to bottom.

The Crucified is the Son of God!

(3) THE GLORIOUS RESURRECTION — Chapter 28.

One short chapter — 20 verses — gives the climax to all that is victorious to our faith. Matthew is not concerned with theological argument of the fact — but only in the fact itself.

- The angel announced the resurrection — 28:1-7.
- The Lord Jesus is seen — V-8-10.
- The Jewish authorities lie about it — V-11-15.
- The commission to the eleven and to us — V-16-20.

8. **Additional Study in Matthew:**

(1) PARABLES — The Lord spoke in Matthew 13 in parables for a reason. Note the question of his disciples in 13:10. His answer explains His use of parables.

Read 13:11 _____

_____

(2) "PETER AND THE CHURCH" — Matthew 16.

Every believer should know that the Church was and is not built on Simon Peter. The actual translation of 16:18 is "Thou art PETROS (a stone) and upon this PETRA (a mighty rock, i.e. CHRIST) I will build My Church." Christ founded the "ecclesia," "the called out ones" on Him, the Rock of our salvation.

(3) THE OLIVET DISCOURSE — Matthew 24 and 25.

This is our Lord's own account of the end time. Studied together with all Scripture references in your Bible margin will help you.

(4) THE SEVEN LAST WORDS OF JESUS ON THE CROSS

(Most people think they are all in one Gospel in order. They are not.) Here are the Seven Last Words.

- Luke 23:34
- Luke 23:43
- John 19:26
- Matthew 27:46
- John 19:28
- John 19:30
- Luke 23:46

HOW MUCH DO YOU REMEMBER?

Q. Matthew presents Christ as the _____.

Q. What are the first three Gospels called?

Q. What is the great theme of Matthew?

Q. Why did Matthew give one genealogy and Luke another?

Q. Matthew presents the ministry of Christ in two regions. Name them.

YOUR ASSIGNMENT FOR NEXT WEEK

1. Read the Book of Mark — 16 Chapters, less than 3 Chapters each day.
2. Review your lesson in Matthew.
3. Mark your Bible from notes made in class.
4. Be present for Mark's Gospel next Lord's Day.

Lesson 29
"The Book of Mark"

(Where lines are provided, please look up Scriptures and fill in the entire Scripture or the main Truth of the passage.)

1. **A Background**

   The four Gospels deal with the same basic material and the first three are called the "Synoptists," meaning "syn" = "together" and "opsis" = "a view" — thus Matthew, Mark and Luke are the Synoptists (giving a like view) while John relates the Divine aspects of our Lord's life.

   Mark, known throughout Scripture as John Mark, wrote for the Romans (primarily). John was his Jewish name while Mark was his Roman name. He was a Jew, the son of a Mary (Acts 12:12). He was a companion of Paul on some of his journeys. He was a learner and a close companion of Peter. It is believed that Peter won Mark to the Lord and that Peter's style and influence is seen throughout this Gospel of Mark (see I Peter 5:13).

2. **Mark**

   Mark presents Christ as the *Servant*. Mark presents what Jesus *did* — Jesus at *work*. The works of Jesus proved who He was. There is no opening genealogy, as in Matthew, nor is there an account of the birth of Christ. Mark reaches in Chapter 1 what Matthew takes eight chapters to cover. Mark omits much of what Jesus *said*.

   Mark gives *work after work* of the Lord — recording twenty miracles in detail. The key word "EUTHEOS" translated "straightway," "immediately," "forthwith." Examples: 1:10, 18, 20, 21, 29, 31, 42, 43 (all in Chapter 1). The word occurs 42 times in Mark — only 7 times in Matthew and only 1 time in Luke.

3. **The Central Message**

   "The Son of Man came not to be ministered unto, but to minister, and to give His life a ransom for many" — Mark 10:45.

   HE IS JEHOVAH'S SERVANT

   Look up Philippians 2:7-8: _____

   _____

   _____

4. **The Structure of the Book**
   - Sanctification (Introduction) — Chapter 1:1-13
   - Service — Chapters 1:14 through 8:30
   - Sacrifice — Chapter 8:31 through 15
   - Resurrection and Ascension — Chapter 16

5. **The Introduction — Sanctification — 1:1-13**

   Mark wastes no time in introducing us to Jesus. He states simply in 1:1, "The beginning of the Gospel of Jesus Christ" — notice Mark does not present the beginning of Jesus but of the Gospel.

   Then four voices announce the Lord Jesus:
   - V-1 — Mark — "Jesus Christ, the SON OF GOD"
   - V-3 — Isaiah — "Prepare ye the way of THE LORD"
   - V-7 — John the Baptist — "There cometh ONE MIGHTIER"

- V-11 — God — "Thou art MY BELOVED SON"

This *One,* the "beginning of the Gospel" is thus introduced, and immediately was tested. Notice V-12 — "the Spirit driveth Him" indicating Divine permission and in V-13 "tempted of Satan" — indicating *real* temptation.

6. **Service — (Works of Jesus) — 1:14 through 8:30**

The ministry of Jesus in Galilee begins by his "preaching the Gospel of the Kingdom" — 1:14-15.

He selected four to become the first of the twelve — 1:16-20.

He *taught* (V-21), the people were *astonished (V-22) at His doctrine, demons* cast out (V-23-26), a *fever* healed (V-30), *invalids* cured (V-34), *leper* healed (V-41) — the people *amazed* at His *authority* (V-27), His *fame* (V-45) spread through Galilee. All this in Chapter 1 — fast, rapid, as you would expect of Mark.

CHAPTER 2 brings quick reaction:
    — from the Scribes — V-7
    — from the Pharisees — V-16 and 24

Notice the perfect answers of Jesus — V-8-11 and 17.

These two Chapters are examples of the mighty works of the Master while in Chapter 3 He ordained the twelve, and faced more opposition — taught in parables in Chapter 4.

The remainder of this part of our Structure of the Book is an accounting of His work with the disciples, more miracles and more opposition. Such miracles revealed the identity of Christ — the like had never been witnessed before in all the earth. This was truly the Son of God — the people flocked to see and hear — the healed, the thankful, the blessed — all applauded Him.

The light dims and the scene changes very suddenly. Just after Peter tells Jesus, "Thou art the Christ" — the Lord began to teach *why* He came. The change is sudden and it is here that the Lord has the *cross* uppermost in His mind.

The Lord says in 8:31:

> "AND HE BEGAN TO TEACH THEM THAT THE SON OF MAN MUST SUFFER MANY THINGS, AND BE REJECTED OF THE ELDERS, AND OF THE CHIEF PRIESTS, AND SCRIBES, AND BE KILLED, AND AFTER THREE DAYS RISE AGAIN." (Note in V-32 — "He spake that saying *openly*" a word Matthew and Luke do not use.)

Yes, the scene changes from *Service* and His works to the tragic *Sacrifice* (in the Structure of the Book).

7. **Sacrifice — Chapters 8:31 through 15**

Repeatedly from our Lord's lips, the cross is mentioned — Look up: Mark 9:12 and 31 (write key phrases about His death)

_____

_____

Mark 10:32-34 _____

_____

Mark 10:45 (the Key Verse of Mark) _____

_____

Mark 14:8 _____

Mark 14:24-25 _____

_____

Instead of a throne, He knew there would be a cross. From Chapter 11 on to the Cross in Chapter 15, Mark vividly portrays the events differently than do Matthew and Luke. For example: The *Olivet Discourse* in Matthew is 97 verses in length while in Mark there are only 37 verses.

There is an absence of indictments in Mark such as occur in the other Gospels. No denunciation of Galilee's impenitent cities (as in Matthew 11), no condemnation of Scribes and Pharisees (Matthew 23 and Luke 11), and other noticeable absences. Why? The omission of such judgments belong to a *King,* as in Matthew and do not befit the *Servant* aspect of our Lord as recorded by Mark.

Again, in like manner, no reference is made in Mark of the promise of the Kingdom to the dying thief on the Cross — no mention of His right to summon legions of angels, if He so willed. These, too, were attributes of a King and not of a Servant.

8. **Resurrection and Ascension — Chapter 16**

The bodily resurrection of Jesus Christ is one of the cardinal doctrines of the Christian faith. *All four Gospels record the fact.* Every sermon in the Book of Acts is a message on the resurrection.

Yet, when we come to Mark 16 — more argument is made over the last twelve verses — as to whether or not they were a part of the original canon of Scripture — and little attention given to the *fact* of the resurrection.

First, the fact of the resurrection is given in Mark. The women, the angel, the stone, the report of the women to the disciples (V-7) as the angel said — the women were amazed and speechless in V-8. (This does not seem to be the right place for Mark to end his Gospel and we will deal with that in a moment.)

Notice the great commission in V-15. Here we do not hear a King say, "All power is given unto me in heaven and in earth," as in Matthew. Here in Mark we see in Jesus' words that His disciples are to take His place and He will serve in and through them. Read and record 16:20:

_____

_____

He is the ascended Lord, the Servant highly exalted — working in and through us. "We are laborers together with Him" — I Cor. 3:9.

(THE LAST TWELVE VERSES — Since the last twelve verses are a part of the inspired Scripture and has been given to us as such, there is little to argue or even discuss.

My own opinion is that Mark's writings were all influenced by the Apostle Peter. At the middle of this chapter, Mark had to write his own rapid like account of the events from V-9 and on. His quick transition from one scene to another is the style of Mark.

The main point is — the last verses give *hope, assurance, help* and *comfort.* They are a part of the Word of God. Accept them as such.

HOW MUCH DO YOU REMEMBER?

Q. What are the first three Gospels called?

Q. What is Mark's other name?

Q. To whom did Mark write primarily?

Q. How does Mark present Christ?

Q. What is the key word in Mark?

   The key verse?

YOUR ASSIGNMENT FOR NEXT WEEK

1. Read entire Book of Luke — only 4 chapters or less each day.
2. Review your notes from Matthew and Mark.
3. Mark your Bible.
4. Be present for the study of Luke next Lord's Day.

Lesson 30
"The Book of Luke"

NOTES

(Where lines are provided, please look up Scriptures and fill in the entire Scripture or the main Truth of the passage.)

1. **Luke The Man**

   In the Book of Matthew, Jesus is presented as *King*. In Mark He is the *Servant*. Now as we come to the Book of Luke, Jesus is presented as the *Son of Man*.

   Remember that Matthew writes to the Hebrew mind; Mark to the Roman mind while Luke writes to the Greek mind.

   Luke, the Physician, wrote Luke and also the Book of Acts. Both Luke and Acts are addressed to the same person — "Theophilus" — (Luke 1:3, Acts 1:1). We know less about Luke than of any other New Testament writer. He never refers to himself in the Gospel — and in the Book of Acts he refers only to himself where the words "we" and "us" are used when he is a part of Paul's group of traveling companions.

   For example — the change from "they" to "we" in Acts 16:10 indicates he became a companion of Paul at Troas. Note also Acts 10:6 — and from that point Luke was with Paul right through to Paul's martyrdom (Col. 4:14; II Timothy 4:11). We know he was a physician from Paul's words in Col. 4:14 — "Luke, the beloved physician, and Demus, greet you." We see traces of his thinking as a physician in his own writing: "He hath sent me to *heal*" — 4:18 (spoken by our Lord). "Physician heal thyself" — 4:23. Like references are found concerning the physical in 5:12; 5:18; 7:2; 13:11.

2. **The Central Message**

   "For the Son of Man is come to seek and to save that which was lost" — Luke 19:10.

   The key phrase of the Book is *"Son of Man"* because Luke deals with the humanity of our Lord.

3. **The Structure of the Book**

   THE NATIVITY, BOYHOOD, MANHOOD OF JESUS — Chapters 1 through 4:13.

   HIS MINISTRY IN GALILEE — Chapters 4:14 through 9:50.

   HIS JOURNEY TO JERUSALEM — Chapters 9:51 through 19:44.

   HIS SACRIFICE AND TRIUMPH — Chapters 19:45 through 24.

4. **The Nativity, Boyhood, Manhood of Jesus — Chapters 1 through 4:13**

   (1) Luke dwells on the birth of Christ and his account has no parallel in the other Gospels. Mark and John tell nothing about His birth at Bethlehem. Matthew gives an account of His birth but he does not describe, as Luke does, the birth, babyhood, boyhood of the Lord and his account is only one quarter the length of Luke's.

   (2) Matthew and Luke both give a genealogy showing the Lord's ancestry. Matthew starts his Book with his genealogy but Luke does not mention it until after the baptism of Jesus. The reason, we believe, is that the first important thing with Matthew is to establish our Lord's Davidic heirship to the throne — whereas, Luke's first concern is the real human birth, growth and *perfect* manhood.

(3) Matthew gives the genealogy through *Joseph* who was *legally,* not physically, the father of Jesus. Luke gives his genealogy through *Mary* who really was the mother of *His* manhood.

Matthew starts at Abraham and traces it down through David — *Kingship.* Luke goes back to Adam and traces Christ to the point of His appearance in the history of the race as a *human* — as the Son of Man. (John goes beyond Adam back into eternity as we shall see in that study.)

(4) This part of His life covers a period of thirty years (3:23). The first two chapters cover the first twelve years (2:42). He grew physically and in wisdom (2:52). After the baptism of Jesus, He was tempted and Luke tells us *"Jesus, being full of the Holy Spirit — was led by the spirit into the wilderness being forty days tempted of the devil"* (4:1). This is to show us that our Lord, tempted, tried, tested was controlled by the Holy Spirit. After His baptism and the accounts surrounding that event — He was placed, as we are after a blessing, in a position of trial and testing.

5. **The Ministry in Galilee — Chapters 4:14 through 9:50**

(1) Luke's account of our Lord's ministry in Galilee is much shorter than either Matthew's or Mark's. The emphasis, as we saw in Matthew, is on what Jesus *said;* in Mark on what Jesus *did,* while in Luke it is on *Jesus Himself.*

(2) The Galilean ministry begins with Jesus in the synagogue at Nazareth (recorded only by Luke) and with emphasis at once on the manhood of Jesus Himself:

Luke 4:18, 21, 22 _____

_____

_____

(3) Only in Luke do we find Him teaching concerning the abundance of fish and Peter's realization of His wonderful power (Chapter 5).

In Chapter 7, only in Luke, He gives life to the son of the widow of Nain.

These are only two examples of Luke's emphasis on His human feelings.

(4) Jesus chose the twelve apostles (4:14 — 6:11) then sent them forth as a multiplied ministry (9:1-17).

Peter's confession (9:18) marks a change and from this point Jesus talks of His coming rejection and death.

(5) The transfiguration (9:27-36) was a Divine attestation of Him as the Son of God. Here in Luke, He is depicted as the Divine Messenger. Notice 9:35, "This is my beloved Son, *hear Him.*"

(6) His last public miracle in Galilee, before going on to Jerusalem, was the release of the demoniac son (9:37-50).

NOTE: It is with these last three events that we find a reference to the Cross:

Read 9:22 _____

_____

9:31 _____

_____

9:44 _____

6. **His Journey to Jerusalem — Chapters 9:51 through 19:44**

(1) In all these Chapters (11) only *five* miracles are reported as compared to *twenty-one* miracles in the few chapters of His ministry in Galilee. In this section there is a great number of *sayings, doings,*

parables, rebukes — all reflecting that MATCHLESS MAN.

(2) Luke has preserved for us some of the priceless treasury of these sayings and incidents which are not recorded by any of the other three Gospel writers. The one thing you should remember is our Lord's art of reply. Note:

13:1-5 _____

13:31-33 _____

17:20-21 _____

(3) This section divides into almost two equal sections — the one ending with Jesus' *first* lament over Jerusalem in 13:34 and the *second* lament at 19:41-44.

Don't forget that this section is concerning His journey to Jerusalem. For your own Scripture marking, read Chapter 13:22-33 and write V-22: _____

_____

and V-33 _____

_____

7. **His Sacrifice and Triumph — Chapters 19:45 through 24**

(1) This last section begins with the Lord in the temple and ends with His *crucifixion, entombment, resurrection* and *ascension.*

(2) His manhood is seen through all this section in His "sweat drops as it were great drops of blood" — (22:44) — in His praying, His torture — But we see more of His Deity in His *answers,* His *submissiveness,* His *resurrection,* His *ministry* as the risen Christ and His *ascension* — then the people "were continually in the temple, praising and blessing God" — (24:53).

8. **Some Things That Distinguish Luke**

I could not leave this Gospel without pointing out the differences in Luke as compared to the other Gospel writers.

(1) JESUS' HUMAN DEPENDENCE UPON PRAYER.

Matthew and Mark also record the prayer in Gethsemane — but beside this our Lord's engagement in prayer occurs only twice in Matthew — Matthew 14:23; 27:46 and twice in Mark 6:46; 15:34. In Luke the prayer life of Jesus is shown over and over again. Look up:

- Luke 3:21 — "Jesus also baptized, and *praying*"
- Luke 5:16 — "He withdrew and *prayed*"
- Luke 6:12 — "He continued all night in *prayer* to God"
- Luke 9:18 — "As He was alone *praying*"
- Luke 9:28 — "He went up into the mountain to *pray*"
- Luke 9:29 — "And as He *prayed*" at transfiguration
- Luke 11:1 — "As He was *praying* in a certain place"
- Luke 22:32 — "I have *prayed* for thee" — for Peter
- Luke 22:44 — "He *prayed* more earnestly"
- Luke 23:34 — His first utterance on the Cross — a *prayer*
- Luke 23:46 — His last utterance on the Cross — a *prayer*

(2) HIS TEACHING ON PRAYER.

- Read Luke 11:9-10 — (a midnight appeal)
- Read Luke 18:1 — ("always pray and not faint")
- Read Luke 18:9-14 — (humility in prayer)
- Read Luke 21:36 — ("pray always")
- Read Luke 22:46 — ("rise and pray")

Many other instances and references to prayer are in Luke and it is sometimes called the Gospel of Prayer.

(3) SO ALSO IN LUKE IS THE PROMINENCE OF THE HOLY SPIRIT.

He is mentioned more in Luke than in Matthew and Mark together and even more than in John.

NOTE: Luke 1:35 — the Holy Spirit and conception of Christ
Luke 4:1 — only Luke says "being full of the Holy Spirit"
Luke 4:14 — only Luke says "He returned in the Power of the Spirit"
Luke 4:18 — only Luke says "The Spirit of the Lord is upon me — anointed me"
Luke 11:13 — only Luke says "How much more shall your heavenly Father give the Holy Spirit"
(See difference in Matthew 7:11)

(4) LUKE STRESSES THE ALL INCLUSIVE MINISTRY OF JESUS.

This can be seen in the parables which occur only in Luke — they emphasize the thoughts of the *Son of Man:*

— the two debtors — 7:41-50
— the good Samaritan — 10:30-37
— the great Supper — 14:16-24
— the lost coin — 15:8-10
— the prodigal son — 15:1-32
— the Pharisee and the publican — 18:9-14

Luke's ministry as presenting Christ as the Son of Man is so evident. This is expressed in the words of Simeon in Luke 2:29-32

Luke alone records our Lord's comments about the Gentile widow of Sidon and the Gentile Syrian, Naaman — (4:26-27).

Luke alone tells of the ten lepers cleansed and one, a *Samaritan,* ran back to give thanks (17:15-16).

(5) LUKE RECORDS THE PROMINENCE GIVEN TO WOMEN BY JESUS.

Luke alone records Jesus forgiving the "woman which was a sinner" — 7:37-50.

The care for Martha and her "trouble about many things" — 10:41.

Luke alone records the incident of healing "the woman which had an infirmity eighteen years" — 13:10-17.

Luke alone records the "woman having ten pieces of silver" — 15:8.

Luke alone records the incident of Jesus telling the women — "weep not for me, daughters of Jerusalem" — 23:28.

Luke alone tells us of John's mother, Elisabeth — 1:5 and of Anna and her adoration of the Lord — 2:36-38.

There are other references to women in Luke but from these examples you can see the places of women in the heart of Jesus.

There is so much left unsaid about this Book — and about Luke. Study carefully the references to Luke's ministry with Paul.

HOW MUCH DO YOU REMEMBER?

Q. What was Luke's profession?
Q. What Books of the New Testament did he write?
Q. What is the key phrase in Luke?
Q. What aspect of Christ does Luke present?

NOTES

YOUR ASSIGNMENT FOR NEXT WEEK
   1. Read the Gospel of John — 21 Chapters — 3 Chapters each day.
   2. Review your notes on the Gospel of Luke.
   3. Mark your Bible from your notes.
   4. Be in class next Lord's Day to study the Gospel of John.

Lesson 31
"The Book of John"

(Where lines are provided, please look up Scriptures and fill in the entire Scripture or the main Truth of the passage.)

1. **The Book**

   The Gospel of John brings to a climax the *full* purpose of God in Christ. In the other three Gospels we have learned what Jesus said — what He did and what He felt. We have seen the high points of His life and ministry —

   - His SUPERNATURAL BIRTH
   - His BAPTISM
   - His TEMPTATION
   - His TRANSFIGURATION
   - His CRUCIFIXION
   - His RESURRECTION
   - His ASCENSION

   In all of the three preceding Gospels we have learned *what* He was and now John presents the completion of *who* He was. The other three are a *presentation* of Christ — John is an *interpretation* of Him. The first three show Jesus *outwardly* and John shows Jesus *inwardly.* John truly exposes the *Divine* — He is *God-Man.* The earlier three writers are mainly concerned with our Lord's public utterances while John majors on His private conversations and thoughts.

2. **The Author**

   John, The Apostle, is the author. He was the son of Zebedee, the brother of James (Matthew 4:21). These two were surnamed by our Lord "The sons of thunder" (Mark 3:17). John wrote three epistles, the Revelation and this Gospel. John was the beloved pastor at Ephesus, and later (95 A.D.), he was exiled to Patmos by the Emperor Domitian where he wrote the Book of Revelation.

3. **The Central Truth**

   "But as many as received Him, to them gave He the power (right or authority) to become the sons of God, even to them that believe on His name" (John 1:12).

   ALSO BLAZING ALL THROUGH THE GOSPEL IS JOHN 20:31:

   "But these are written, that ye might believe that Jesus is the Christ, the Son of God; and that believing ye might have life through His name."

4. **The Structure of the Book**

   (1) THE PROLOGUE — 1:1-18
   (2) HIS PUBLIC MINISTRY — 1:19 through 12:50
   (3) HIS PRIVATE MINISTRY — Chapters 13 through 17
   (4) HIS SUFFERING AND DEATH — Chapters 18 and 19
   (5) VICTORY OVER DEATH — Chapters 20 and 21

5. **The Prologue — 1:1-18**

   (1) In the prologue there are so many things to capture our attention. Notice, however, four names or designations of our Lord: "WORD" — "LIFE" — "LIGHT" — "SON." (Notice V-1, 3, 9, 18)

NOTES

through the Bible in one year

(2) In relation to the Father, He is the *Word* and the *Son*.

Our Lord Jesus is *the Word* (V-1), the expression of God toward all men and also the expression of God before all of creation (V-2 & 3). Jesus was not *from* the beginning, He was *in* the beginning — He was not only *with* God — He *was* God — (V-1).

Jesus is the *Son,* "in the bosom" of the Father . . . there can be no eternal Fatherhood without eternal Sonship.

(3) In relation to *us,* He is *Life* and Light. From Him radiates all illumination, both intellectual and spiritual — (V-4-9). These two words, *Life* and *Light* go together, or correspond with the *Word* and Son.

As the *Word,* He, Jesus is the expresser, revealer, illuminator, the *Light*.

As the *Son,* He, Jesus is the quickener, the imparter of Life — God in the flesh (Incarnate).

(4) Along with these titles there are two other words you should note — "grace" and "truth" (V-14 & 16). The incarnate One (the made flesh One) is "full of *grace and truth*" — full of "grace" to *redeem* man, and full of "truth" to *reveal* God — because His is the God-Man, Revealer, Redeemer.

(5) So you won't forget the facts of the prologue you may remember this diagram by comparing V-1 with V-14:

VERSE 1	VERSE 14
in the beginning was the WORD	and the WORD was made flesh
and the WORD was with GOD	and dwelt among us
and the WORD was GOD	full of grace and truth

(6) Note especially V-18 — "No man hath seen God at any time, the only begotten Son, which is in the bosom of the Father, He hath declared (made manifest — in full view or revelation) Him."

(7) Jesus, the Word, was in the beginning with God.

Look up Col. 1:15-19 _____

_____

_____

Look up I John 5:7 _____

_____

6. **His Public Ministry — 1:19 through 12:50**

(1) John records seven signs or miracles which prove that Jesus is the Son of God. Nicodemus states this in John 3:2:

_____

_____

The seven miracles were:
- Turning water into wine — 2:1-11
- Healing the nobleman's son — 4:46-54
- Healing the man at Bethesda — 5:1-18
- Feeding the 5,000 — 6:1-14
- Walking on the water — 6:15-21
- Healing the blind man — 9:1-41
- Raising of Lazarus — 11:1-57

(2) John records the "new birth" chapter and Jesus' conversation with Nicodemus — Chapter 3.

Read especially — V-3 through 18 — Underline your Bible.

(3) John records the incident with the Samaritan woman in 4:1-42. He

reveals that He is "the water of life." What did the woman do? V-39: _____

_____

(4) The Fourfold Witness of Christ — 5:32-47.

In answering the Jews about His miracles, Jesus gives four witnesses of His Messiahship —

     1. John the Baptist — 5:33-35
     2. His works — 5:36
     3. The Father — 5:37-38
     4. The Scriptures — 5:39-47

(5) The healing of the blind man in Chapter 9 — Jesus gave the great discourse on the Good Shepherd in Chapter 10. Read especially V-14 and V-27-30. _____

_____

_____

_____

(6) The raising of Lazarus is the last "sign" (Chapter 11) in John's Gospel. He had been dead four days, but that made no difference. Notice Martha's reference to "the resurrection at the last day." Here then is recorded the great words of Jesus on resurrection, death and life — Read V-25 and 26: _____

_____

_____

_____

7. His Private Ministry — Chapters 13 through 17

(1) Here we see the heart of Jesus. He teaches by every word and act, His disciples and us.

CHAPTER 13 — Humility — V-5; cleansing — V-10; love — V-34.

CHAPTER 14 — Comfort, His second coming — V-1-6; promise of the Holy Spirit — Read V-16-18 and 26:

_____

_____

_____

CHAPTER 15 — Abiding in Christ — V-7-9; Another promise of the Holy Spirit — V-26-27:

_____

_____

_____

CHAPTER 16 — The work of the Spirit — V-7-11; new truth revealed by the Holy Spirit — V-12-14:

_____

_____

_____

CHAPTER 17 — Our Lord's Prayer — Note V-11, 17, 21, 24.

(2) Notice in all this section that Jesus promises the coming of the Holy Spirit, whom Jesus will send after he ascends, as the Comforter who comes from the Father. The Holy Spirit always

glorifies Jesus, not Himself (the Holy Spirit). The Holy Spirit is our teacher, our guide, our Comforter — (Chapters 13-17).

8. **His Suffering and Death — Chapters 18 and 19**

(1) From the prayer of Chapter 17, Jesus goes to the Garden of Gethsemane (Chapter 18:1 "a garden") followed by His arrest — trials — scourging — crucifixion — death.

Not one of these experiences did Jesus try to delay or avoid. The "Man of Sorrows and acquainted with grief" was "obedient unto death, even the death of the cross" — Phil. 2:8.

(2) His Jewish Trial before Annas, the High Priest — 18:12-14; 19-23

His Roman Trial before Pilate — 18:28-38

- before Herod — Luke 23:6-12
- before Pilate again — John 18:39 — 19:36

(3) His death — you should remember these six things:

1. His identity — 19:19
2. His garments — 19:23
3. His mother — 19:25-27
4. His death — 19:28-30
5. His death verified — 19:36 (from Old Testament)
6. His body buried — 19:38-42 (Note Nicodemus is mentioned in V-39)

Only John records *It is finished.*

9. **Victory Over Death — Chapters 20 and 21**

(1) On the third day the tomb was empty and He came out of the grave with a spiritual body. He appeared *ten* different times after His resurrection — the seventh one being to Thomas (Read John 20:28).

(2) His last word of instruction is to Peter and to us "Follow thou me — till I come" — (21:22).

10. **The Major Differences in John's Gospel**

(1) OMISSIONS in the Gospel of John:

- No genealogy is recorded at all (as Matthew and Luke)
- No account of His birth — because He was "in the beginning"
- Nothing about His boyhood
- Nothing about His temptation
- Nothing about His transfiguration
- No account of the ascension
- No great commission
  (Read Chapter 21:25 and see how much is not written)

(2) The THREE KEYS to John's Gospel —

John 20:31 _____

_____

John 16:28 _____

_____

John 1:12 _____

_____

(3) A REMARKABLE PARALLEL

There is a remarkable parallel between the furniture of the tabernacle and the Gospel of John. The approach to God is one and the same in both. John leads us in exactly the same order as those seven articles of furniture, to the great spiritual realities which they typify.

He begins in Chapter 1 by leading us to the BRAZEN ALTAR of sacrifice — "Behold the Lamb of God, etc." — V-29.

In Chapter 3 he takes us to the LAVER OF CLEANSING AND RENEWAL — "Except a man be born of water and of the Spirit" — V-5.

In Chapters 4-6 he takes us to the TABLE OF SHEWBREAD with its food and drink concerning "living water" — 4:14 and "the living Bread" — 6:51.

In Chapters 8 and 9 John takes us to the GOLDEN CANDLESTICK for twice we hear Jesus say, "I am the Light of the world" — 8:12 and 9:5.

In Chapters 14-16 we are at the golden ALTAR OF INCENSE learning to pray — prayers like a fragrant incense when breathed in the name of Him, Our Lord — 14:13-14; 16:23-24.

In the 17th Chapter — the great intercessory prayer of Jesus, our High Priest, we are taken through the "veil" into the Holy of Holies — all of Chapter 17.

In Chapters 18 and 19 we see Calvary — how Jesus is the ARK OF THE COVENANT and the MERCY SEAT sprinkled with His own blood — promising in Chapter 20 to return to His Father and our Father and to His God and our God.

So you will not forget this Old Testament teaching in reference to Christ – we diagram it for you:

FURNITURE OF TABERNACLE	SYMBOLICAL MEANING IN O.T.	TYPICAL MEANING
1. The Brazen Altar	Atonement thru sacrifice	Atonement of Christ on Cross
2. The Laver	Spiritual renewal	Christ cleansing us of "spot & wrinkle"
3. Table of Shewbread	Spiritual nourishment	Christ as our Living Bread
4. Golden Candlestick	Illumination	Christ — our Light
5. Altar of Incense	To ask humbly	Prayer in Name of Jesus
6. The Ark	Access only thru High Priest	Christ our Access to God
7. The Mercy Seat	Vindication thru Blood Sacrifice	Christ is Mercy Seat — "Propitiation" — Romans 3:25

(4) THE SEVEN "I AM'S"

Jesus reveals His deity — His God nature in these sayings:

1. "I AM the bread of life" — 6:35
2. "I AM the light of the world" — 8:12
3. "Before Abraham was, I AM" — 8:58
4. "I AM the Good Shepherd" — 10:11
5. "I AM the resurrection and the life" — 11:25
6. "I AM the way, the truth and the life" — 14:6
7. "I AM the true vine" — 15:1

There is so much we have had to leave out of this lesson — but may I encourage you to read and mark your Bible from the material in this lesson.

HOW MUCH DO YOU REMEMBER?

Q. How does John present Christ?

Q. Did Jesus begin at Bethlehem?

Q. Give three other names for Jesus.

Q. What does "incarnate" mean?

Q. Where is the Lord's Intercessory Prayer found?

YOUR ASSIGNMENT FOR NEXT WEEK

1. Read the first twelve chapters of the Book of Acts — less than two chapters each day. We shall divide the Book of Acts into two studies — two weeks — the first being Acts 1 through 12 and the second being Acts 13 through 28.
2. Review your notes on the Book of John.
3. Mark your Bible in the Book of John.
4. Prepare and be present next Lord's Day study in the all important Book of Acts.

Lesson 32
"The Book of Acts — Part I"
(Acts 1 through 12)

(Where lines are provided, please look up Scriptures and fill in the entire Scripture or the main Truth of the passage.)

1. The Book

Luke, the writer of the third Gospel is also the author of the "Acts of the Apostles." We know this because the ascension of our Lord was the closing scene in Luke (Luke 24:49-51) and it is the opening words of Luke in Acts (1:10-11). Luke opens both Books in similar ways, addressing them to Theophilus.

"The Acts of the Apostles" has also been called *The Acts of the Holy Spirit.* All of the twelve disciples are named in the first chapter and they are collectively referred to some *twenty-three* times in Acts — however, the detailed account of only two are given in the Books of Acts — Peter and Paul.

2. The Central Message (both Part 1 and 2 of Acts)

Acts 1:8 — "Ye shall receive power after that the Holy Ghost has come upon you, and ye shall be *witnesses* unto Me, both in Jerusalem and in all Judea and in Samaria, and unto the uttermost part of the earth."

The TRUTH, then is, POWER-WITNESS-EVERYWHERE.

3. The Structure of the Book

The Book of Acts divides itself into two parts:

    PART I — Chapters 1 through 12 (this lesson)
    PART II — Chapters 13 through 28 (next lesson)

The Structure of *both* will be given for comparison:

PART I — (1 through 12)	PART II — (13 through 28)
• JERUSALEM — the center	• ANTIOCH — the center
• PETER — main character	• PAUL — main character
• GOSPEL — To Jerusalem, Judea Samaria	• GOSPEL — to "uttermost" part," Rome
• PETER IMPRISONED	• PAUL IMPRISONED

(The First Part will be this week's lesson.)

4. The Resurrection Ministry and Ascension of Christ — Chapter 1

The *fifty* days from the Lord's resurrection to the day of Pentecost is divided into *40* days and *10* days. The 40 days of the Lord's resurrection ministry (in Chapter 1:3) and the ten days is indicated in 1:4-5. We arrive at the ten days from the fact that Jesus was "seen forty days" and He told His disciples to tarry, wait for the power of the Holy Spirit in a few days. They waited in the Upper Room until "the Day of Pentecost was fully come." PENTECOST MEANS "50."

    He was seen in His resurrection body 40 days —

    He ascended into Glory

Copyrighted. Unauthorized reproduction prohibited by law.

141

The coming of the Holy Spirit on 50th day
(See Lev. 23:15-16 after Feast of First Fruits)

Acts 1:4-5 speaks of "ye shall be baptized with the Holy Ghost." In comparing Scripture with Scripture we see that Jesus means exactly what Scripture says. By Spirit baptism we are joined to the body of Christ — *placed* in His glorious body, the Church.

> Look up I Cor. 12:13:   Eph. 4:5:
> Romans 6:3-5:   Col. 2:12:
> Gal. 3:27:   I Peter 3:21:

The Spirit is the baptizer placing us in "the body" of Christ — *"a building" – "the bride"* — at the moment of our acceptance of Christ.

Note that the *Power* was to come and *then* they were to be witnesses — (1:8-9).

So in Chapter 1 we have all that Christ had promised and taught coming to a climax.

5. **The Holy Spirit at Pentecost — Chapter 2**

(1) THE SPIRIT DESCENDED — fell on them — V-1-3.

The Spirit *filled* them — V-4.

The Spirit worked through them — V-41-47.

(2) THE DAY OF PENTECOST — Chapter. 2. There can only be *one* Day of Pentecost — just as there can only be one Calvary, one resurrection, one second coming. It will never be repeated.

(3) THE DIFFERENCE PENTECOST MADE

a. At Pentecost the Holy Spirit entered into a new temple. The tabernacle was an empty tent until Exodus 40:34-35:

_____

_____

The temple of Solomon was an empty shell until I Kings 8:10-11:

_____

_____

In the New Testament, the Lord God is choosing a new temple — not made with skins and tapestries — nor of stone and fine ornaments. This new temple is built on the foundation of Christ out of *living stones* who are regenerated believers in the Lord (I Peter 2:5).

On the Day of Pentecost *the Holy Spirit came to indwell the Church of God* — all of us who believe — just as the Shekinah Glory of God had invested the tabernacle and temple with His glorious presence. So the Holy Spirit abides in His Church.

b. The SECOND difference Pentecost made is that the Holy Spirit came to dwell *in* every believer, personally, individually.

Look up John 14:17 _____

_____

Look up I Cor. 6:19 _____

_____

Each one of us who is saved is *a temple indwelt* by the Person of the Holy Spirit.

c. A THIRD Pentecostal difference lies in the fact that the gift of the Holy Spirit, after the Ascension of Jesus into heaven, is a *personal indwelling* in every believer and is *never withdrawn*. In the Old Testament the Holy Spirit came and departed as God willed.

d. Why these differences before and after Pentecost? *One answer – Jesus said so.* Look up and underline in your Bible the following Scriptures:

- John 14:16-17
- John 14:26
- John 15:26
- John 16:7
- John 16:12-14

(4) THE SIGNS — MIRACLES OF PENTECOST — 2:1-8.

What was the purpose — what do they mean — these signs and miracles of Pentecost? Should we pray for these gifts? Can we expect duplications in our day?

Besides the chapters of creation and besides the marvelous period of consummation in Revelation — there are *three periods* of miracles in the Bible:

FIRST, the days of Moses in the introduction of the law.

SECOND, the days of Elijah and Elisha in the times of the apostasy of Israel.

THIRD, the days of Jesus and the apostles in the introduction of the new dispensation of grace.

All of these periods had something in common. It is simply this: without exception the purpose of the miracle or sign is that of *authentication*. God is introducing *His* servant with *His* message by *His* sign from heaven. Read Exodus 4:1-9 and I Kings 18:36-37.

The *signs* of Pentecost are: (2:1-4)

- *All* in one accord — one place.
- *Sound* as of a mighty wind —
- *Appeared* — tongues — like as of fire.
- *All filled* with the Holy Spirit —
- *Other tongues* as Spirit gave.

The experience came from the Holy Spirit filling them. The tongues here were not *"unknown tongues,"* but the Holy Spirit gave the ability to speak to people of other tongues (like me speaking Chinese, a known tongue). These experiences will be covered more as we go through the Book of Acts and the Epistles.

(5) PETER'S SERMON AND THE FIRST CHURCH — 2:14-47.

Peter quotes Joel 2:28-29 and that relates to this age of grace. He quotes Joel 2:30-31 and that relates to the consummation of this age and the return of Christ. The sermon is simply "Jesus, a man approved of God."

Note V-41 — 3,000 souls added.

Note V-42-47 — Happy, praising God — and the Lord added to the Church daily.

The Church is the "Ekklesia" in Greek, meaning "called out ones." (Ecclesia — English)

(6) THE FIRST APOSTALIC MIRACLE OF THE CHURCH AND PETER'S SECOND SERMON — Chapter 3.

Note especially V-13-15 _____

_____

_____

6. **Five Thousand Saved — The First Persecution — Chapter 4**

Note in V-4 "They *heard, believed, 5000 men*" saved. After their release from prison, Peter and John went back to the Church and they prayed — Note V-31.

7. **The Tests and Victories of the Early Church — Chapter 5**

Note the *tests* in V-1-11, V-17, V-27-28 and V-33-40. Along with the tests — God gives victories in V-12-16; 19-26; 29-32; 41-42.

8. **Stephen Martyred — A Deacon Who Spoke With Power — Chapters 6-7**

   Read 7:51-53. He was the first martyr but it took his death for Paul to be challenged by the faith of Stephen. Notice the words of Stephen in 7:55-56. _____

   _____

   Saul (Paul) is mentioned in V-58 _____

   _____

9. **The Church As Jesus Said in Acts 1:8 — Chapter 8**

   With great persecution of the Church at Jerusalem, the Church was scattered to Judea and Samaria (8:1 and 4). Peter, the possessor of the keys, laid hands on believers and they were filled as in Acts 1:8 and Acts 2:38 (Promised by Jesus to Peter in Matt. 16:19).

10. **The Conversion of Saul — Paul — Chapter 9**

    He was saved on Damascus road — became a chosen vessel of God — V-15 — began preaching immediately.

11. **The Gospel to the Gentiles — Chapter 10**

    The chapter is God's approval on the salvation of all, Jew or Gentile. Verses 44-48 has been called the "Gentile Pentecost." At Pentecost, Peter had used the *"keys of the kingdom"* to open the door of the Gospel to the Jews. Here Peter uses the keys to open the door of the Gospel to the Gentiles. They spake in tongues, understandable, and not an unknown tongue.

12. **Antioch Becomes Center of Gentile Church — Chapter 11**

    The Jerusalem Church demanded to know about Peter's conduct in establishing a church in Antioch. He only says what the Holy Spirit had revealed. Read V-14-18.

    Barnabas is sent to Antioch as Pastor by the Jerusalem Church — V-22-24, and he wants Paul to help — V-25.

    Read that significant Verse 26 _____

    _____

13. **Persecution Again — But the Word Multiplied — Chapter 12**
    - James, the brother of John is executed — Peter imprisoned.
    - The Church prayed for Peter — V-5.
    - Herod dies — God smote him — V-23.
    - But in face of all this the Church grew and multiplied — V-24.

    So the first section of the Book of Acts closes with the Gospel having been carried out exactly as Jesus instructed in Acts 1:8. Peter's ministry is over except a brief defense of himself in Acts 15. Peter was the sovereign choice of God through whom the gift of the keys of the kingdom was given and the people were filled with the Holy Spirit.

    The early church in Jerusalem grew rapidly – notice:
    - Acts 1:14-15 — 120 in first group
    - Acts 2:41 — 3,000 souls added (1 day old)
    - Acts 4:4 — 5,000 men plus women and children
    - Acts 5:14 — more added
    - Acts 6:1-7 — multiplied greatly

    History tells us the Jerusalem Church exceeded 100,000 after only seven years.

HOW MUCH DO YOU REMEMBER?

Q. Who is the author of Acts?

Q. Who is the main character in this first lesson on Acts?

Q. Did Jesus give a geographic plan of evangelism? If so, can you name the plan?

Q. What does Pentecost mean?

Q. Name one of the many differences Pentecost made.

YOUR ASSIGNMENT FOR NEXT WEEK

1. Read the remainder of the Book of Acts — Chapters 13 through 28 — only 16 chapters.
2. Review the first study of Acts from your outline.
3. Mark your Bible — especially those Scriptures referring to "baptism" and "filling" of the Holy Spirit.
4. Be present next Lord's Day to complete the Book of Acts.

Lesson 33
"The Book of Acts — Part II"
(Acts 13 through 28)

through the Bible in one year

(Where lines are provided, please look up Scriptures and fill in the entire Scripture or the main Truth of the passage.)

1. **Paul**

   This lesson will mainly concern the life and ministry of Paul the Apostle. In the last lesson (Chapter 9) we saw the conversion of Saul (who is called Paul — 13:9). He was present at the stoning and martyrdom of Stephen (7:59 — 8:3). His conversion was caused by what he had done against the Christians and Jesus said, "Why persecutest thou me — I am Jesus whom thou persecuted — it is hard for thee to kick against your conscience" — 9:4-5.

   Paul was providentially prepared for his ministry — he was a Jew by birth — a Roman citizen — educated in Greek culture and trained in the Scripture by the Holy Spirit and at Jerusalem.

2. **The Central Message (same as Part I)**

   Acts 1:8 — especially in this lesson "ye shall be witnesses — unto the uttermost part of the earth."

3. **The Structure of This Lesson**
   - ANTIOCH — the center
   - PAUL — the main character
   - GOSPEL — to "uttermost part"
   - PAUL IMPRISONED

   Also in this lesson we see the evangelization by Paul on his three missionary journeys.

   This section of Acts may be visually remembered as follows:

THE CHURCH EXTENDED — (Chapters 13 — 21:17)			
FIRST MISSIONARY JOURNEY 13:1 - 14:28	JERUSALEM COUNCIL 15:1 - 15:35	SECOND JOURNEY 15:36 - 18:22	THIRD JOURNEY 18:23 - 21:17

PAUL AS A PRISONER (Chapters 21:18 — 28:31)				
BEFORE THE MOB 21:18 - 22:29	BEFORE THE COUNCIL 22:30 - 23:30	BEFORE GOVERNORS FELIX AND FESTUS 23:31-25:12	BEFORE KING AGRIPPA 25:13 - 26:32	AWAITING TRIAL IN ROME 27:1 - 28:31
AT JERUSALEM		AT CAESAREA		AT ROME

4. **The First Missionary Journey — Chapters 13:1 — 14:28**
   (1) "Separate me Barnabas and Saul for the work I have called them" — 13:2. The Holy Spirit called. They were ordained and sent on their way — 13:3.

(2) Journey started at Antioch — 13:1.
- to Seleucia — V-4 — to Salamis on Cypress — V-5 —
- to Paphos — V-6 — to Perga — V-13 — to Antioch in Pisidia — V-14 —
- to Iconium — V-51 — to Lystra — 14:6 — to Derbe — 14:6 —
- back to Lystra — 14:21 — back to Iconium — 14:21 —
- back to Antioch in Pisidia — 14:21 — to Attalia — 14:25 — back to Antioch where they started (V-26).

That was the first missionary journey. The churches are the churches of the ancient Roman province of Galatia. Thus, Paul wrote back to these churches and the Book is the Book of Galatians.

5. **The Jerusalem Council — 15:1-35**

There is given in this chapter a history of that conference but Paul gives the outcome of that conference in Galatians 1 and 2. The outcome was this — that Peter and James and John would preach to the Jew, and Paul and Barnabas — and others would go to the Gentiles — Gal. 2:1-9.

6. **The Second Missionary Journey — 15:36 — 18:22**

(1) Paul and Barnabas disagreed over John Mark and they divide. Paul chose Silas and they went back to visit the churches in Galatia and he finds Timothy (16:1).

(2) Paul wanted to go east (16:6-7) but the Holy Spirit wouldn't let him and they went west to Troas, by the sea, and God gave Paul the Macedonian vision.

Luke, the author, joins them there and you notice it is *"we"* (V-10) from this point on.

(3) They cross to Neapolis — 16:11 — to Philippi — 16:12 — to Apollonia 17:1 — to Thessalonica 17:1 — to Berea 17:10 — to Athens 17:15 — to Corinth 18:1 — to Ephesus 18:19 — to Caesarea 18:22 — up to Jerusalem and back down to Antioch.

That is the *second* journey of Paul.

7. **The Third Missionary Journey — 18:23 — 21:17**

(1) Paul revisited the places of the first journey strengthening the churches — 18:23 — and the points of the second journey also 20:3. He goes from Ephesus to Tyre 21:3 — to Caesarea 21:8 (Holy Spirit forbids Paul to go to Jerusalem just yet) but in 21:14-17 Paul goes to Jerusalem anyway.

(2) This is the third journey in miniature.

8. **Paul arrested in Jerusalem — the mob — 21:18 — 22:29**

(1) Acts 21:18-26 makes it clear that meat nor things commend us to God. Paul also wrote of the same thing in I Corinthians 7:17-18 and I Corinthians 9:19-23.

(2) In 21:27-40 Paul is mobbed and beaten in the temple. Paul identifies himself to the chief captain who grants him permission to address the mob (V-39-40).

(3) Paul's defense before the multitide — 22:1-29.

NOTE: *From Chapter 21 to the end of the Book Paul is in bonds.*

9. **Paul Before the Council (Sanhedrin) at Jerusalem — 22:30 — 23:30**

(1) The Sanhedrin was the highest Jewish tribunal of that day (called "council" in most Bibles). The Sanhedrin was made up of Pharisees and Sadducees. The Pharisees held to tradition in addition to the written law. The Sadducees accepted only the law. Note especially:

23:8 _____

_____

(2) Note the assurance of the Lord to Paul — 23:11: _____

_____

_____

10. **Paul Before the Governors — 23:31 — 25:12**

    (1) Felix and Festus were the Judean governors to whom Paul was next to appear for trial.

    (2) In Chapter 24 he testifies before Felix in Caesarea. The result was that Felix left him bound two years (V-27).

    (3) In Chapter 25 Paul is before Festus at the judgment seat (V-6) and is asked to go to Jerusalem and appeal his case to Caesar (V-9-10).

11. **Paul Before King Agrippa — 25:13 — 26:32**

    (1) Festus, the governor, mentioned his problem with Paul to King Agrippa — an expert in Jewish custom and law (26:3) and requested the opportunity to hear Paul's testimony. Paul *preached* to all three, Festus, Bernice and Agrippa, and notice Paul just gave his testimony — 26:1-28.

    (2) The king could find no fault in Paul and would have liberated him if he had not appealed to Caesar (V-32).

12. **Paul Awaiting Trial in Rome — 27:1 — 28:31**

    (1) The Lord had said in Acts 23:11 that Paul would bear witness of Him in Rome. Even through the perils of the voyage, Paul was assured of a safe arrival. Paul arrives in Rome by the Appian Way and is allowed to dwell by himself with a soldier that guarded him.

    (2) He stayed there two years and preached to everyone that came to see him — (28:30-31).

THE BOOK OF ACTS ENDS HERE.

CONCLUDING THOUGHTS

Luke wrote the Book of Acts about 64 A.D. Almost certainly Paul was liberated sometime after the first imprisonment. During his imprisonments Paul wrote Philippians, Ephesians, Colossians, Philemon.

Seemingly, you cannot place the Pastoral Epistles in the Book of Acts (I & II Timothy and Titus), but we do know from II Timothy 4 just before his martyrdom, that he wrote the Second Letter to Timothy. He was there in the Mamertine dungeon about 68 A.D. He could have written I Timothy from prison or just before his last trip to Jerusalem.

The record stops there at the end of Acts and has no conclusion because the Acts of the Holy Spirit continue to work in and through us, His Body, the Church, to be concluded at the coming of Christ for His Church.

HOW MUCH DO YOU REMEMBER?

Q. How was Paul providentially prepared for his ministry?

Q. Who went with Paul on his first journey?

Q. What was the outcome of the Jerusalem Council in Acts 15?

Q. Did Luke, the author, ever join Paul on his trips?

Q. What did Paul always do – before governors, kings, or in prison?

YOUR ASSIGNMENT FOR NEXT WEEK

    1. Read the Book of Romans — 16 Chapters (slightly over 2 Chapters each day).

    2. Review your notes from the two lessons in Acts.

    3. Mark the Scriptures in your Bible.

    4. Be present for the great Book of Romans next Lord's Day.

Lesson 34
"The Book of Romans"

(Where lines are provided, please look up Scriptures and fill in the entire Scripture or the main Truth of the passage.)

1. **The Epistles**

   We come now to the Epistles of the New Testament and we find first, there are *nine* Epistles written by the Apostle Paul to *seven* Gentile churches — in ROME, CORINTH, GALATIA, EPHESUS, PHILIPPI, COLOSSE, and THESSALONICA.

   These epistles develop the doctrine of the Church. They give instruction as to her unique purpose in the purposes of God. The Church, you will remember, was "the mystery which from the beginning of the world hath been hid in God" — Eph. 3:9.

2. **The Church**

   "Through Paul alone we know that the Church is not an organization, but an organism, the Body of Christ; instinct with His life, and heavenly in calling, promise, and destiny. Through him alone we know the nature, purpose, and form of the organization of local churches, and the right conduct of such gatherings."

   "Paul, converted by the personal ministry of the Lord in glory, is distinctively the witness to a glorified Christ, Head over all things to the Church, which is His body, as the eleven were to Christ in the flesh, the Son of Abraham and of David" — (Scofield Bible).

3. **The Book of Romans**

   The Epistle to the Romans was written by Paul from Corinth during his third visit to that city. When Paul wrote it, the Gospel had been preached through the Roman world for about a quarter of a century and many groups of Christians had come into existence. Many questions had come out of these groups such as — *"God's grace – the Gospel and the Law – the Abrahamic Covenant"* — and many other such questions. Paul had not yet been to Rome when he wrote this Epistle.

4. **The Central Message**

   Romans 1:16-17 — "For I am not ashamed of *the Gospel* of Christ: for it is *the power of God unto salvation* to *everyone* that *believeth;* to the Jew first, and also to the Greek. For therein is the *righteousness* of God revealed from faith to faith, as it is written, the just shall live by faith."

   (The italicized words indicate the great themes to be considered through the Epistle.)

5. **The Structure of the Book**

   - How the Gospel Saves — Chapters 1 through 8.
   - How the Gospel Relates to Israel — Chapters 9 through 11.
   - How the Gospel Affects Conduct — Chapters 12 through 16.

6. **How the Gospel Saves — Chapters 1 through 8**

   (1) These first eight chapters are *doctrinal* because they teach the basic doctrines of the Gospel. After a brief introduction (V-1-15) Paul immediately begins a doctrinal discussion on *"how the Gospel saves."*

   From Chapter 1:18 to 3:20, we see man's need for the Gospel:

FIRST, The pagan man — (Gentile) — 1:18-32.

Note V-21-24 especially. Note also the times you read "God gave them up" from V-24-28.

SECOND, The moral man (hypocrite) — 2:1-16.

This refers to both Jew and Gentile — V-11-12.

THIRD, The religious man — (Jew) — 2:17 through 3:8.

FOURTH, *ALL* are in sin — Jew and Gentile — 3:9-20.

We see then that all *have* sinned — acts of sin — and that all are *in* sin — an inward condition — 3:23.

(2) "But now" — Justification — 3:21 — 5:21.

Where you read the word *"justify"* in Scriptures, associate the word *"righteous"* for they come from the same root of the Greek.

Note 3:24, 26, 28. In justification God declares a sinner righteous on the *basis of his faith in Jesus Christ*.

"Redemption" (3:24) means "to deliver, or save, by paying a price." So He paid the price for our salvation, our justification. Look up I Cor. 6:20:

_____

_____

"Propitiation" (3:25) means simply *"satisfaction."* Christ is our propitiation, a satisfactory sacrifice, if we accept His shed blood. Look up Hebrews 2:17. The same word translated *"mercy seat"* is the same as *"propitiation."*

CHAPTER 4 — Paul selects one man out of Israel's past to show us an illustration of justification — the man, Abraham. God's justification is timeless, and He justified men before and after Christ. Read 4:3 and compare with Gen. 15:6 and we see that he was justified and he was 85 years old (Gen. 16:16). In Genesis 17:24, we are told of the circumcision at the age of 99. So he was justified 14 years before proving that justification is entirely independent of, and apart from, ordinances. He was not justified because of circumcision, but he was circumcised as a seal of his faith (4:13). He was accepted of God and promised to be heir to the world, not through the law (4:13), but through faith. This promise was given to Abraham 430 years before the Mosaic law was given — Gal. 3:17

_____

_____

Abraham believed — Romans 4:20-24:_____

_____

_____

CHAPTER 5 — The fruits of justification are peace V-1 — access to His grace, rejoice in hope V-2 — rejoicing in tribulations — patience, hope V-3-4—The *free gift* of God is spotlighted in V-12-21.

Note V-18 _____

_____

Adam was the root of sin in man — sins are the fruit of the problem caused by self-will.

CHAPTER 6 — The verb tenses in this chapter are all in the *past* —example is V-6 — should read "our old man *was* crucified." The expression "old man — body of sin" refers to the Adamic race as a whole.

What beautiful riches are in this chapter — Remember *three* words

in this chapter —
    "Know" — V-3, 6, 9.
    "Reckon" — V-11.
    "Yield" — V-13.

CHAPTERS 7 AND 8 — Paul shows us how the Gospel deals with the sin problems in the actual experience of the believer — the acute problem of 7:17-20 — "sin that dwelleth in me." Then Chapter 8 gives the glorious answer. Paul shows that the new life and law and liberty of the Spirit in the believer are the ample answer to the cry, "Who shall deliver me?" The Holy Spirit is mentioned in this chapter no less than *nineteen* times.

Read and note 8:1 _____

_____

8:14 and 16_____

_____

_____

Read again 8:26-27.
Memorize 8:28.
Do you know that if you are saved you are secure forever? Read 8:35-39. Nothing can separate us from the love we have in Christ Jesus. AMEN! AMEN!

7. **How the Gospel Relates to Israel — Chapters 9-11**

(1) CHAPTER 9 — Israel's Selection in the Past.

Paul states that the Gospel to the whole world does not annul God's special purpose for Israel and he proves it from Israel's own history and God's sovereignty:

- V-6-9 — Isaac selected.
- V-10-13 — Jacob selected (namely Israel).
- V-14-23 — God's mercy with Israel and Pharaoh.
- V-24-26 — God's mercy to Gentiles as prophecied in Hosea.
- V-27-29 — Isaiah's prophecy.

NOTE V-27_____

_____

V-30-33 PAUL'S CONCLUSION — Gentiles had attained righteousness through faith — while Israel, through the law, had not attained righteousness even after seeking it (V-32).

(2) CHAPTER 10 — Israel's Present and Their Rejection of Messiah.

Note — V-1-8 — Paul says to Israel, "The word is nigh thee, even in thy mouth and heart, that is the word of faith, which we preach" — V-8.

V-9-13 — The simple plan of salvation for Jew and Gentile. Write in V-9: _____

_____

_____

V-14-21 — The call to evangelize and Paul quotes David, Moses and Isaiah — predicting this sad rejection.

(3) CHAPTER 11 — Israel's Future Restoration.

Paul states that the Gospel, besides fulfilling the promise to Israel, confirms the great prospect for Israel — that all Israel shall be saved (V-25-29). God has not cast away Israel as a nation.

Through the unbelief of Israel — the Gentiles have been blessed (V-11-12). *Underline Verse 11.*

The "fullness of the Gentiles" in V-25 refers to the completion of the body of Christ made up of both Jew and Gentile — from Pentecost to the rapture.

Israel shall be saved — when the Deliverer (Jesus) comes, and turns away sin from Jacob (Israel) because this was God's covenant with them — V-25-26. *(Read these verses and underline.)*

Read Paul's gracious benediction in V-33-36.

8. CHAPTERS 12-16 — How the Gospel Affects Conduct.

(1) IN CHAPTER 12 — the appeal to consecration and transformation (V-1-2).

In the rest of the Chapter we see the appeal to *service* as a result of V-1 and 2. This is the *Christian life*.

(2) CHAPTER 13 — The Christian and his civil duties to government (V-1-7) and to neighbors (V-8-14).

(3) CHAPTER 14 — The Christian and weaker believers. We should not judge nor cause a weaker person to stumble — (V-13 and 19).

(4) CHAPTER 15 — Gentile and Jewish believers are one in Christ. Note V-4: _____

_____

Paul gives a preview of his planned ministry to go to Rome — (V-29-32).

(5) CHAPTER 16 — Paul's commendation and greetings to twenty-eight individuals by name. At the beginning of Romans, Paul says, "I make mention of you always in my prayers" — (1:9). Here he names some of them, men, women, Jew, Gentile.

Paul's closing prayer (16:25-27) is a masterful benediction in which he again mentions "the Gospel — according to the revelation of the *mystery* which was kept secret since the world began, but is made manifest (known) by the Scriptures of the prophets —."

CONCLUSION

In the Book of Romans, God is saying to Jew and Gentile — "righteousness may be received only through faith in Jesus Christ." The Book is applicable in our day because the human heart has not changed. This is the Book that shook Martin Luther (1:17) which started the Reformation. Luther said of Romans, "The chief Book of the New Testament — it deserves to be known by heart — word for word."

HOW MUCH DO YOU REMEMBER?

Q. Why was Romans written?

Q. What is the Central Message? Answer from memory if possible.

Q. Can you recall three verses that should be used in presenting the plan of salvation? If not, look up Romans 2:23 – Romans 6:23 – Romans 10:9-10.

Q. What does "justify" mean?

Q. What does "redemption" mean?

YOUR ASSIGNMENT FOR NEXT WEEK

1. Read I Corinthians (16 chapters) — little over two chapters each day.
2. Review the Book of Romans from your notes.
3. Mark your Bible from your notes.
4. Be present next Lord's Day for the study of I Corinthians.

Lesson 35
"The Book of
I Corinthians"

(Where lines are provided, please look up Scriptures and fill in the entire Scripture or the main Truth of the passage.)

1. **The Book**

   This letter is obviously Paul's answer to a letter he had received (I Cor. 7:1) in which questions were asked concerning the church in Corinth. Paul's reply is a letter of correction of errors and confirmation of truth.

   Paul wrote I Corinthians from Ephesus (Acts 20:31; I Cor. 16:5-8). This Book deals with factions in the church at that time and — amazing as it may seem — many of the same things remain in the church today. This Book is one of the vital parts of Scripture which should be taught in all churches — for *"doctrine"* and *"reproof"* and *"correction."*

2. **Corinth**

   The city of Corinth was the "sin center" of the Roman Empire in Paul's day. It was located about forty miles west of Athens. It was the commercial center of the Roman Empire with three great harbors.

   The ruins of the old city of Corinth can be seen today. To go there and see the background and the setting helps one to understand the preaching and teaching of Paul.

3. **The Central Message**

   "The Wisdom of God" — I Corinthians 1:24, 30; 2:4-8.
   (Note especially 1:30 and 2:7.)

4. **The Structure of the Book**

   Salutation and Thanksgiving — 1:1-9

   Correction Concerning Divisions in the Church — 1:10 — Chapter 6

   Answers Concerning Problems — Chapters 7-16

5. **Salutation and Thanksgiving — 1:1-9**

   In these first nine verses the Lord Jesus Christ is mentioned *six* times. Notice how Paul affirms the fact that the people in the Corinthian Church were *saved*, "sanctified"; "called to be saints"; "grace of God given you by Jesus Christ"; and on and on Paul affirms the fact of their faith. So Paul is not writing to unbelievers but he is writing to a church whom Paul says "are yet carnal" and "babes in Christ" — (3:1-4).

   So, Paul says these glorious things about their faith and about the grace of God "in them" before he starts correcting them.

6. **Correction Concerning Divisions in the Church — 1:10 through Chapter 6**

   (1) Paul says first — "There are contentions among you" — (1:11). The contentions (divisions, strife) were caused by the people exalting certain men instead of the Lord Jesus.

   NOTICE IN V-12 — some followers of Paul

   — some followers of Apollos (see Acts 18:24-28)

   — some followers of Cephas (Peter)

— some followers of Christ

So we have four divisions: (1) THE BRAGGING GROUP, who followed Paul about bragging of their Gospel freedom; (2) THE APOLLOS GROUP, the intellectuals, swayed by his personality and brilliance; (3) THE CEPHAS GROUP, who said their leader (Peter) was the authority of the apostles; and (4) THE "CHRIST" GROUP, who used the term "I am of Christ" in a way that implied inferiority of all the others.

Seem silly? *It still exists.*

Paul reproves them — Chapter 1:18-31. Man exalting schemes that cause division in the church are wrong, because salvation by the cross sets aside foolish things of man. God uses "the foolishness of preaching" to save.

CHAPTER 2 — Paul teaches that true wisdom is of God. No man can understand spiritual things until the Holy Spirit teaches him (V-11-12).

Now read 2:13-14 and underline these verses in your Bible. ("Comparing spiritual things with spiritual things" is simply — "comparing Scripture with Scripture.")

CHAPTER 3 — We have seen three full Chapters of teaching the folly of leaning wrongly on men instead of the Lord. In Chapter 3:5 — Ministers are "servants."

Read 3:6 and write it down:_____

_____

(2) The *only* foundation on which to build — 3:9-23.

    • the foundation is Christ — V-11.

    • rewards are given on the kind of foundation one builds — V-12-15.

    • fire tests every man's work — gold, silver, precious stone will stand the test; wood, hay, stubble are burned.

In other words, if a Christian builds on spiritual things (represented as gold, silver, precious stone), he will receive a reward (V-14); but if one builds on self-glory, self-satisfaction (wood, hay, stubble), his work shall be burned; "but he shall be saved, yet so as by fire." Rewards are given to the saved; they are earned in the service of the Lord. Loss of rewards does not mean loss of salvation.

(3) CHAPTER 4 — The ministers of Christ are *"stewards of the mysteries of God."* They should be examples of humility and faith (4:9-10).

(4) CHAPTER 5 — Scandals in the church at Corinth (5:1 — 6:20). The evils of incest (V-1) with a stepmother — the church ignored it. In V-4-5 Paul means to *"put him out of fellowship until repentance"* — destruction of sinful nature — not annihilation.

"Purge out the old leaven" — get rid of sin — V-7.

(5) CHAPTER 6 — Differences between believers should be settled within the fold of believers. Believers should not take believers to a court of law to be judged by unbelievers — (V-6).

Note V-11: _____

_____

V-19-20 — We are the temple of the Holy Spirit.

7. **Answers Concerning Problems — Chapters 7-16**

(1) Answers of Paul indicates in 7:1 — *"Now concerning the things whereof ye wrote unto me."*

The first answer is *concerning marriage.* The passage is clear — one wife for one man — if one is an unbeliever the believing mate should stay and try to win the other (V-10-40).

(2) In Chapters 8, 9 and 10 we see that they go together and *answer the questions concerning conduct and Christian liberty.*

Note 8:1, 8, 9 and especially V-13.

These Chapters deal with Christian conduct and its affect on weaker brethren. Five times in these three Chapters we find the expression of consideration for the weaker brother:

> 8:9 — *"them that are weak"*
>
> 8:13 — *"make my brother stumble"*
>
> 9:22 — *"that I might gain the weak"*
>
> 10:24 — *"let no man seek his own advantage, but of others"*
>
> 10:32 — *"give none offence"*

NOTE 10:13 AND TRY TO MEMORIZE THIS VERSE:

(3) CHAPTER 11 — Paul answers *concerning women and the Lord's Table*.

In 11:5 we find a verse that has been grossly misconstrued. The principle of the woman's place is stated in Verse 3:

- THE HEAD OF MAN IS CHRIST
- THE HEAD OF WOMAN IS MAN
- THE HEAD OF CHRIST IS GOD

The application of the principle is in V-4-6. The women certainly did "prophesy" (i.e., teach, speak, exhort, comfort) in that church of Corinth. In this passage Paul's concern is solely that of *head dress* in taking part in public worship. V-10 is the badge of "authority" she was to wear to have the right to speak or pray.

Paul was actually a champion for women and he has been misinterpreted terribly.

The Lord's Table is the subject of V-17-34. The Lord's Supper is recorded in detail by all four gospel writers — thus, it is important to all believers.

In V-17-22 the early church had a meal before celebrating the Lord's Supper. The meal was called an "agape," a love feast. Disorders had arisen and now Paul commands that those disorders be discontinued.

In V-23-26 — Paul was given these instructions directly from the Lord (V-23). Paul spells out the meaning and simplicity of the Lord's Supper — *"do this in remembrance of me"* – *"ye do show forth the Lord's death till he come."*

(4) CHAPTERS 12, 13, 14 — *Concerning Spiritual Gifts.*

The three Chapters should be taken together as one. There are gifts given to every man as *He* wills.

IN CHAPTER 12 —

- Diversity of gifts but one Spirit — V-4-11
- Many members but one body — V-12-27
- Many types of service but one Church — V-28-31

IN CHAPTER 13 — *"I show you more excellent way"* (12:31)

Without love, all of Chapter 12 would be as sounding brass. With all the gifts, if one does not have Godly love, they are useless.

IN CHAPTER 14 — *"Follow after love"* — (V-1)

This is the famous chapter on "tongues" and we shall not argue the point — just state the facts in relation to Chapters 12 and 13.

The important gift is prophecy — (V-1). The word *"unknown"* is italicized which means it was not in the original text. There is no such thing as an "unknown" tongue. Tongues are existing languages, not previously learned, but the ability to speak in another language was given in the apostolic church only for God's glory and not for man's — (V-4).

The modern day teaching on tongues is that it is a sign of the "baptism of the Holy Spirit" which is not Paul's teaching in I Corinthians 12:13.

The verse most talked about is V-34. Here, if taken in context, the women were not to speak in tongues in the church. Paul did not change his mind between 11:5 and this verse.

The emphasis in Chapter 14 is on prophesying, edifying the church, convincing unbelievers — (V-22-25).

Read V-40: _____

_____

(5) CHAPTER 15 — *Concerning the Resurrection.*

Paul begins with the *Cross* — V-3-4. "Christ died, for our sins, buried, He rose again."

Proofs of His resurrection — V-5-19.

NAME THE ONES WHO SAW HIM:

   (1) _____ (2) _____

   (3) _____ (4) _____

   (5) _____ (6) _____

The order of the resurrections — V-20-28. The order is self-explanatory.

The pattern or the features of our resurrection. V-42-50 — *There are seven:*

(1) "SOWN IN CORRUPTION; RAISED IN INCORRUPTION" — V-42.

(2) "SOWN IN DISHONOR; RAISED IN GLORY" — V-43.

(3) "SOWN IN WEAKNESS; RAISED IN POWER" — V-43.

(4) "SOWN A NATURAL BODY; RAISED A SPIRITUAL BODY" — V-44.

(5) "SOWN AN EARTHY BODY; RAISED A HEAVENLY BODY" — V-49.

(6) SOWN A "FLESH AND BLOOD" BODY; RAISED A CHANGED BODY — V-50-52.

(7) SOWN A "MORTAL" BODY; RAISED AN "IMMORTAL" BODY — V-53.

   THE TOWERING CHALLENGE OF PAUL — V-58.

(6) CHAPTER 16 — *Concerning the Collection.*

Note — when — where — how much — V-2.

The remainder of the Chapter is personal and Paul's final exhortations and benediction.

(Note — giving to the Lord is a "gift" — Romans 12:8. It should be a willing service for every believer.)

HOW MUCH DO YOU REMEMBER?

Q. Paul wrote first about _____ in the church.

Q. What was one of the major divisions in Corinth?

Q. What was the second reason Paul wrote this letter?

Q. Name only three things that stand out in your mind about I Corinthians.

YOUR ASSIGNMENT FOR NEXT WEEK

   1. Read the Book of II Corinthians (13 Chapters — less than two Chapters each day).

   2. Review your notes on I Corinthians.

   3. Mark your Bible from your notes.

   4. Be present for II Corinthians next Lord's Day.

Lesson 36
"The Book of
II Corinthians"

(Where lines are provided, please look up Scriptures and fill in the entire Scripture or the main Truth of the passage.)

1. **The Book**

   The first letter of Paul to the church at Corinth was written from Ephesus (II Cor. 1:8) while *this* letter was written from Philippi. Paul had sent Titus to Corinth because he could not go himself. Titus was to have met Paul and Timothy at Troas with a report on the church at Corinth, but Titus did not arrive (II Cor. 2:12-13). When Titus did not come, Paul and Timothy went on to Philippi where Titus brought good news from Corinth (II Cor. 7:5-11). Paul gives more of his personal history and his own feelings in this letter than in any other of his writings.

2. **The Central Message**

   "The Comfort of God Through Christ" — (1:3; 13:11).

3. **The Structure of the Book**

   - THE COMFORT OF GOD — Chapters 1 through 7.
   - CHRISTIAN GIVING — Chapters 8 and 9.
   - PAUL'S DEFENSE OF HIS APOSTLESHIP — Chapters 10 through 13.

4. **The Comfort of God — Chapters 1 through 7**

   (1) CHAPTER 1 — Paul's sufferings in Ephesus (Asia) were serious. His condition was such that *"we had the sentence of death in ourselves, that we should not trust in ourselves, but in God"* — (1:9).

   In V-3-7 the words *"comfort"* and *"consolation"* are used 10 times in five verses. It is the same word used for the Holy Spirit — "THE COMFORTER."

   Paul uses his own sufferings as a testimony to Corinth that God sustains and comforts so that he might comfort others — (V-8-14). His desire and plan is to go to Corinth but God changed his plans. Read V-15-24.

   NOTE: • the Holy Spirit *"establishes"* the believer — V-21

            • the Holy Spirit *"anoints"* the believer — V-21

            • the Holy Spirit *"seals"* the believer — V-22

            • the Holy Spirit is the *"earnest"* — the *"pledge"* of more to come — V-22

   (2) CHAPTER 2 — A reference to a sinning person of I Cor. 5 is in V-5-13. Paul had commanded discipline. Now we find that the person had repented and now Paul urges them to restore him in the fellowship (note V-8). Refusal to forgive him would give Satan an advantage (V-11).

   In V-14-17 — The triumphant Christian life is outlined. *(Underline V-14)*.

   (3) CHAPTERS 3 AND 4 — We see the OLD Covenant versus the NEW.

        • the Old Covenant was of the *"letter"* — (law) — the New is that of the Spirit written in *"freshly tables of the heart"* —

V-3 and 6.

- the Old Covenant "killeth" — the New *giveth life* — V-6.
- the Old Covenant was one of *"condemnation"* — the New of *righteousness* — V-9.
- the Old Covenant though *"done away,* WAS *glorious"* — the New IS glorious ("that which remaineth") — V-11.
- the Old Covenant in the *face of Moses* — the New shines from the *face of Jesus Christ* — (3:13 and 4:6).
- the symbol of the Old Covenant was a *veil* — the New is a *mirror* (3:13-18). Write in V-17: _____

_____

_____

So we see the differences between the Old and New Covenants. We are made mirrors to reflect the glory of the Lord. (Note 4:3-6). Write in V-6: _____

_____

_____

What comfort we should find in 4:7-10. We are but clay vessels (V-7) and the vessels must be broken for the light to shine out — "that the power may be of God, and not of us."

NOTE NOW V-8-9: "troubled — not distressed"

"perplexed — not in despair"

"persecuted — not forsaken"

"cast down — not destroyed"

Then V-16 — "our outward man perish — inward man is renewed."

What comfort! Suffering in this life for Christ "worketh an eternal weight of glory" — (V-17-18).

(4) CHAPTER 5 — COMFORT IN DEATH.

Physical death means the departure from the body (tabernacle). The bodies we have are temporary and they suffer (V-1-5). Death means that we leave these bodies and are *immediately* in the presence of the Lord.

Note V-8 _____

_____

In V-9-13 the believer appears before the judgment seat of Christ to receive *rewards* — or no rewards. Salvation was settled at the time one accepted Christ — this is not the judgment of sin but of works done for Christ.

In V-14-21 — The aim of Paul's ministry was that men be reconciled to God.

Note V-17 and *underline in your Bible* — also V-20-21.

(5) Chapter 6 — Paul lists 18 trying experiences of the ministry in V-4-7. (Can you find them?)

Then he lists 9 contrasts — covering all of life in V-8-10. (Find them, if you can.)

In V-11-18 you read a personal appeal to the Christians at Corinth to be separated from the world.

Note V-14 and write it here_____

_____

_____

_____

(6) Chapter 7 — The Comfort of God in the heart of Paul is found in V-4, 6, 7, 13.

Note V-10 and underline.

5. **Christian Giving — Chapters 8 and 9**

These two chapters give us detailed instructions for Christian giving.

V-1-6 — Giving is a grace. God wants you before your gift (V-5).

V-7-15 — Principles of Christian giving — NOT RULES.

> NOTE: • We should give *proportionately* — V-12-14.
>
> • We should give *bountifully* — 9:6.
>
> • We should give *cheerfully* — 9:7.

Note 8:9: _____

_____

_____

Look up Luke 6:38 _____

_____

Giving is a "gift" — Romans 12:8_____

_____

6. **Paul's Defense of His Apostleship — Chapters 10-13**

In this section Paul is forced to answer in reference to his own apostleship.

Paul's "boasting" was in the Lord and not for his own edification — (10:8).

Look up 10:12 and underline.

Paul's defense in CHAPTER 11 is very personal. He paid his own way (11:9). His life is given in graphic detail in 11:16-33. How would you go through such things if they came your way? Note V-22-28.

In CHAPTER 12:1-10 we see the inner life of the great champion of faith. In V-2-7, Paul says, "above fourteen years ago . . . caught up to the third heaven — heard unspeakable words — lest I should be exalted through revelations — there was given to me a thorn in the flesh, the messenger of Satan to buffet me."

Just think, Paul had not mentioned this for fourteen years. Three times he had pleaded with the Lord that the "thorn" be removed but God had a better plan. Note 12:9: _____

_____

_____

REMEMBER: "MY" — means God

"GRACE" — unearned favor

"IS" — the present

"SUFFICIENT" — more than enough

Paul gladly "gloried in the infirmities that the power of Christ may rest upon me."

Finally in CHAPTER 13 — "Examine yourselves, whether ye be in the faith, prove your own selves" — V-5. Paul concludes this letter where he began — "the comfort of God" — V-11. Then the beautiful benediction which is so familiar — V-14.

HOW MUCH DO YOU REMEMBER?

Q. What is the Central Message of II Corinthians?

Q. Why does God allow suffering and tribulation? (Read 1:3-4)

Q. Where does the Christian go at death?

Q. What does Paul teach about separation for the Christian?

Q. Giving is a _____. *Does God want your money or you?*

YOUR ASSIGNMENT FOR NEXT WEEK
1. Read the Book of Galatians (six Chapters).
2. Review your notes on II Corinthians.
3. Underline in your Bible the verses that mean the most to you.
4. Be present next Lord's Day for the study of the Book of Galatians.

Lesson 37
"The Book of Galatians"

(Where lines are provided, please look up Scriptures and fill in the entire Scripture or the main Truth of the passage.)

1. The Book

In this Book the Apostle Paul is struggling to preserve the purity of the gospel from those who would present "another gospel: which is not another; but there be some that trouble you and would pervert the gospel of Christ."

We notice in Chapter 4, Verse 13, "I preached the gospel unto you the first time," that he had visited Galatia twice before he wrote the epistle. The record in the Book of Acts tells us that Paul first went to Galatia on his second missionary journey (Acts 16:6) and that he paid a second visit there during the third missionary journey, some three years later (Acts 18:23).

The Galatians themselves were an emotional and intense people. They were a branch of the Gauls originally from the north of the Baltic Sea.

J. Vernon McGee says, "The Book of Galatians is a stern, severe, solemn message. It does not correct conduct as the Corinthian letters do, but it is corrective.

"This is the only time in all of Paul's writings in which he does not express his thankfulness. This is the only church of whom he does not ask prayers. There is no word of commendation nor praise and there is no mention of their standing in Christ. No one with him is mentioned by name.

"The heart of Paul the Apostle is laid bare; there is deep emotion and strong feeling. This is Paul's fighting epistle.

"Galatians is the declaration of emancipation from legalism of any type. This was Martin Luther's favorite epistle and it was on the masthead of the reformation.

"It is the strongest declaration of defense of the Doctrine of Justification By Faith in or out of Scripture."

2. The Central Message

"Stand fast therefore in the liberty wherewith Christ hath made us free" — Galatians 5:1.

3. The Structure of the Book

- INTRODUCTION — Chapter 1:1-10
- PERSONAL — A Testimony — Chapters 1 and 2
- DOCTRINAL — Justification By Faith — Chapters 3 and 4
- PRACTICAL — Liberty In Christ — Chapters 5 and 6

4. The Introduction — Chapter 1:1-10

Paul gives a cool greeting because first, he qualifies his apostleship which was not *from* men, that is, not legalistic. Nor was it *by* men — meaning that it was not ritualistic. But his apostleship was "through Jesus Christ." Jesus called him and set him apart for the office — Acts 9:15-16. The greeting here is very cool, brief and formal.

You'll notice in Verses 6-10 Paul states the subject — there is only one gospel and Paul warns them not to listen to what was called "another gospel." The Judaizers had sought to add the law to grace — FAITH PLUS LAW — in other words. Paul calls this a *"perversion of the gospel of Christ."* — Verse 7

5. **Personal — A Testimony — Chapters 1 and 2**

When you first read these two Chapters you might get the idea that Paul is defending his apostleship. Paul is here proving his genuineness and the authenticity of the gospel which he preached. He had already told them in Verse 1 that his apostleship was neither from men nor through men and you will notice in Verses 11 and 12 that what he preached came by *direct revelation* from the Lord Jesus Christ. After he had received this *direct revelation* and commission he had "conferred not with flesh and blood" — Verse 16. Nor had he gone up to Jerusalem to see those men who were apostles before him, but instead went into Arabia — Verse 17. (Write V-16.)

_____

_____

After three years he went up to Jerusalem to see Peter and to stay with him 15 days (Verse 18), and he didn't see any of the other apostles except James (Verses 18 and 19). So the purpose here in this first Chapter *is to show that the gospel which he preached was genuine as to its origin because it did not come from man, but was a direct revelation of Jesus Christ.*

In Chapter 2 Paul went to Jerusalem along with Barnabas and Titus (Verses 1-10). It had been 14 years since his first visit to Jerusalem. He took Barnabas and Titus, and there they had an understanding between him and those present (Verses 6-10). Their understanding dealt with the Central Doctrine of Salvation — *solely and wholly by* GRACE — so that when Peter and others on a later occasion in Antioch lapsed into Judaistic behavior, Paul rebuked him on the very basis of that common understanding (Verses 11-21). Here, then, we find in these two Chapters the *basic identity of the gospel* preached by Paul, Peter and other apostles.

Of special attention is the fact that Paul silently rebukes Peter for allowing the Judaizers to pressure him into withdrawing from all Gentile believers upon the arrival of some influential Jews from Jerusalem. This is indeed difficult for the church of Rome to interpret because Paul, a tentmaker, was rebuking Peter, who was supposed to be "the first Pope."

Note Chapter 2, Verse 20 *and underline in your Bible.*

6. **Doctrinal — Justification By Faith — Chapters 3 and 4**

Paul expresses an attitude of sheer surprise here because he speaks as though it is incredible to him that anyone should be able to turn back from the glorious liberty and the wonderful gospel to the bondage of legalism. His first words are *"O foolish Galatians, who did bewitch you?"* as though he could only contribute what had happened to some strange hypnotic spell. You will find that word *"foolish"* again in Verse 3.

All through these two Chapters Paul is showing the superiority of the gospel over Judaism;

- of faith OVER works (3:2)
- of the spirit OVER the flesh (Verse 3)
- of being justified OVER being held by law (Verses 8 and 11)
- of being blessed OVER being cursed (Verses 9 and 10)
- of the "promise" in Abraham OVER the command through Moses (Verses 12-14)
- of the Abrahamic Covenant OVER the Mosaic Covenant (Verses

16-22) and on and on we could go.

One of the important lessons for all believers today is to understand Paul's legal illustration beginning at Chapter 3, Verse 6. Abraham received his righteousness by faith in God long before the law was given (3:6, 17). God told Abraham in Genesis 12:3 that Gentiles would also receive the righteousness by faith (Chapter 3:8 and 9). God not only pardons sinners by faith, but then preserves them by faith because "the just shall live by faith" (3:11). This statement is taken from Habakkuk 2:4 and is used here as well as in Romans 1:17 and Hebrews 10:38.

In Verse 10 we're told that if the Old Testament law is broken at all ("cursed is everyone that continueth not in *all* things which are written in the Book of the law") the entire law is broken.

The law was given to Israel 430 years *after* the promise (justification by faith) was given. We studied this period of time back in the study of Genesis and you will recall from that study that the 430 years is the time from God's confirmation of His promise to Jacob until the giving of the law at Sinai. The giving of the law was an insertion, given because of sin. *"It was added because of sin or transgression."* It was ordained by angels in the hand of a mediator (3:19).

It thus acted as Israel's school master because "the law was our school master to bring us unto Christ" (3:24). The law, in a sense, should shock us into a sense of our need of Christ that we might be justified by faith in Him (3:24). So the giving of the law did not override the Abrahamic Promise. The Chapter closes with a special emphasis: "Ye are all sons of God through faith in Jesus Christ" — Verse 26. "If ye are Christ's, then are ye Abraham's seed" — Verse 29.

Notice especially Verses 27 and 28 of Chapter 3. Christ unified *all* repenting sinners in His body because "there is now neither Jew nor Greek, neither bond nor free, neither male nor female for ye are all one in Christ Jesus."

In Chapter 4 Paul continued what he began in Chapter 3. He guarantees our full adoption as sons of God in Verses 1-7. You will notice in Verses 6 and 7 that we enter into the privileges of adult sonship in a real spiritual sense because "God hath sent forth the spirit of His Son into our hearts . . . wherefore thou art no more a servant but a son; and if a son, then an heir of God through Christ."

Note especially Verses 4 and 5 because here we find these two verses explaining how we are redeemed from under the law.

Paul gives an allegorical illustration in Verses 21-31. He is simply using the Old Testament doctrinal events to make the point.

THE FACTS OF PAUL'S ALLEGORY:

Abraham had two sons and two wives. One, Ishmael, was born by Haggar. The other, Isaac, was born *supernaturally* by Sarah — V-22-23.

THE APPLICATION OF PAUL'S ALLEGORY ARE:

Haggar represents the LAW while Sarah speaks of GRACE.

Isaac refers to the spirit and to those who would look to Jesus thus becoming free sons.

Haggar represents MT. SINAI while Sarah represents the MT. OF OLIVES — V-25.

For a believer to miss "LAW AND GRACE" is to suffer persecution and ridicule as did Isaac from Ishmael (Verses 28-29).

7. **Practical — Liberty In Christ — Chapters 5 and 6**

In the last two Chapters we have Paul's exhortation to the Galatians. As

165

rich as it is we cannot take it verse by verse, but only the highlights. First, does Verse 4 mean falling from grace? The verse does not mean that they had lost their salvation because Paul calls these same Galatians "brethren" nine times and he also calls them "children of God" in 3:26 and "sons of God" in 4:6 and "heirs of the promise" in 3:29.

The Greek word here for "fallen" is found in Acts 27:17, 26, 29 and 32 where it refers to a ship not under control. This is the meaning here in Galatians. It means a *"falling away"* or in our day it would be *"backsliding."*

NOTE VERSE 13 AND UNDERLINE.

After you have read Verse 13 notice how Paul lists some 17 works of the flesh resulting from an illegal usage of the law (Verses 19-21). Can you find the 17 works of the flesh?

THE FRUIT OF THE SPIRIT — VERSES 22 AND 23.

The Spirit always produces living fruit, which is —

1. LOVE — divine concern for others.
2. JOY — inward peace.
3. PEACE — a confidence and quietness.
4. LONGSUFFERING — patience, endurance.
5. GENTLENESS — kindness.
6. GOODNESS — love in action.
7. FAITH — things not seen.
8. MEEKNESS — subdued strength.
9. TEMPERANCE — self-control.

There are duties and liberties that we have as believers and you will find these listed in CHAPTER 6. We have a liberty of a service and a love toward those in need and you will find this emphasized in the first few verses in Chapter 6.

Even the last few verses are packed with striking words from the lips of Paul, but we call your attention only to the *last two verses.* "from henceforth let no man trouble me: for I bear in my body the marks of the Lord Jesus." The marks of the Lord Jesus which Paul had on his body were the marks of people who had been branded as slaves (a mark of ownership), soldiers (a mark of allegiance), devotees (as a mark of consequences), criminals (as a mark of exposure), and the abhorred (as a mark of reproach).

PAUL HAD ALL FIVE OF THESE. He had been battered and bruised in such a way that his body had permanent scars. He had been stoned at Lystra, dragged outside the city and left for dead. He had been whipped five times by the Jews and had three floggings by the Roman soldiers. He had been assaulted by the mobs and ambushed by enemies.

All of these left marks on Paul's body. But why does he mention these brands at the end of the Galatian letter? One reason is indicated by the fact that the "I" is emphatic: "I bear in my body the brands of the Lord Jesus." Paul here draws a contrast between himself and the Judaizing teachers who were subverting the Galatian believers. These men were big talkers but they did not bear any brand marks of the Lord Jesus in their person as Paul did.

A SECOND REASON why Paul mentions these brand marks is found in the emphasis that they are the brand marks of "the Lord Jesus Christ." He is *drawing a contrast between* the marks of Jesus and the mark of Moses which is circumcision. Circumcision is the mark of Moses and speaks of servitude to a legal system. The marks of the Lord Jesus are those of a glad, free, voluntary service.

A THIRD REASON why Paul speaks here of these brand marks is found in the words "from henceforth let no man trouble me." All of the trouble had come thus far in this Book from the false teachers who were perverting the young faith of Paul's converts. In these words Paul is saying that if any of these false teachers have any sense of honesty or honor they will at least drop their tricks of trying to destroy the faith that Paul has preached.

We should bear the marks of the Lord Jesus in ourselves and never be ashamed of bearing some reproach for Christ's sake — never be afraid of bearing some marks in our bodies.

HOW MUCH DO YOU REMEMBER?

Q. What is the Central Message of the Book?

Q. The Galatians were a branch of _____.

Q. Does the Galation epistle contain any word of praise or thanksgiving or commendation?

Q. What did Paul call the Galatians?

Q. What did Paul bear in his body?

YOUR ASSIGNMENT FOR NEXT WEEK

1. Read the six Chapters of the Book of Ephesians.
2. Review your study of the Book of Galatians.
3. Underline in your Bible those important verses in Galatians.
4. Be ready for the study of the Book of Ephesians next Lord's Day.

Lesson 38
"The Book of Ephesians"

through the Bible in one year

(Where lines are provided, please look up Scriptures and fill in the entire Scripture or the main Truth of the passage.)

1. **Background**

   Ephesians was written from Rome and is the first in the order of the Prison Epistles. Paul was forbidden by the Holy Spirit to enter Asia, where Ephesus was the center (Acts 16:6). He was called by a vision to Macedonia. He was led by the Spirit into Europe as far as Corinth, after which he returned by way of Ephesus (Acts 18:19). He was so impressed that he promised to return and he did on his third missionary journey. He stayed there two years — longer than at any other place (Acts 19:8-10).

   READ I CORINTHIANS 16:8-9.

   Paul loved this church even in face of great opposition (Acts 19). His last meeting with the Ephesian elders was a tender farewell (Acts 20:17-38).

2. **The Central Message**

   "Blessed be the God and Father of our Lord Jesus Christ, who hath blessed us with all spiritual blessings in heavenly places in Christ: According as He hath chosen us in Him before the foundation of the world —" — Ephesians 1:3-4.

3. **The Structure of the Book**

   Doctrinal — Our Heavenly Calling — Chapters 1 through 3.
   Practical — Our Earthly Conduct — Chapters 4 through 6.

4. **Doctrinal — Our Heavenly Calling — Chapters 1 through 3**

   (1) THE CHURCH IS A BODY — Chapter 1.

   Paul begins with a great outpouring of *praise* for our possessions in Christ — V-1-14.

   (a) We are *"in* Christ" — V-1.

   (b) We are *"blessed* with spiritual blessings" — V-3.

   (c) "He has *chosen* us in Him" — V-4.

   (d) "The *adoption* of us by Jesus Christ" — V-5.

   (e) We are *"accepted* in the beloved" — V-6.

   (f) We have *"redemption* through His blood" — V-7
   ("redemption" means "we are bought with a price").

   (g) We have the "forgiveness of sins" — V-7.

   (h) He has *made known* the mystery of His will" — V-9.

   (i) "He will gather *together in one* all things in Christ — V-10.

   (j) "We have *obtained an inheritance"* in Him — V-11.

   (k) We are "the *praise* of His glory" — V-12.

   (l) We are *"sealed* with the Holy Spirit" — V-13.

   (m) We are guaranteed this: "the *earnest* of our inheritance *until the redemption* of the purchased possession" — V-14.

(a) "Give unto you the spirit of wisdom and revelation in knowledge of Him" — V-17.

(b) "that you may know the hope of His calling" — V-18.

(c) "the exceeding greatness of His power to us-ward who believe" — V-19-20. This is the "power wrought in Christ when He was raised from the dead and is at the right hand of God in heavenly places."

The exalted Christ is above all and is the head over the Church, which is His body. Paul gives thanks that we, the Church, are the fullness (complement) of Him — V-20-23.

(2) THE CHURCH IS THE HOUSEHOLD OF GOD — Chapter 2.

The new condition in Christ — V-1-10.

In the first three verses we see our condition before we were saved:

(a) We were "dead in trespasses and sins" — V-1.
We were dead spiritually — apart from God.

(b) "We walked according to the course of this world — children of disobedience" — V-2.
"That the spirit now works in unbelievers."

(c) We lived "in the lusts of the flesh fulfilling the desires of the flesh and of the mind: and were by nature the children of wrath" — V-3.

But at V-4 there is a break and it begins with the words *"But God."*
Our *new condition* is stated in four characteristics:

(a) "He hath quickened us together with Christ" — V-5. Quite a contrast to V-1 (quickened means made alive).

(b) God has "raised us up together and made us sit together *in* heavenly places *in* Christ Jesus." — V-6. We are present possessors of that life in Christ Jesus.

(c) "In ages to come He (God) might show the riches of His grace in His kindness toward us through Jesus Christ" — V-7.

(d) "By grace are ye saved through faith — for we are His workmanship created in Christ Jesus unto good works" — V-8-10.
(Divine grace, not human merit at all.)

Now Paul gives our new relationship since we changed our old condition — V-11-22. Paul reviews some things in our past in V-11-12. We were ALIENS — WITHOUT CHRIST — STRANGERS — NO HOPE — WITHOUT GOD.

In V-13-18 Paul says again, "BUT NOW," and here is the new relationshp in Christ:

(a) "Made nigh by the blood of Christ" — V-13.

(b) "He is our peace — and hath broken down the middle wall of partition between us" — (Jew and Gentile) — V-14.

(c) "He abolished the enmity — making peace" — V-15.

(d) He made "in Himself *one* new man" — V-15 thus destroying distinction between Jew and Gentile if we are in Christ — His Body.

In V-19-22 we see that we are the temple of God — the household of faith. Note these things:

(a) "We are fellow citizens" — V-19.

(b) We are "of the household of God" — V-19.

(c) We are "built on one foundation" — V-20.

(d) We are "the building framed together — unto a holy temple in the Lord" — V-21.

(e) We are indwelt by the Spirit — V-22.

(3) THE CHURCH IS A DIVINE MYSTERY — Chapter 3.

We come now to one of the profound passages in the Bible. In the first part Paul reveals the divine mystery — V-1-12.

(a) The mystery was made known and committed to Paul — V-1-3.

(b) The mystery was not made known to the Old Testament saints — V-5.

(c) The mystery is then totally revealed in V-6-10.

"That the Gentiles should be fellow-heirs and of the same body, and partakers of His promise in Christ by the Gospel" — V-6.

In the Old Testament, Gentile salvation was known but not in this manner — (salvation without becoming Jews by proselytism).

Look up Isaiah 11:10 _____

_____

Isaiah 42:6 _____

_____

_____

Isaiah 60:3 _____

_____

_____

The Scofield Bible note says — "The mystery hid in God was the divine purpose to make the Jew and Gentile a wholly new thing — the Church, which is His (Christ's) body, formed by the baptism of the Holy Spirit (I Cor. 12:13) and in which the earthly distinction of Jew and Gentile disappears (Eph. 2:14-15; Col. 3:10-11). The revelation of this mystery, which was foretold but not explained by Christ (Matt. 16:18), was committed to Paul. In His writings ALONE we find the *doctrine, position, walk,* and *destiny* of the Church." (Scofield note on Eph. 3:6).

SO, THE MYSTERY THEN IS "THE CHURCH" — THE BODY OF CHRIST — ALL OF US WHO ARE SAVED.)

The Old Testament prophets could never see this dispensation of the Church (See V-9 and 10 again.)

In this present age, an elect people, should be called out (saved) regardless of nationality to form the Church.

In the second part of this Chapter Paul prays for three things in V-13-21:

(a) "That He would grant you according to the riches of His glory, to be strengthened with might by His Spirit" — V-16.

(b) "That ye be rooted and grounded in love" — V-17.

(c) "That ye may be able to comprehend — the breadth, length, depth, and height — that he might be filled with all the fulness of God — V-18-19.

Look up Col. 1:19 _____

_____

Col. 2:9-10 _____

_____

The Doxology of Paul is glorious! Read and underline 3:20-21.

5. Practical — Our Earthly Conduct — Chapters 4 through 6

(1) Chapter 4 — We are to *walk worthy* of our calling — keeping the unity of peace in the Body. We are unified by seven great stabilizers:

(a) ONE BODY (Christ's Body — the Church — I Cor. 12:12)

(b) ONE SPIRIT (the Holy Spirit — see I Cor. 12:4)

(c) ONE HOPE (Blessed — Titus 2:13; Eternal — Titus 3:7)

(d) ONE LORD (The Saviour — I Cor. 12:5)

(e) ONE FAITH (I Cor. 16:13; II Tim. 4:7)

(f) ONE BAPTISM (Into Christ's Body — I Cor. 12:13)

(g) ONE GOD (The Father — I Cor. 12:6)

Compare 4:7-10 with Psalm 68:18.

 The ministry gifts of Christ to the Church — V-11.

 The purpose of the gifts — V-12-16.

In V-17-32 — We see how we are to walk and talk as "new men."

Note also that this *Practical* section looks back to the Doctrinal section (Chapters 1-3). EXAMPLE: In 1:13 we are taught that the Holy Spirit *seals* us. Now in 4:30 we are told "grieve not the Holy Spirit."

(2) THE CHURCH WILL BE THE BRIDE — Chapter 5.

 (a) We are to be separated — V-1-13.

 (b) We are to serve — V-14-17.
   Note V-16_____

 (c) We are to be Spirit-filled — V-18.

 (d) We are to be happy and thankful — V-19-20.

 (e) God chose the human relationship — the love of a man for his wife — to illustrate Christ's love for the Church — V-21-25.

   Note V-25_____

 (f) His love consummated at the Rapture — V-26-27.
   Note V-26 — "cleanse it with the washing by the Word."

 (g) Note V-32 — The Mystery is stated.

(3) THE CHURCH IS A WARRIOR IN THIS WORLD — Chapter 6.

 (a) There is an orderly way to train children. The parents have a spiritual responsibility — V-1-4.

 (b) Servants and masters are to serve as unto Christ — for God is no respector of persons — V-5-9.

 (c) The equipment we are to have — V-10-17. Note the pieces of armor:

  • "girdle of truth" — V-14

  • "the breastplate of righteousness" — V-14

  • "the sandals of the Gospel" — V-15

  • "shield of faith" — V-16

  • "helmet of salvation" — V-17

  • "sword of the Spirit, *which is the Word of God*" — V-17

 (d) Finally we are to pray and watch and speak boldly — V-18-19.

What a glorious letter. Every verse so rich. We have gone far over our space — but still we have left out so much.

HOW MUCH DO YOU REMEMBER?

Q. What are the two main divisions of the Book?

Q. Can you name 5 possessions we have in Christ?

Q. How does Paul describe Christ's love for the Church?

Q. Was the Church made known to the Old Testament?

YOUR ASSIGNMENT FOR NEXT WEEK
1. Read the Book of Philippians — only 4 Chapters.
2. Review the rich study of Ephesians.
3. Mark your Bible from your notes.
4. Be present next Lord's Day for the study of Philippians.

Lesson 39
"The Book of Philippians"

(Where lines are provided, please look up Scriptures and fill in the entire Scripture or the main Truth of the passage.)

1. **Background of the Book**

   This epistle of Paul was written in 62 A.D. while Paul was a prisoner in Rome. We know this from the reference to "Caesar's household" in 4:22. The church was born out of the vision Paul received at Troas in Acts 16:6-13 — "Come over into Macedonia and help us." Philippi was the chief city of Macedonia and it was the first European city to receive the Gospel.

   This letter was written some ten years after Paul's visit there. The first convert in Europe was a woman, Lydia, a seller of purple, from Thyatira. He expelled a demon from a slave girl — and the Philippian jailer was converted. These three were the first to believe and they were the potential of that church (Acts 16:14-34).

   Learning of Paul's imprisonment, the Philippian church sent Epaphroditus to Rome to convey their love and gifts for him (4:18). Epaphroditus was taken seriously ill on his journey to Rome and Paul was thankful for the mercy of God in restoring him to health (2:25-30). In sending Epaphroditus back, Paul sends this epistle with him.

2. **The Central Message**

   "For me to live is Christ, and to die is gain" — (1:21).

   ("Joy in Christ" could easily be another Central message — Note: 1:4, 18, 25; 2:16, 17, 18, 28; 3:1, 3; 4:1, 4.)

3. **The Structure of the Book**

   - Christ, THE PURPOSE OF LIFE — Chapter 1
   - Christ, OUR PATTERN FOR LIVING — Chapter 2
   - Christ, OUR GOAL IN LIFE — Chapter 3
   - Christ, OUR POWER (STRENGTH) IN LIFE — Chapter 4

4. **Christ, the Purpose of Life — Chapter 1**

   The *Key Verse* of Chapter 1 is V-21, "For me to live is Christ, and to die is gain."

   The first seven verses are a salutation and are so precious to the Christian. Note V-3 and underline.

   Memorize and underline V-6. ALL BELIEVERS SHOULD KNOW THIS VERSE.

   We find seven expressions that Christ is the purpose of life in Chapter 1:

   (1) The Christian should have *the feelings of Christ* — "I long after you all in the affections of Christ" — V-8 ("bowels" means "affection").

   (2) We should have *the same interests as Christ* — "The things which happened to me have caused the spreading of the Gospel — Christ is preached and therein I do rejoice" — V-12-18.

   (3) The very *Spirit of Jesus Christ* is ours — "For I know that this shall

turn to my freedom through your prayer, and the supply of the *Spirit of Jesus Christ,"* V-19. His inmost life is ours.

(4) Our one supreme concern should be Christ because *He is our life* — "Christ shall be magnified in my body, whether it be by life or by death" — V-20.

(5) *Christ is,* and should be, *our longing desire* — V-21 and 23. Paul longs for Christ "which is far better."

(6) *Our conduct should be controlled by Christ* — "Let your manner of life (conversation) be as it becomes the Gospel of Christ" — V-27.

(7) *We may suffer for Christ – the badge of a Christian* — and we should be strong and willing — "but also to suffer for His sake" — V-29 (Read V-27-30).

Look up John 16:33b_____

_____

5. **Christ, Our Pattern For Living — Chapter 2**

The key verse of Chapter 2 is V-5 — "Let this mind be in you, which was also in Christ Jesus."

(1) THE MIND OF CHRIST

Here in this Chapter we see the *"mind of Christ"* which should be the controlling factor of the Christian mind:

Note: V-2 — "BE LIKEMINDED"

V-2 — "OF ONE MIND"

V-3 — "LOWLINESS OF MIND"

V-5 — "LET THIS MIND BE IN YOU —" the impartation of the mind of Christ by the Holy Spirit.

(2) THE SELF-HUMBLING OF OUR LORD — V-5-8 (seven steps):

(a) "Being in the form of God thought it not robbery to be equal with God" — He was God, the Son, regardless.

(b) "Made Himself of no reputation" — emptied Himself.

(c) "Took upon Him the form of a servant." He came through the line of David — but Isaiah 11:1 says, "He shall come out of the stem of Jesse." Why? Because at the time of His birth, Jesse, the father of David, was a peasant farmer — "He took the form of a servant."

(d) "Was made in the likeness of men" — see John 1:14.

(e) "He humbled Himself" — See I Peter 2:21-24.

(f) "Became obedient unto death" — see John 10:18.

(g) "Even the death of the Cross."

(3) THE EXALTATION OF CHRIST BY GOD, THE FATHER — V-9-11.

This is the work of the Father — that "every tongue should confess that Jesus Christ is Lord."

(4) MIND OF PAUL — V-12-18.

Note V-12-13. We are not to "work out" salvation. Paul means here that the Christian life is not a series of "ups and downs" but "ins and outs." God works *in;* we are to work *out* (now read V-13 again).

Paul reminds them — "Do all things without murmurings and disputings" — V-14.

"Holding forth the Word of life" — should be our motto.

(5) MIND OF TIMOTHY — V-19-24.

- Paul plans to send Timothy to Philippi — V-19.
- Timothy was likeminded as Paul — V-20.
- Timothy compared to others — 21-23.

(6) MIND OF EPAPHRODITUS — V-25-30.

"For the work of Christ, he was nigh unto death." He had one goal — the Lord Jesus.

6. **Christ, Our Goal in Life — Chapter 3**

The key verse of Chapter 3 is V-10. "That I may know Him —."

(1) Paul warns of those who would lead astray. V-1-3 — "Beware of dogs, evil workers, of the concision." They were like snapping dogs toward the Gospel and they were evil and believed in "mutilation" — circumcision necessary for salvation. God's real circumcision is in:

Col. 2:11 _____

_____

_____

Paul says "We have no confidence in the flesh."

(2) If anyone had reason to glory in the flesh, Paul had — V-4-6.

Note what Paul "counted loss" gladly to serve Christ:

- "CIRCUMCISED THE EIGHTH DAY" — Israelite by birth.
- "OF THE STOCK OF ISRAEL" — Parents were Hebrews.
- "OF THE TRIBE OF BENJAMIN" — the tribe which gave Israel the first king.
- "AN HEBREW OF THE HEBREWS" — kept Hebrew customs.
- "AS TOUCHING THE LAW, A PHARISEE" — the strict view of the law.
- "CONCERNING ZEAL, PERSECUTING THE CHURCH" — a zealous Pharisee.
- "TOUCHING THE RIGHTEOUSNESS IN THE LAW, BLAMELESS" — Paul kept all the practices of the law.

(3) The prize Paul gained — V-7-21 (Gains and Losses).

(a) He gained new KNOWLEDGE — V-7-8.

(b) He gained new RIGHTEOUSNESS — V-9.

(c) He gained new POWER ("power of His resurrection") — V-10.

(d) He gained a new GOAL — V-11-17. Notice especially "this one thing I do" — V-13.

Look up Mark 10:21 for contrast _____

_____

Note also — "reaching forth to those things which are before." See I Corinthians 9:24-27.

The prize is in V-14 — Christ is the prize, Paul appeals for them to have the same goal — V-15-19.

(e) He gained a *new* hope — V-20-21.

"Look for the Saviour, the Lord Jesus Christ, who shall change our vile body —."

Look up I Corinthians 15:51-54.

Also I John 3:2 _____

_____

7. **Christ, Our Power (Strength) in Life — Chapter 4**

The key verse is V-13 — "I can do all things through (in) Christ which strengtheneth me."

(1) JOY the source of power — V-1-4.

The Philippians were a joy to Paul — V-1.

Two women had a fuss and Paul says they should have the same mind (get right with each other) — V-2.

Notice the prominence of women in the church — V-3.

Joy is a command — "Rejoice in the Lord alway" — V-4.

(2) PRAYER — the secret of power — V-5-7.

"Be anxious for nothing, but in *everything* by prayer and supplication with *thanksgiving* let your requests be made known unto God" — V-6.

This brings the peace of God. Underline V-6-7.

(3) RIGHT THINKING — for strength and peace — V-8-9.

Notice we are to think on things that are:

"TRUE " — "HONEST" — "JUST" — "PURE" — "LOVELY" — "GOOD REPORT" —

Do the things you have "LEARNED" — "RECEIVED" — "HEARD" — "SEEN" — "DO."

(4) THE POWER OF CHRIST SATISFIES — V-10-12 — "therewith to be content" — regardless of conditions.

Don't fret over things. Christ is enough.

(5) THE POWER OF CHRIST SUPPLIES — V-13-23.

"I can do all things through Christ" — V-13.

The prepositions used by Paul in this Book are important:

- to be *in* Christ means salvation.
- to work *through* Christ means sanctification.
- to live *for* Christ means dedication.
- to surrender *to* Christ means consecration.
- to be *with* Christ means glorification.

Paul ends this glorious letter with a gracious reminder —

"But my God shall supply all your needs according to His riches in glory by Christ Jesus" — V-19.

HOW MUCH DO YOU REMEMBER?

Q. Where was Paul when he wrote this epistle?

Q. Can you give the Central Message?

Q. What is another prevailing theme in the Book?

Q. Where would you turn for help in talking to someone emotionally upset?

YOUR ASSIGNMENT FOR NEXT WEEK

1. Read the Book of Colossians — (only 4 Chapters).
2. Review your notes on Philippians.
3. Have you marked your Bible — the verses in Philippians you should remember?
4. Be in class next Lord's Day for the study of Colossians.

Lesson 40
"The Book of Colossians"

NOTES

(Where lines are provided, please look up Scriptures and fill in the entire Scripture or the main Truth of the passage.)

1. **Background of the Book**

   This epistle was written during Paul's imprisonment in Rome, about 62 A.D. Although Paul never visited Colosse (2:1) he did spend two years teaching the Word at Ephesus. Colosse was about 90 miles east of Ephesus. Apparently visitors from Colosse had heard Paul and had come to know Christ. Epaphras (the pastor at Colosse) and Philemon were probably two of them.

   Colosse was only 12 miles from Laodicea. It was infected with *Judaistic Gnosticism*. This philosophy consisted of the following *(with Paul's answer in the Scripture reference)*:

JUDAISTIC GNOSTICISM	PAUL'S ANSWER
• Salvation could be obtained only through wisdom.	Col. 1:28
• That God did not create the universe directly — but through creating one creature who in turn created another, etc. Christ was just another of these creatures.	Col. 1:15-19; 2:18
• Asceticism — avoiding joy of life and practicing self-denial.	Col. 2:16, 23
• Licentiousness — Unrestrained immorality.	Col. 3:5-9

2. **The Central Message**

   "For in Him (Jesus) dwelleth all the fulness of the Godhead bodily" — (2:9).

3. **The Structure of the Book**

   DOCTRINAL: "That ye may be filled" — Chapters 1 and 2.

   PRACTICAL: "Set your affection on things above" — Chapters 3 and 4.

4. **Doctrinal: "That ye may be filled" — Chapters 1 and 2**

   (1) CHAPTER 1 — THE PRE-EMINENCE OF CHRIST.

   (a) THE INTRODUCTION — V-1-8.

   Note that Paul links the trinity of graces for believers — V-4-5.

   • FAITH — Past Tense
   • LOVE — Present
   • HOPE — Future

   Epaphras was a dear fellowservant and minister of Christ.

   (b) PAUL'S PRAYER — V-9-14.

   Note • "that ye might be filled with the knowledge of His will" — V-9.

   • "that ye might walk worthy" — V-10

- "strengthened — unto all patience" — V-11.
- "partakers of the *inheritance* of the saints" — V-12.
- "who hath *delivered* us from the power of darkness" — V-13.
- "and has *translated* us unto the kingdom of His Son" — V-13.
- "in whom we have *redemption* through His blood" — V-14.
- "even the *forgiveness* of sins" — V-14.

(Note: the five italicized words — expressing fivefold salvation in this prayer.)

(c) THE PERSON OF CHRIST — V-15-18.

Paul gives his *full length portrait* of our Lord. It will help you to remember if we list the *seven* features:

1. "The image (visible form) of the invisible God" — V-15.
2. "The first born of all creation" — V-15.
3. "By Him were ALL things created" — V-16.
4. "He IS before all things" — V-17.
5. "By Him all things consist" — V-17.
6. "He is the Head of the body, the Church" — V-18.
7. "The first born from among the dead" — V-18.

This was the Christ which had been preached to the Colossians. Christ alone, unites all of these aspects Paul gives in his prayer — "that in all things He might have the pre-eminence" — V-18.

(d) THREE ASPECTS OF OUR LORD — V-19-27.

1. "In Him should all fulness dwell . . ." — V-19.
2. "Having made peace through the blood of his Cross — V-20.
3. "His body — the Church — the mystery which had been hid" — V-24-27.

The "FULNESS" comprehends the Godhead — the "CROSS" comprehends the universe — the "MYSTERY" comprehends all ages — "but now is made manifest to his saints." That "MYSTERY" is "CHRIST IN YOU, THE HOPE OF GLORY" — V-27.

(2) CHAPTER 2 — THE DANGERS OF PHILOSOPHY AND RITUAL

(a) Christ is the answer to philosophy — V-1-15.

There were at least five errors that endangered the Church at Colosse:

1. ENTICING WORDS — V-4.
2. PHILOSOPHY — V-8.
3. LEGALISM — V-14-17.
4. MYSTICISM — V-18-19.
5. ASCETICISM — V-20-23.

Paul answered each of these errors:

- *Know* who Jesus is! — V-3 and 9.
- *Know* what He has done for you — V-13 and 15.
- *Know* who you are as Christians — V-10 and 12.
- *Know* what you are to do for Him — V-6-7.

(There is so much doctrine in these first two Chapters. The heart of the epistle is in V-9-10. And let me paraphrase: "In Him dwelleth all the FULNESS of the Godhead bodily; and ye are FILLED FULL in Him."

5. **Practical — "Set your affection on things above" — Chapters 3 and 4**

In these two Chapters we see the duty of the believer in relation to all areas of life. Paul minces no words. The Scriptures speak for themselves:

(1) In relation to the Son of God — 3:1-4.

(2) In relation to our personal life — 3:5-12.

(3) In relation to other believers — 3:13-14.

(4) In relation to the Word of God — 3:16 — write in this verse:

_____

_____

_____

(5) In relation to the work of God — 3:17. _____

_____

_____

(6) In relation to the home — 3:18-21 (Notice that Paul mentions *Wives, Husbands, Children, Fathers.*)

(7) In relation to your service — 3:22-25. (Write in V-23.)

_____

_____

(8) In relation to prayer life — 4:2-4. (Write in V-2.)

_____

_____

(9) In relation to the unsaved — 4:5-6. (Write in V-5.)

_____

_____

(10) In relation to other Christian leaders — 4:7-18.

Paul closes the letter by listing nine leaders associated with his ministry:

1. TYCHICUS — took the letter to Colosse.
2. ONESIMUS — the runaway slave of Philemon.
3. ARISTARCHUS — a fellow prisoner with Paul.
4. JOHN MARK — See Acts 15:37.
5. JUSTUS — a co-worker with Paul.
6. EPAPHRAS — the pastor at Colosse (imprisoned).
7. LUKE — the physician and author of Luke and Acts.
8. DEMUS — A co-worker that eventually forsook Paul (II Timothy 4:10).
9. ARCHIPPUS — the one who assumed the pastorate at Colosse when Epaphras was imprisoned.

"Remember my bonds" — V-18. Paul, in prison, wrote this masterpiece — what grace!

HOW MUCH DO YOU REMEMBER?

Q. How did the Word get to Colosse?

Q. Why did Epaphras go to Rome to see Paul?

Q. What is the Central Truth of Colossians?

Q. Paul's full length portrait of Christ is in 1:15-18. Have you marked these aspects in your Bible?

YOUR ASSIGNMENT FOR NEXT WEEK
1. Read I Thessalonians — (only 5 Chapters).
2. Review your notes on Colossians.
3. Mark your Bible from your notes.
4. Be present next Lord's Day for I Thessalonians.

Lesson 41
"The Book of
I Thessalonians"

(Where lines are provided, please look up Scriptures and fill in the entire Scripture or the main Truth of the passage.)

1. **Background**

The first letter to the Thessalonian Church was written from Corinth about 53 A.D. The historical background of the Church at Thessalonica is given in Acts 17:1-14. Notice from this Scripture that Paul wasted no time in establishing a church there:

- He preached in the synagogue of the Jews — V-1-2.
- He preached from the Scriptures — V-2.
- He preached basic truths: Christ had to suffer and die; He had to rise from the dead. This Jesus whom Paul preached WAS Christ (these truths are in 17:3).
- Immediate results are given — V-4-5. (Note Greeks, women, Jews.)
- Paul was forced to leave the city — V-10.

With Paul on this second missionary journey were Silas (Silvanus) and Timothy. After preaching in Thessalonica, he was compelled to flee and went to Berea only to be pursued by the opposition from Thessalonica — the unbelieving Jews. (Acts 17:13-14). Paul had to move on — this time to Athens. After preaching in Athens on Mars Hill, Paul went on to Corinth, where this epistle was written. Paul had wanted to go back to Thessalonica (2:17-18), but was hindered from visiting them. He sent Timothy back to minister to them (3:1-5). After he received word from Timothy about the church (3:6-13) he wrote this letter to them.

2. **The Central Message**

"I pray God your whole spirit and soul and body be preserved blameless unto the coming of our Lord Jesus Christ" — (5:23b).

3. **The Structure of the Book**

(2) Looking Back — Personal and Historical — Chapters 1-3.

(2) Looking Forward — How They Should Live — Chapters 4-5.

4. **Looking Back — Personal and Historical — Chapters 1-3**

(1) A MODEL CHURCH — Chapter 1.

Notice — the Thessalonian Church was IN God the Father and IN the Lord Jesus Christ — V-1.

"Grace" and *"Peace"* — Paul uses both words in his salutation to all the churches. The word "grace" was the western Gentile greeting, while *"peace"* or *"Shalom"* was the eastern Jewish greeting — V-1.

Paul looks back in V-3 when he uses the word *"remembering."* From this point to the end of Chapter 3, Paul is reminiscent.

The remainder of Chapter 1 is a looking back to the conversion of those in Thessalonica.

V-3 — Paul always puts these Christian graces together:
"FAITH — HOPE — LOVE."

V-4 — "Election of God" is the sovereign act of God in grace whereby He chose in Christ Jesus for salvation all those whom he foreknew would accept Him. (See Romans 8:29-30.)

V-5 — They had been saved *"in the power."*

V-6-7 — They had become *"examples."*

V-8 — They *"sounded out"* or ECHOED the Gospel.

V-9-10 — We see the three tenses of the believers life:

PAST — "ye turned to God from idols" —

PRESENT — "to serve the living and true God."

FUTURE — "to wait for His Son from heaven."

We have covered Chapter 1, verse by verse to point out to you *two things:*

(a) In this one Chapter Paul teaches this young church SIX major doctrines — setting the example that the new Christian should be taught some sound doctrine, namely:

    1. ELECTION — 1:4

    2. HOLY SPIRIT — 1:5-6

    3. ASSURANCE — 1:5

    4. TRINITY — 1:1, 5, 6

    5. CONVERSION — 1:9

    6. SECOND COMING OF CHRIST — 1:10

(b) Paul presses the theme — *"the coming of the Lord"* from the first to the last. Each of the five Chapters ends with a reference to the Lord's return. Notice in this Chapter V-10 — "wait for the Son from heaven — even Jesus — which delivered us from the wrath to come." (Tribulation) We are NOT to wait for wrath but for Christ.

(2) THE SERVANT OF THE LORD — Chapter 2.

The backward look is continued — and Paul talks about himself and Silas and Timothy.

In V-1-6 we see the MOTIVE and METHOD of Paul. He was there less than one month (about three weeks) and:

- it was not in *"vain"* (without results) — (V-1)
- they were *"bold"* in spite of *"contention"* (conflict) — (V-2)
- our preaching was not *"deceit"* — error — (V-3)
- approved of God — (V-4)
- He used no *"flattering words"* — (V-5)
- sought no glory from men — (V-6)

In V-7-12 we read of their CONDUCT as preachers:

- *"gentle"* as a *"nurse"* — V-7 — (a mother's love).
- *"affectionate"* and *"dear"* — V-8 — Paul loved them.
- *"laboring night and day"* — V-9. Hurry, waste no time.
- *"unblameably"* — V-10 — Paul set the example.
- *"exhorted"* — (helped). *"Comforted,"* *"charged"* (cautioned). *"As a father does his children."*

In V-13-16 — the MESSAGE of Paul and Silas and Timothy:

- *"the Word of God, received as truth and it works in you"* — V-13.
- the churches in Judea had suffered — so would they — V-14.
- Paul identified those that killed Christ and the prophets as the same as those persecuting him and forbidding him to preach — V-15-16.

In V-17-20 — the REWARD of a Christian:

V-17 — Paul desired to see them again in Thessalonica.

V-18 — Satan hindered him (kept him from going).

V-19 — *"Crown of rejoicing"* — is given as a reward for those who win others.

V-20 — Paul's joy was to know they would meet Christ at His coming.

(3) PAUL'S CARE FOR THE YOUNG CHURCH — Chapter 3.
(We shall not go into a verse by verse look at this Chapter for it is such a masterpiece, it speaks for itself.)

NOTE: — V-1-5 — Paul's deep concern for them.

V-6-8 — Timothy's good report about them.

V-9-13 — Paul prays for them *"night and day."*

5. **Looking Forward — How They Should Live — Chapters 4-5**

(1) THE BELIEVER'S WALK AND HOPE — Chapter 4.

In the first twelve verses, Paul urges purity in their Christian lives.

"The will of God is your sanctification" — V-3.

Sanctification is a separation FROM evil and a consecration UNTO righteousness. It is the complete work of God, when He glorifies the believer at the coming of Christ — (3:13).

The will of God should also be looked up in I Thess. 5:18:

_____

_____

Note especially V-11-12 — "STUDY *to be quiet,"* *"mind your own business," "work with your own hands," "that ye may walk honestly."*

NOW, THE BLESSED HOPE, THE RAPTURE OF THE CHURCH — 4:13-18.

This is one of the most profound of all Scriptures. Paul covers the Rapture, but the question he is answering is about believers who die before the rapture (the calling out of the Church).

He starts by saying, "I would not have you be ignorant concerning them which are asleep" — meaning asleep in Christ — physical death. Look up II Cor. 5:8: _____

_____

V-14 means those Christians in the grave asleep in Jesus and they will come with Christ.

V-15 — *"we which are alive and remain"* — in other words, all living Christians — *"shall not precede* (instead of prevent) *them which are asleep."*

V-16 — "SHOUT" is a command.

"VOICE" — the voice of the shout is *like* an archangel.

"Trump of God" — the voice of the Lord is *like* a trumpet (no reference to Gabriel). It is the same as Revelations 1:10: _____

_____

This is the ONE voice of the Lord Jesus — not a trio.

V-16-17 — "The dead in Christ" go first — "then we who are alive shall be caught up (raptured)."

Note — *"to meet the Lord* IN THE AIR."

Look up Acts 1:11 and Matthew 24:30.

V-18 — This is a comfort to believers.

PRAISE GOD! THERE IS A CALLING OUT — A RAPTURE!

(2) THEREFORE, AWAKE AND DO — Chapter 5.

The first part of this Chapter explains the fact that the *"Day of the Lord comes as a thief in the night."* The world will think it is entering the millennium but in reality they are entering *"sudden destruction"* — V-3. We are children of light (Phil. 2:15). In V-9 *"God hath not appointed us to wrath,"* I believe stands in context showing that the Church will not be on earth during the Great Tribulation.

Beginning at V-11 to the end of the Chapter we see 22 THINGS THAT CHRISTIANS SHOULD DO:

1. V-11 — ''Comfort (encourage) yourselves.''
2. V-11 — ''Edify (build up) one another.''
3. V-12 — ''Understand those who teach (labor) the Word.''
4. V-13 — ''Esteem the preacher or teacher.''
5. V-13 — ''Be at peace.''
6. V-14 — ''Warn the unruly.''
7. V-14 — ''Comfort the feebleminded'' (faint-hearted).
8. V-14 — ''Support the weak.''
9. V-14 — ''Be patient toward all men'' — Don't lose temper.
10. V-15 — ''Don't fight one another.''
11. V-15 — ''Follow that which is good.''
12. V-16 — ''Rejoice always.''
13. V-17 — ''Pray without ceasing.''
14. V-18 — ''In everything give thanks.''
15. V-19 — ''Quench not the Spirit.''
16. V-20 — ''Despise not the Word.''
17. V-21 — ''Prove all things'' — don't be taken in by flattery.
18. V-21 — ''Hold fast that which is good.''
19. V-22 — ''Abstain from all appearance of evil.''
20. V-25 — ''Pray for us.''
21. V-26 — ''Greet with a holy kiss'' — We shake hands in our day.
22. V-27 — ''This epistle be read to all brethren.''

These are the 22 commandments for us to perform as we wait for His coming.

NOTE: *Paul closes every Chapter with a reference to the coming of the Lord – underline these: 1:10; 2:19; 3:13; 4:17; 5:23.*

HOW MUCH DO YOU REMEMBER?

Q. Where and when did Paul write I Thessalonians?

Q. Who was with Paul at Thessalonica?

Q. What is the theme of the Book?

Q. What has this Book meant to you?

YOUR ASSIGNMENT FOR NEXT WEEK

1. Read II Thessalonians (3 Chapters) at least twice.
2. Review your notes from I Thessalonians.
3. Mark your Bible.
4. Be present next Lord's Day for II Thessalonians.

Lesson 42
"The Book of
II Thessalonians"

(Where lines are provided, please look up Scriptures and fill in the entire Scripture or the main Truth of the passage.)

1. **Background**

   A few months after Paul had written his first letter to the Thessalonians, he decided to write another epistle. Paul had received word that there were those who misunderstood his first letter. This was partially brought about by some "forged" letter supposedly coming from the hand of Paul (II Thess. 2:2) and the people had "been shaken in mind." The negative report came back to Paul that the Christians were believing the false word that the rapture of the Church had already come because of the persecution they were then suffering. This caused some of the believers to think that they were then living in judgment of the "day of the Lord."

   Before we proceed with the rest of the Book — it may be well for us to review two phrases that might have you confused by now. They are:

   (1) "THE DAY OF CHRIST" — relates wholly to the blessing and reward of the saved at His coming. Look up I Cor. 1:8; I Cor. 5:5; II Cor. 1:14; Phil. 1:6; 10; Phil. 2:16. (II Thess. 2:2 has "day of Christ" INCORRECTLY for the Day of the Lord.)

   (2) "THE DAY OF THE LORD" is connected with judgment. It occurs in the writings of the Old Testament prophets where it relates to the future kingdom promised in the Old Testament. Isaiah 2:12; Mal. 4:5; Joel 2:1-12. It starts with the beginning of the tribulation (Acts 2:20; II Peter 3:10).

2. **The Central Message**

   "Stand fast, and hold the traditions which ye have been taught —" — 2:15.

3. **The Structure of the Book**

   (1) Persecution of Believers — Chapter 1.
   (2) Prophecy and Correction — Chapter 2.
   (3) Instruction to the Believers — Chapter 3.

4. **Persecution of Believers — Chapter 1**

   The same salutation is given as in I Thessalonians. In the midst of severe persecution, they were growing and abounding, increasing in faith and love. They were an example to other churches. (In V-4 and 6 the word "tribulation" appears. This should not be confused with the "tribulation period" but does refer here to trials and persecution the believers had to endure — V-1-6.)

   In V-7-12 Paul assures us that God will take care of the ungodly. We are "to rest" because "the Lord Jesus shall be revealed from heaven." He will avenge — those "who know not God" and "obey not the Gospel."

   V-9 is a definition of hell — (underline and memorize). The coming of the Lord will bring glory both to Christ and to the Church — V-10-12.

5. **Prophecy and Correction — Chapter 2.**

through
the
Bible
in one
year

NOTES

Paul starts this great Chapter with a re-emphasis of the rapture — "The coming of our Lord Jesus Christ and by our gathering together unto Him." This is the same emphasis of I Thessalonians 4:13-18.

In V-2 there is an unfortunate translation. It should be "day of the Lord." (See page 1 of this lesson.) The Thessalonian believers had a false report, supposedly from Paul's writing that the day of the Lord had already come, which would have meant that they had missed the rapture.

In V-3 it states two things plainly in that the "day of the Lord" will not come until two things happen: FIRST, the falling away — apostasy; SECOND, the revealing of the "man of sin."

Now, that *"man of sin"* is a person, not a system. Notice in V-3 and 4 he is a "man," "he," "himself," "son of perdition" — all denote a person. The "man of sin" is the ANTI-CHRIST. He actually assumes the place of God — as God in the Temple. This one is:

- the little horn of Daniel 7:8; 8:9
- the willful king of Daniel 11:36

_____

- the Anti-Christ of I John 2:18

_____

- the beast out of the sea — Rev. 13:1-10

V-5-8 — The personal pronoun "until HE be gone" refers to the Holy Spirit operating through every believer who is a temple of the Holy Spirit. So the "man of sin" is being restrained, hindered, by the presence of the Holy Spirit in His body, the Church. He cannot have full control "until He be taken out of the way" — meaning the rapture of the Church. The "man of sin" — "that wicked one" (V-8) — will be revealed "then" (after the Church is called out). He is the one "whom the Lord shall destroy."

V-9-12 — The Anti-Christ will be a miracle worker and have power, signs and lying wonders. God shall send strong delusions for those to believe a lie who have heard the Gospel and "received not the love of truth that they might be saved."

In V-13-17 we have instruction and a review of what Christ has done in our hearts. Notice the steps:

- "Chosen you to salvation"
- "Sanctification by the Spirit"
- "Belief of the truth" (growth)
- "Obtaining the glory" — See I John 3:2

_____

6. **Instruction to Believers — Chapter 3**

In this Chapter Paul passes out some instruction in a firm and loving manner. He uses the word "command" four times (V-4, 6, 10, 12).

Paul is desiring that "the Word of the Lord may have free course" — so that the Lord can direct their hearts so that they will do the Lord's will (V-1-4). They were to wait patiently for the coming of the Lord — (V-5). The believer should not associate with the disorderly — but should follow the example Paul had given (V-6-7).

In the last section (V-8-18) Paul stresses the needs of everyday life. They should work (V-8-9); no work, no food (V-10).

Some are busybodies (V-11); they should work quietly (V-12); believers should not grow weary in working for Christ (V-13); obey the words of *this* epistle, *noting* the man who doesn't (V-14).

Try to win a wayward brother (V-15), Paul's benediction is in V-16-18.

We set forth a table of differences in I and II Thessalonians:

I THESSALONIANS	II THESSALONIANS
How the Thessalonians received Word of God	Mentions their progress in faith, love, and patience
Teaches the imminent return of the Lord	Corrects false teaching about His coming
Comforts and encourages the saints	Assures coming judgment on Christ's foes
Concerns the Church	Concerns Satan, Anti-Christ, the world
Presents great passage on end time (4:13-18)	Presents great passage on end time (2:1-2)
Presents the Day of Christ — (4:13-18)	Presents the Day of the Lord — (2:2)

The two phases of the end time and the return of Christ:

FIRST PHASE (RAPTURE)	SECOND PHASE (REVELATION)
Christ comes to claim His bride, the Church	Christ returns with the bride
Christ comes in the air	Christ returns to the earth
the tribulation begins	the millennial kingdom is established
translation is imminent	a multitude of signs precede
a message of comfort is given	a message of judgment is given
the program for the church is emphasized	the program for Israel and the world is emphasized
translation is a mystery	revelation is predicted in both Testaments
believers are judged	Gentiles and Israel are judged
Israel's covenants are not yet fulfilled	all of Israel's covenants are fulfilled
believers only are affected	all people are affected
the church is taken into the Lord's presence	Israel is brought into the kingdom

There is so much in this short Book. Please read it over and over. Run Scripture references from the margin of your Bible.

HOW MUCH DO YOU REMEMBER?

Q. Why did Paul write this second epistle?

Q. The Day of the Lord is connected with _____.

Q. Who is restraining the work of Satan and the revelation of the Anit-Christ?

Q. What is the "man of sin" – a system or a person?

Q. When will he be revealed?

YOUR ASSIGNMENT FOR NEXT WEEK

1. Read the Book of I Timothy — 6 Chapters.
2. Review your notes on the Thessalonian letters.
3. Mark the Scriptures in your Bible.
4. Be present next Lord's Day for the beginning of Paul's writings to individuals.

Lesson 43
"The Book of
I Timothy"

(Where lines are provided, please look up Scriptures and fill in the entire Scripture or the main Truth of the passage.)

NOTES

1. Background

We come now to the Pastoral Epistles — those letters written to individuals who had the care of "the flocks of God." Timothy was serving in the Ephesian Church when Paul wrote this first epistle to him. Paul wrote this letter after his release from prison in Rome the first time. The second epistle to Timothy was written during Paul's second imprisonment in Rome.

Timothy is one of the most devoted Christians in the New Testament. He was Paul's closest friend to the very end. Paul calls him a "man of God" (I Tim. 6:11). His name appears twenty-four times in the New Testament — we list only a few:

- Acts 16:1
- Acts 17:14-15
- Acts 18:5
- Romans 16:21
- I Corinthians 4:17
- II Corinthians 1:1,19
- Philippians 1:1

Timothy was a native of Derbe (Acts 16:1), the son of a Gentile father and a Jewish mother (Acts 16:1-3). His mother and grandmother are mentioned by name in II Timothy 1:5 — Eunice and Lois. Paul was thirty-five years old when Timothy was born, which means that at the time of the writing of this epistle, Paul was twice Timothy's age.

From his childhood, Timothy was taught the Old Testament Scriptures by his mother (II Timothy 1:5 and 3:15). His name means "honored by God." He was highly recommended by the Christians in and around Derbe to Paul, and Paul responded and accepted him as a co-laborer (Acts 16:1-2). Timothy was circumcised and ordained to the ministry of the Word (Acts 16:3-5). (Read the first part of Acts 16.)

Acts 16:5 says: _____

_____

2. The Central Message

"That thou may know how thou ought to behave in the house of God, which is the Church of the living God, the pillar and ground of the truth" — I Timothy 3:15.

3. The Structure of the Book

(1) Legalism; Heresy Rebuked; Charge Given — Chapter 1.

(2) The Church and Its Conduct — Chapters 2 and 3.

(3) The Minister and His Conduct — Chapters 4 through 6.

4. Legalism; Heresy Rebuked; Charge Given — Chapter 1

The first Chapter was written to encourage and instruct Timothy on how to handle false teaching. In V-3 Paul left Timothy at Ephesus to "charge" them to teach no other doctrine except Christ which produces love and not empty chatter — "vain jangling" — V-5 and 6. The church should teach sound doctrine according to the glorious Gospel of God — V-10-11.

After Paul repeats his personal testimony (V-11-17) he gives Timothy A CHARGE (V-18) — "that thou might war a good warfare." The details of Paul's charge (instruction) to Timothy begins at Chapter 2 and continues through the epistle.

5. **The Church and Its Conduct — Chapters 2-3**

(1) CONCERNING ORDER IN THE CHURCH — Chapter 2.

Here Paul discusses the public worship services where some problems existed. Prayer is the first concern:

- V-1-3 — "Supplications" are petitions — "Intercession" to intercede on their behalf of the kings and those in authority — this is the will of God.
- V-4-5 — His desire is that all be saved and grow in knowledge of the Word.
- Write V-5 and memorize _____

  _____

- V-7 — Paul was ordained (appointed) a preacher, and an apostle.
- V-8 — How men ought to pray — Lifting up hands was a custom in that day. "Without wrath" means sins have been confessed.
- V-9-10 — "In like manner" means the women are to pray but they are to dress modestly.
- V-11 — Paul cautions *again* that women are not to speak in tongues publicly (I Corinthians 14:34).
- V-12 — The woman should not be over the man in spiritual matters. This should be an incentive for men to be the spiritual leaders — not asserting authority as a dictator. (Might I add, were it not for women, few homes would have any spiritual guidance. Paul is NOT speaking against women — he is trying to get the men to take the lead. Women taught in the early church — Acts 18:26; I Corinthians 11:5; Titus 2:3-4.)
- V-13-14 — It was the sin of Eve that brought sin into the world. It was the birth of Jesus to a woman, Mary, that brought the Saviour into the world. No man provided a Saviour — a *woman* did.

(2) CONCERNING OFFICES IN THE CHURCH — Chapter 3.

A "bishop" is an overseer — "elder" can be the same person. "Elder" is the word applied to the person; "bishop" is applied to the office. V-2-7 states the qualifications for this office. These men are called "pastors" in our day.

V-8-13 set forth the requirements of a deacon. In today's churches, we need to restudy Chapter 3 in detail. The Pastor and Deacon have the same requirements. Read them and underline the qualifications for each.

In V-14-16, Paul says he sent this letter ahead to guide Timothy until he could go to Ephesus. This letter would be the "RULES OF ORDER" for the church in Paul's absence.

V-16 is one of the great verses in the Bible. Better wording would be the "mystery of Godlikeness" or the "mystery of the Christian life." It can only be lived because of the incarnation, His example, His life, His death. (Write in V-16.)

_____

_____

6. **The Minister and His Conduct — Chapters 4-6**

(1) THE ANTIDOTE FOR FALSE TEACHING — Chapter 4.

The Spirit spoke through Paul that in the last days some will depart from the faith and follow all sorts of false teaching (V-1-3).

Timothy is to remind the brethren of this and teach only SOUND DOCTRINE — a mark of a "good minister." Timothy was young but he was to be an "example in word, in conversation, in love, in spirit, in faith, in purity" (V-12). He was to READ the Word, COMFORT and TEACH (V-6-13).

Timothy had a special gift of the Spirit to do these things. Paul reminds him to take heed of himself and the doctrine — be faithful (V-14-16).

(2) DUTIES OF THE OFFICERS IN THE CHURCH — Chapters 5-6.

One of the values of the Word of God is that it has an answer for every need. The same principles are to be followed in our day. A minister must deal wisely and be fair to each of his flock. Elders must be honored, widows cared for (5:1-25).

The slaves were to be taught and treated right. The passage 6:6-16 Paul gives a guide for all of us who are believers. Read and underline the things that apply to us today.

Paul closes the Book by telling his young friend, "keep that which is committed to thy trust" (V-20).

Now, let us observe that this letter is a "CHARGE" (a command, instruction). Paul wanted Timothy to remember what he had been told verbally. Notice the following:

- "That thou might CHARGE some that they teach, etc." — (1:3).
- "Now the end of the commandment (CHARGE) is love out of a pure heart" — (1:5).
- "This CHARGE I commit unto thee" — (1:18).
- "These things CHARGE, and teach" — (4:11).
- "These things also CHARGE, that they may be blameless" — (5:7).
- "I CHARGE thee before God and the Lord Jesus Christ" — (5:21).
- "I CHARGE thee in the sight of God" — (6:13).
- "CHARGE them that are rich" — (6:17).

Now we see that Paul had to write this letter so that they *might know how to behave in the House of God."* I Timothy 3:15 is one of the verses you should remember from this study.

HOW MUCH DO YOU REMEMBER?

Q. Where was Timothy serving when he received this letter?

Q. Who was Timothy's mother?

Grandmother?

Q. What was Paul's main concern in this epistle?

Q. What did this letter become to the Ephesian church?

YOUR ASSIGNMENT FOR NEXT WEEK

1. Read II Timothy — 4 Chapters.
2. Review your notes from I Timothy.
3. Mark your Bibles.
4. Be present for next Lord's Day and the second epistle to Timothy.

Lesson 44
"The Book of II Timothy"

(Where lines are provided, please look up Scriptures and fill in the entire Scripture or the main Truth of the passage.)

1. This second epistle (letter) to Timothy was written from the Mamertine Prison in Rome. Paul writes his most personal letter, and we see more of his thoughts and feelings.

   Paul speaks in this letter of a great apostasy which will almost blot out the "faith" and this is in complete harmony with the words of our Lord when He said, "When the Son of Man cometh, shall He find faith in the earth?" — Luke 18:8. This may be the result of so many "professors" but not "possessors" of the faith. The exponents of "social gospel" who expect to transform the world by better programs and human know-how seldom turn to this Book because it makes all men stop and reflect.

   This is Paul's last writing. He was facing death — martyrdom. He had to say much in a little time. Some of the great verses of the Bible are in this Book.

2. **The Central Message**

   "I know whom I have believed, and am persuaded that He is able to keep that which I have committed (deposited) unto Him against that day" — (1:12).

   Also II Timothy 2:15 (You should know — write it in)

   _____

   _____

   _____

3. **The Structure of the Book**

   (1) Paul the PREACHER — Chapter 1.

   (2) Paul, the EXAMPLE — Chapter 2.

   (3) Paul, the PROPHET — Chapter 3.

   (4) Paul, the PRISONER — Chapter 4.

4. **Paul the Preacher — Chapter 1**

   (1) • Paul's son in the Gospel was Timothy — V-2.

   • Paul prayed for him day and night — V-3.

   • Paul longed to see Timothy — V-4.

   • He had full confidence in Timothy — V-5.

   • He told him to stir up his gift — V-6.

   • Paul inserts a verse here which every Christian should memorize:

   V-7 _____

   _____

   _____

   • Timothy is not to be ashamed of the message or messengers of

Christ — V-8.

- He reminds Timothy of his calling — V-9.
- Timothy is to hold on to sound doctrine — V-13.
- He is to remain true to the ministry — V-14.

(2) Note some things Paul says about himself:

- an apostle — V-1 and 11.
- a preacher — V-11.
- a teacher — V-11.
- then in V-12 he rings out what every Christian should KNOW FROM MEMORY. This is a verse of assurance and one that teaches security in Christ — notice Paul says — "I am NOT ASHAMED — for I KNOW — I have COMMITTED."

The final verses of Chapter 1 reveal that Paul had been forsaken by so-called friends. He had been helped by one — Onesiphorus — (V-16-18).

5. Paul the Example — Chapter 2

In this Chapter Paul uses seven figures of speech to describe the duty and activity of a believer:

(1) A SON — he should follow the example and teach others, so they may teach others — V-1-2.

(2) A SOLDIER — he is to "endure hardness" or hardships and avoid the entanglements of the world — to please the One who made him a soldier — V-3-4.

(3) AN ATHLETE — he is to contend for the reward. He is to abide by the rules — V-5.

(4) A FARMER — Must labor before he partakes of the fruit — V-6.

(5) A STUDENT — V-15 — (you should know).

(6) A VESSEL — a vessel must be clean to be usable — V-20-21.

(7) A SERVANT — a believer is a servant, gentle, apt to teach, patient — V-24.

6. Paul the Prophet — Chapter 3

"This know also, that in the last days, perilous times shall come" — V-1. This means the last days of the Church (see I Timothy 4:1; II Peter 3:3; Jude 18).

In V-2 through 13, Paul uses 22 words or phrases to describe last days:

(1) "lovers of their own selves"

(2) "covetous" — get what one wants

(3) "boasters" — braggart

(4) "proud" — haughty

(5) "blasphemers" — using God's name in vain

(6) "disobedient"

(7) "unthankful"

(8) "unholy" — profane

(9) "without natural affection"

(10) "truce-breakers" — promises mean nothing

(11) "false accusers"

(12) "incontinent" — without self-control

(13) "fierce" — is savage

(14) "despisers of those that are good"

(15) "traitors" — or betrayers

(16) "heady" — reckless

(17) "high-minded" — drunk with pride

(18) "lovers of pleasure more than lovers of God"

(19) "have a form" — denying the power of God

(20) "ever learning" — never able to discern truth

(21) "seducers" — sorcerers

(22) "deceiving and being deceived"

In V-14-17 the only thing that will help is the authority of the Word in the last days. Paul says, "But continue thou in the things which thou hast learned and been assured of, knowing of whom thou hast learned them" etc. — V-14.

In this remarkable passage — V-16 — Paul claims that:

"all Scripture" (every part, every word)

"is given by inspiration" (God breathed)

"is profitable for DOCTRINE" (better teaching)

"for reproof" (conviction)

"for correction" (setting right)

"for instruction" (discipline)

7. **Paul the Prisoner — Chapter 4**

(1) HIS FINAL CHARGE — V-1, 2, 5.

- "at His appearing" (meaning the calling out of the Church)
- "preach the Word"
- "be diligent all the time"
- "reprove, rebuke, exhort"
- "watch thou (be alert) in all things"
- "endure afflictions"
- "do the work of an evangelist"
- "make full proof of the ministry"

(What a "charge" or command to a preacher.)

(2) HIS FINAL WARNING — V-3-4.

In the last days men will not listen to doctrine.
They will try to satisfy their own lusts.
They will find teachers — false ones.
They will turn away from truth — believe fables.

(3) HIS FINAL TESTIMONY — V-6-8.

"For I am now ready to be offered, and my departure is at hand. I have fought a good fight, I have finished my course, I have kept the faith: henceforth there is laid up for me a crown of righteousness, which the Lord, the righteous judge, shall give me at that day; and not to me only but unto *all them* also that love *His appearing.*"

This has been called the death-bed testimony of Paul. It says a lot to us today. Paul spoke these words from that prison in Rome. What a testimony! Notice he will receive a "crown." For other references to "crowns" ("rewards") see the following:

I Cor. 9:25 _____

_____

Phil. 4:1 _____

_____

I Thess. 2:19 _____

_____

James 1:12 _____

_____

Rev. 3:11_____

_____

(4) HIS LAST WORDS — V-9-22.

Timothy was to try to go see him — V-9.

"Demas" — short for Demetrius — an apostate — V-10.

Only Luke was with Paul. He requested Mark to come to Rome — V-11.

Tychicus was evidently a minister in Ephesus — V-12.

He requested his coat to keep him warm in the damp Mamertine Prison. Timothy was to bring Paul's books and the "parchments" — which were the Old Testament Scriptures — V-13.

Alexander had persecuted him — V-14-15 (See Acts 19:33).

"At my first *answer*" (his first trial) "the Lord stood with me . . . that all Gentiles might hear" — V-16-17.

This, I think, took place in Nero's palace. His last message he stood alone — only the Lord stood with him and he preached the Gospel.

The last few verses are personal greetings and Paul's final benediction.

HOW MUCH DO YOU REMEMBER?

Q. Where was Paul when he wrote this letter?

Q. Can you name one of the Scriptures which is the Central Message?

Q. Who did Paul want to see and what did he want brought to him?

Q. What do you think of this man, Paul?

YOUR ASSIGNMENT FOR NEXT WEEK

1. Read Titus and Philemon — 4 Chapters.
2. Read ahead into the Book of Hebrews.
3. Review your notes on II Timothy.
4. Mark your Bible from your notes.
5. Be present next Lord's Day.

Lesson 45
"The Books of Titus and Philemon"

"THE BOOK OF TITUS"

(Where lines are provided, please look up Scriptures and fill in the entire Scripture or the main Truth of the passage.)

1. Background

Titus was a Gentile (Greek) and one of Paul's converts. This epistle was written about the same time as First Timothy. Titus had proved to be a loyal co-worker with Paul and he had become very close to Paul. Look up Galatians 2:1-3 and you see that Titus was with Paul and Barnabas at the Jerusalem Council of Acts 15. For other references to Titus and Paul look up:

    II Corinthians 2:13:

    II Corinthians 7:6:

    II Corinthians 8:1-6, 16, 17:

At the time of this epistle, Titus was on the Island of Crete. The Cretans were kin to the Philistines and they had a reputation of being "liars, evil beasts, lazy gluttons" (Titus 1:12). Titus was to strengthen the work in the church which had been established there.

In I and II Timothy Paul stresses doctrine.

In Titus he stresses duty. The doctrine of the first two is to be adorned by doing in Titus.

He is last mentioned by Paul in II Timothy 4:10 where Paul indicates that he has sent Titus to Dalmatia (known to us as Yugoslavia).

2. Central Message

    "Be careful to maintain good works" — 3:8 and 14.

3. The Structure of the Book

    "Put things in order" — Chapter 1.

    "Adorn the doctrine" — Chapter 2.

    "Maintain good works" — Chapter 3.

4. "Put Things In Order" — Chapter 1

The New Testament teaches that each church was to be autonomous (self-governing). In the first days of the early church, there was the authority of the apostles in control.

This is still the authority as written in the epistles of the New Testament and they teach the principle that each local church is self-governed by a simple plan.

Here Titus was to "set things in order" — V-5. There was to be the appointment of elders — and they were "wanting" because they had not been appointed. Titus was to correct this and "ordain elders in every city" (in every church on Crete). Elders were to be the "overseers" by the direction of the Holy Spirit (Acts 20:28). They were the local pastors who were to "feed the flock." (As we taught in I Timothy 3 — "elder" and "bishop" designate the same office. "Elder" is the word applied to the person and "bishop" is applied to the function of the office.)

We learn from this letter to Titus that there is to be adequate, but simple, organization. We should notice that the qualifications for the office of "elder" are *spiritual,* rather than *natural* gifts.

Paul names *fourteen* qualifications — V-6-8:

    (1) Blameless

    (2) The husband of one wife

    (3) Have faithful children (control over them)

    (4) Not self-willed (God's will must be first)

    (5) Not soon angry

    (6) Not given to wine

    (7) No striker (not violent)

    (8) Not given to filthy lucre (not materialistic)

    (9) A lover of hospitality

    (10) A lover of good men

    (11) Sober

    (12) Just

    (13) Holy (set apart — unpolluted)

    (14) Temperate — (self-control)

Then Paul spells out the duties of these leaders — V-9-16:

    (1) To know the truths of God's Word — V-9

    (2) To exhort — V-9

    (3) To convince — V-9

This was because of the talkers and deceivers within and without the church. Paul does not use kind language but direct, hard words that something had to be done. Read V-10-16.

The lesson: It takes good spiritual leadership to develop a good spiritual membership.

5. **"Adorn the Doctrine" — Chapter 2**

"Sound doctrine" includes the teaching of all ages.

NOTICE: FIRST, "senior citizens" — men and women — V-2-3

          SECOND, "young women" — V-4-5

          THIRD, "young men" — V-6-8

          FOURTH, "servants — to adorn the doctrine" — V-9-10 (we as servants of the Lord are to do the same).

We are to "adorn the doctrine" because:

- of "the grace of God" — V-11
- of "the glorious appearing of the great God and our Saviour Jesus Christ" — V-13
- "He gave Himself — that He might redeem us" — V-14

Paul gives a word of sound advice — V-15: _____

_____

_____

(Note the words "with all authority.")

6. **"Maintain Good Works" — Chapter 3**

- We are to obey the laws of the land and be "ready to every good work," not to speak evil, but we are to be gentle, etc. — V-1-2.
- What we once were and the wonder of our conversion — V-4-6. Underline V-5.
- We are *now* heirs of eternal life — V-7.
- Good works should be a part of every Christian life: Note V-8 — "Maintain good works" and then again "maintain good works" — V-14.

- We are not to spend time on foolish questions, arguments, heretics — V-9-11.
- This letter is a lesson in practical Christian living. Its final injunction is, *"Maintain good works."*

"THE BOOK OF PHILEMON"

1. Background

This is a personal note from Paul to Philemon written from prison in Rome. It is very intimate and conveys a message for us today.

The background for these twenty-five verses is easy to remember. Onesimus was a domestic slave of Philemon. He had stolen from his master and made his way to Rome. He thought that he would never see Colosse again (hometown of Philemon — Col. 4:9). While in Rome, Onesimus came under the influence of Paul and was saved.

The letter is a great illustration of the truth of *imputation* (the act of settling the account of another). It also should teach us the value of letter writing — it can be a ministry.

2. The Central Message

"Put that on mine account" — V-18.

3. The Structure of the Book

- Salutation — V-1-3
- Praise For Philemon — V-4-7
- Paul's Plea for Onesimus — V-8-16
- Paul's Assurance and Pledge — V-17-25

4. The Salutation — V-1-3

This is a greeting to Philemon and his family in Colosse, "Philemon our dearly beloved and fellow-laborer." Timothy is with Paul — V-1.

"Apphia" was the wife of Philemon, while "Archippus" was his son and also the pastor of the church of Colosse. The church met in the home — V-2.

5. Praise For Philemon — V-4-7

Philemon had a good reputation. His love was toward the Lord Jesus; so was his faith; therefore, he had the same feeling toward Christians. This attitude would affect others. The life of Philemon was a testimony.

The hearts ("bowels" is wrong) of the believers were refreshed by Philemon.

6. Paul's Pleas For Onesimus — V-8-16

Paul now comes to the purpose of his writing this letter and he is a diplomat in his approach — V-8.

Paul gives the reasons for his request: "for love's sake" — "Paul the aged" — "a prisoner of Jesus Christ" — V-9.

His plea now begins for Onesimus. The slave had accepted Christ. His name means "profitable." In years past he had been "unprofitable," but now he is a believer and is "profitable" to Philemon, Paul and Christ. Paul had to send him back — V-10-12.

Paul would have kept Onesimus but he wanted Philemon to decide — V-13-14.

Since Onesimus had become a Christian, he had a new relationship to Philemon. He is now more than a slave, he is "a brother beloved" — V-15-16.

7. Paul's Assurance and Pledge — V-17-25

This is one of the great illustrations of imputation and substitution. Behind the plea of Paul, is the plea of Christ to the Father for the sinner who will trust Christ as Lord and Saviour. The sinner is received on the same standing that Christ is received. The saved individual has *His* right to heaven because of his faith in Christ. The reason the saved person is accepted is because Christ took upon Himself the sins of all of us who will believe — V-17-18.

Look up James 2:23 _____

_____

This story in Philemon and the Scripture in James are illustrations of "imputation."

Paul pledges to pay the entire debt. Paul says I.O.U. — "I will repay it" — then adds U.O.Me — "how you owe me even yourself" — V-19.

Paul pleads for Onesimus and tells Philemon he expects more than his request — V-20-21.

The last four verses are for prayer for release so he could lodge with Philemon — concluding with greetings to others.

CONCLUSION

This letter teaches the lesson that social issues are corrected when the heart is corrected. Onesimus was a slave; Philemon his owner. On the basis of faith in Christ, Philemon was obliged to accept Onesimus back in Christ. Onsimus would become "profitable."

We also learn the value of a person — a thief, a running coward, a slave. Such teachings as this eventually abolished slavery in our land.

The Book is rich in practical lessons on reconciliation.

HOW MUCH DO YOU REMEMBER?

Q. Where was Titus when he received the letter from Paul?

Q. What is the Central Message of Titus?

Q. What was Titus to do in Crete?

Q. Who was Onesimus?

Q. Who was Philemon?

YOUR ASSIGNMENT FOR NEXT WEEK
   1. Read the Book of Hebrews — 13 Chapters.
   2. Review your notes on Titus and Philemon.
   3. Mark your Bible.
   4. Be present next Lord's Day for the study of Hebrews.

Lesson 46
"The Book of Hebrews"

(Where lines are provided, please look up Scriptures and fill in the entire Scripture or the main Truth of the passage.)

1. **Background**

   We shall try to write this lesson as simply as possible because of so much theological dissent through the ages. There are many, many theories based on Hebrews, thus we shall be guided by the Holy Spirit as we approach the Book with the lay pupil and lay teacher in mind.

   The epistle to the Hebrews is exactly that — a letter to the Hebrews. It was written before the destruction of the temple in 70 A.D. (Hebrews 10:11).

   The author is questionable but from the evidence in Scripture it must have been Paul, the Apostle. The writer had been in bonds (10:34) — he wrote from Italy (13:24) — his companion was Timothy (13:23). Peter identifies Paul as the writer (II Peter 3:15, 16). Who but Paul would say, "Pray for us — do this that I may be restored to you sooner," (13:18-19). The main thing is the fact that it is in the canon of Scripture for us.

2. **The Central Message**

   "For by one offering, He hath perfected forever them that are sanctified — there is no more offering for sin" — Hebrews 10:14 and 18b.

3. **The Structure of the Book**

   (1) THE SUPERIORITY OF THE PERSON OF CHRIST — Chapters 1 through 8:5.
   - Jesus, Better Than the Prophets — 1:1-3
   - Jesus, Better Than the Angels — 1:4 — 2:18
   - Jesus, Better Than Moses — Chapter 3
   - Jesus, Better Than Joshua — Chapter 4
   - Jesus, Better Than Aaron as Priest — 5:1 through 8:5

   (2) THE SUPERIORITY OF THE NEW AND BETTER COVENANT — Chapters 8:6 through 10:18.
   - The New Covenant Better Than the Old — 8:7-13
   - The New Covenant Opens a Better Tabernacle — 9:1-15
   - The New Covenant Is Sealed by a Better Sacrifice — 9:15-28
   - The New Covenant Settles Forever Our Salvation — 10:1-18

   (3) THE SUPERIORITY OF THE LIFE IN CHRIST — 10:19 — 13:25.
   - It Gives Assurance of Faith — 10:19-39
   - It Gives Us a Working Faith — Chapter 11
   - It Gives Us Patience and Direction — 12:1-13
   - It Gives Us Instruction in Our Walk and Worship — 12:14 — 13:25

("The Structure of the Book" is long, but it gives you an outline of the Book of Hebrews. We shall highlight the three main sections — not having space for a verse-by-verse treatment.)

4. **The Superiority of the Person of Christ — Chapters 1 — 8:5**

This Book, written to Hebrew Christians since some tempted to look back to Judaism, is concerned with the superiority of Christ and the new covenant, over against the old, without minimizing the old covenant. The new covenant in Christ honors the old by fulfilling it. Notice:

(1) JESUS, GOD'S SON, BETTER THAN THE PROPHETS — 1:1-3.

> "Jesus is the brightness of God's glory and express image of God's person nature" — V-3. One of the great parts of Scripture.

(2) JESUS BETTER THAN THE ANGELS — 1:4 — 2:18.

> Angels are messengers and ministering spirits — while Jesus is the SON, the CREATOR, RULER of the age to come.

> (Notice the *warning* in 2:1-4. The Hebrew Christians are warned to obey the Word of God. Underline V-3.)

(3) JESUS IS BETTER THAN MOSES — Chapter 3.

> Moses was a servant, Christ is the beloved Son — the Apostle — the High Priest.

> (Notice another warning here about doubting God's Word — 3:7-19.)

(4) JESUS IS BETTER THAN JOSHUA — 4:1-16.

> The word "Jesus" in V-8 should be "Joshua." Jesus is better than Joshua, because His rest is eternal, whereas Joshua's rest was only temporary. *Our rest* is in Jesus Christ — tempted as we are tempted, yet without sin so now we can "come boldly" to Him in time of need.

(5) JESUS IS BETTER THAN AARON AS PRIEST — 5:1 — 8:5.

> Aaron was taken from among men and was called of God — (5:1-4).

> Jesus was made a high priest by God the Father, because He was God's Son — (5:5).

> His Priesthood is after the order of Melchizedek who was a King-Priest (Gen. 14) who was a king of peace and righteousness — with no successor.

> Jesus is the "author of eternal salvation — called of God a high priest after the order of Melchizedek" — (5:9-10).

> *(Note: From 5:11 to 6:20 is parenthetical. The priesthood is resumed at 7:1. We will take up the parenthetical part at the end of the discussion of the priesthood.)*

> Christ is a priest after the order of Melchizedek, who is described in 7:1-3. Notice that tithes were paid to him by Abraham. Melchizedek was a type of Christ and Christ was "a priest forever after the order of Melchizedek" — (7:21).

> The Aaronic priests died but Christ would continue forever with an unchangeable priesthood (7:23-24).

> Jesus was given an all inclusive priesthood, our intercessor for all who come to God by Him, because He offered Himself as our sacrifice ONCE (7:25-28).

> Jesus is our High Priest on the right hand of God — note in 8:1, "WE HAVE." Jesus was a fulfillment of the shadow — pictured in the Aaronic priesthood (8:1-5).

> (Now the *parenthetical section* of 5:11 to 6:20. This is a warning, again, about departing from the Word of God.)

> We must remember that this was written to Jewish people, the

same kind we find in Acts 15 at the Jerusalem Council. Some of them argued that part of the old Jewish customs were necessary to be saved to the Christian faith. This was one of Peter's main subjects — that Jewish ceremony was not necessary. James declared the same thing. (Read again Acts 15.)

Now to the Scripture: 5:11 – 6:20.

There was a low standard of understanding spiritual things. There was an apathetic attitude (5:11).

Some of those Jewish believers should have already been teaching but they wanted to stay on the bottle and drink milk and not eat good food, such as the meat of the Word (5:12).

The people who stay on the bottle never mature and grow above the basic principles of salvation (5:13-14).

"Therefore, *let us go on* unto maturity" (6:1). Move from the mere FOUNDATION of the six facts carried over from the Old Testament which all prefigured Christ:

(a) "Repentance from dead works"

(b) "Faith toward God"

(c) "Doctrine of baptisms"

(d) "Laying on of hands"

(e) "Resurrection from the dead"

(f) "Eternal judgment"

NOW, 6:4-5 Read and underline. These are genuine believers — dull but not dead. "Impossible" — for men, but not for God. The author describes them:

• "for those once enlightened"

• "tasted of the heavenly gift"

• "partakers of the Holy Spirit"

• "tasted of the good Word of God"

• "tasted the powers of the world to come"

• "and having fallen away" (there is no "if").

• "fallen away" means — fall down, stumble. Peter fell down but he was not lost.

• "to renew them to *repentance*" — not salvation.

• "they crucify to themselves the Son of God afresh."

Read V-7-9 and you notice "rejected" in V-8. V-9 says, "things that accompany salvation."

Now, to explain. There are as many theories as there are books. I list only two or three:

FIRST VIEW: That one can fall from grace and can never be saved.

SECOND VIEW: That these Jews were "professors" of Christ but not "possessors" of Christ. This would be impossible if they had experienced the six things of V-4-5.

THIRD VIEW: This passage is not talking about losing salvation, but *repentance;* therefore it would be possible for a believer to be *set aside, rejected* in the sense of I Cor. 9:27 — "a castaway," useless. A person who has sinned willfully without repentance will not lose his salvation but will lose the rewards in glory.

In no way does this passage contradict the glorious guarantee of eternal preservation in Romans 8:28-29.

Note V-9 again — "we are persuaded better things of you, and things that *accompany salvation*." This is a pivotal verse — proving once again that the writer was talking to Jewish *believers.*

V-10-12 — "work and labor of love" is not salvation but the fruit of salvation.

V-13-20 — The promises of the Father are outlined for Abraham and for us — "lay hold of the *hope* set before us: which *hope we have* as an *anchor* of the *soul* . . . which entereth into that within the veil . . . even Jesus, made an high priest forever after the order of Melchizedek."

We resume the "priesthood" beginning at 7:1 to 8:5:

Chapter 7 begins with the Melchizedek priesthood again. He is a type of Christ in every way as we have already explained. (Refer to Gen. 14:17-24.)

V-5-12. Levi was in the loins of Abraham and was descended from Abraham which shows that Melchizedek is greater than the Levitical Priesthood. Aaron's priesthood belonged to the Mosaic Law and Christ has delivered us from the law.

V-13-16. Since Jesus did not come from Levi, the priesthood had to be changed. So Christ was made a priest after the order of Melchizedek and he was made this by the "power of an endless life" — V-16.

Please underline 7:24, 25, 26, 27. AMEN!

8:1 is *the sum of it all."*

5. **The Superiority of the New and Better Covenant — 8:6 — 10:18**

(1) THE NEW COVENANT IS BETTER THAN THE OLD — 8:7-13.

There are two covenants — the Old Testament and the New Testament (8:6).

The first covenant was not adequate — God found fault with the people, not the covenant.

So God gave them a NEW COVENANT — 8:8.

Look up Jeremiah 31:31-34 — (underline in your Bible).

(2) THE NEW COVENANT OPENS A BETTER TABERNACLE — 9:1-15.

In Chapter 9 we see contrasts. In V-1-5 we see what the tabernacle was; V-6-10 what was done in the tabernacle and why; V-11-12 the greater ministry of Christ. In this section is a wonderful study of "types" (pictures of what the Old Covenant revealed in the New).

Read and underline 9:11-15.

(3) THE NEW COVENANT IS SEALED BY A BETTER SACRIFICE — 9:15-28.

Compare V-19 with V-26. Underline V-27.

(4) THE NEW COVENANT SETTLES FOREVER OUR SALVATION — 10:1-18.

Write in 10:10_____

_____

_____

Notice in this section on the New Covenant:

WITHOUT SPOT 9:14; OF NECESSITY 9:16; NO REMISSION 9:22; ONCE FOR ALL 9:26; CAN NEVER 10:1; NOT POSSIBLE 10:4.

6. **The Superiority of the Life in Christ — 10:19 — 13:25**

(1) IT GIVES ASSURANCE OF FAITH — 10:19-39.

"Having therefore, brethren, boldness to enter into the holiest by the blood of Jesus." Read V-19-22. It is Jesus that allows us to pray to God because of His sacrifice.

(2) IT GIVES A WORKING FAITH — Chapter 11.

Here is the "Hall of Fame" for the Old Testament characters of faith.

Learn the definition of faith (11:1). So we should be able, by faith, to act on things not seen.

You find in this Chapter only some of the "faith" people of the Old Testament. Count and underline — "By faith."

(3) IT GIVES US PATIENCE AND DIRECTION — 12:1-13.

Because of the great faith people of Chapter 11 — let us "look unto Jesus the author and finisher of our faith."

The Lord directs us because He loves us and chastens us. Note:

V-6-7: _____

_____

and V-11: _____

_____

(4) IT GIVES US INSTRUCTION IN WALK AND WORSHIP 12:14 — 13:25.

The believer now approaches the Mount Zion, the city of God — 12:22 — not Sinai representing the law. As Christians we are already citizens of that glorious place. We are called by name, "Church of the firstborn" — V-23.

The Book closes in Chapter 13 with its most important teachings in V-20-21; the power of God; the death of Christ; His resurrection; His present work; the everlasting covenant; the object of Christ's work to restore that which is well pleasing in God's sight.

CONCLUSION

Hebrews should be studied in connection with the Book of Exodus. There are so many types, pictures and teachings which we had to pass over. Please, in your own study, go back over the Scripture again.

What a rich treasure this Book is to the believer!

HOW MUCH DO YOU REMEMBER?

Q. To whom was the Book written?

Q. Jesus is better than: 1. _____

2. _____ *3.* _____

Q. Christ is a priest after the order of _____.

Q. What is the New Covenant?

YOUR ASSIGNMENT FOR NEXT WEEK

1. Read the Book of James — 5 Chapters.
2. Review twice the Book of Hebrews.
3, Underline in your Bible.
4. Be present next Lord's Day for the study of James.

Lesson 47
"The Book of James"

(Where lines are provided, please look up Scriptures and fill in the entire Scripture or the main Truth of the passage.)

1. **The Book**

   The Book of James is a very Jewish Book. It is probably the earliest epistle of the New Testament, written about A.D. 45. It is often referred to as the Proverbs of the New Testament — the practical learning experience for the child of God.

   James was the "half" brother of our Lord and the brother of Jude. Look up Mark 6:3. James was an unbeliever until after the resurrection of our Lord (John 7:3-10). Christ appeared to him in His glorified body (I Cor. 15:7). James was among the 120 in the Upper Room and he had won his brothers (Acts 1:14). When Paul talks of his conversion in A.D. 37, he goes up to Jerusalem and confers with James (Gal. 1:19). James became the pastor of the church at Jerusalem (Acts 12:17; Acts 15:13). James presided over the first Jerusalem conference in Acts 15 and declares the results of that conference (read V-13-18). He was one of the great heroes of the first Christian church. He is sometimes referred to as James, the Just.

   James wrote this letter to Hebrew Christians. We must not forget that these same people had not ceased to be Jews. The epistle is addressed "to the twelve tribes scattered abroad." These were Jews of the dispersion, in places other than Palestine.

2. **True Faith**

   James and Paul seem to contradict each other but that is far from the truth. Note:

   > James says 2:24 — "by works a man is justified," etc.
   > Paul says — Eph. 2:8-9 — "by grace — not of works."

   Paul speaks of justification before God.

   James describes justification before man.

   We are justified by faith, says Paul.

   We are justified for works, says James.

   Paul stresses the root of justification.

   James stresses the fruit of justification.

   The theme of the Book could be entitled, "the proofs of true faith in Christ," with James stressing the product of faith.

3. **The Central Message**

   > "Be ye doers of the Word and not hearers only, deceiving your ownselves" — James 1:22.

4. **The Structure of the Book**
   - The Testing of Faith — Chapter 1
   - Faith and Works — Chapter 2
   - Control of the Tongue — Chapter 3
   - Submission to God — Chapter 4
   - Patient and Expectant Faith — Chapter 5

5. **The Testing of Faith — Chapter 1**

   James wrote to the "twelve tribes scattered abroad" (V-1).

through the Bible in one year

NOTES

They were scattered throughout the Roman Empire.

James knew they were undergoing trials (temptations) but they were to go through the testings and count it as a joy (V-2).

When faith is put on trial, the result should be patience (V-3-5).

Look up Romans 5:3-5: _____

_____

_____

When trials come to the Christian, they can be transformed by praying and asking wisdom (V-5-8); accept being poor and rejoice in it for Christ's sake because with the trials and material loss, there is a reward, *"the crown of life,"* for enduring these things in life (V-9-12).

The origin of temptation is never from God if it pertains to evil (V-13). Temptation comes by allowing lust and worldly desire to come into our lives. We should not stray away (V-14-16). Look up:

I Cor. 10:13: _____

_____

_____

God never sends evil. His gifts are good because of "His own will He brought us forth by the Word of truth that we might be a kind of firstfruits of His creation" (V-17-18). For this reason we should be swift to hear and slow to speak, slow to anger (V-19). The anger of a man is contrary to the will of God. The implanted Word is a preventative against the sins of the flesh (V-20-21).

We are to be "doers of the Word and not hearers only" (V-22). This is the safest guard we can build around us because the Word is like a mirror and reveals the natural man. It gives us liberty and a blessedness, simply by doing what God says (V-23-25).

The test of true faith is in V-26-27.

6. **Faith and Works — Chapter 2**

In V-1-13, James takes up the attitude we should have toward people. We are not to discriminate between the rich and poor in the "assembly" — the house of the Lord. James is rough *on the rich. We are to love everyone. That is even a part of the royal law and the teachings of our Lord* — (Matt. 22:39).

Now, faith is tested by works — V-14-26.

This is the battleground for many students of the Word. Let us look at it in general. *Paul* says in Romans 4:1-4 that Abraham was justified by *faith. James says,* "was not Abraham our father justified by *works* when he offered up Isaac his son?" The very reference to Isaac should guard us from any misunderstanding. Abraham's justification by *faith* was before the seal of the covenant, circumcision. His offering up Isaac was twenty years later; so that the man who was justified by *works* had already been justified by *faith* for twenty years. If James had thought of this as a contradiction, he would not have quoted the very verse that tells of Abraham's justification by faith. You find this in James 2:23 and Genesis 15:6.

SO FROM THIS WE SEE THAT *faith* JUSTIFIES THE MAN AND *works* JUSTIFIES THE FAITH.

Write in V-26: _____

_____

7. **Control of the Tongue — Chapter 3**

The tongue should be controlled by faith. James says in this chapter that the tongue is a dynamic instrument that can control almost anything.

He gives us seven illustrations of this:

(1) A horses "BIT" — V-3. It can make the horse go any direction.

(2) A rudder or "HELM" of a ship — V-3. That small rudder can control a large ship.

(3) "A FIRE" — V-5 — what a great fire a match can kindle.

(4) An untamed "BEAST" — man can tame most beasts but not his tongue. — V-7

(5) "POISON" — is what an untamed tongue puts out. — V-8

(6) "FOUNTAIN" — tongue should not give both bitter and sweet water. — V-11

(7) "FIG TREE" — cannot give olives and should not. — V-12.

So, the tongue is the instrument by which we praise God and it is used by some to curse God. James says, "My brethren, these things ought not be" — V-10.

Look up Proverbs 15:1-2: _____

_____

_____

The solution is found in James 3:13, 17, 18.

8. **Submission to God — Chapter 4**

The key verse is V-7 — "Submit yourselves, therefore, to God."

When we submit to God and draw nigh to Him as in V-8 — then we are able to combat:

      — the flesh — V-1-3

      — the world — V-4-5

      — the devil — V-7

We are then able to enjoy:

      — God's grace — V-6

      — God's nearness — V-8

      — God's goodness — V-10

      — God's guidance — V-13-15

This is a very practical Chapter. You should underline and try to memorize these verses: V-3, 7, 8, 10, 15, 17.

9. **Patient and Expectant Faith — Chapter 5**

James again speaks strongly about the rich. Look up:

Matthew 6:19-20: _____

_____

There is nothing wrong with making money — it is the ABUSE and MISUSE of it that is the subject here. The power that goes along with money is criticized.

James turns from money to the great subject of the coming of Christ. Notice V-7 — "Be *patient,* therefore, brethren unto the coming of the Lord."

He is not talking to the corrupt rich folks but to his "brethren." The coming of Christ — just the prospect of His coming — should give us patience and a loving spirit toward each other (V-8-9). Examples from the past, the prophets, give us patience and hope (V-10-11).

A Christian's word should be enough (V-12).

Now, for that section on praying for the sick (V-13-15):

"Is any among you afflicted? Is any sick among you?" James says we are to do two things: pray and use means, i.e. both pray and anoint with oil. Oil was, and is, a medicine. The Bible always follows this same teaching.

In Verse 34 of the parable of the good Samaritan (Luke 10:30-37), the

Samaritan went to the man and poured oil and wine on his wounds. Jesus said, "Go and do thou likewise."

That is why we should pray for the sick AND use means at our disposal — the pharmacist, the doctor, and then "the prayer of *faith* will save the sick — and his sins forgiven."

Then the question, "Is it ever God's will for a believer to have a prolonged illness?" Sometimes God allows us to be sick for the glory of God. II Timothy 4:20; II Corinthians 12:7-10; John 9:1-3; John 11:4 (write this verse here).

_____

_____

_____

Now V-16 says, "Confess your FAULTS one to another." Remember we are to confess our SINS to God.

Elijah is an Old Testament example of effective prayer (V-17-18).

V-19-20 closes the Book. This refers to a child of God ("brethren, if any of you err") who has gone astray. If he can be "converted" (meaning turn around or turn back to right path). In so doing, the one who turns him around "saves a soul from death," physical death. Sometimes God will shorten a life — I John 5:16-17.

Do you have a faith that works?

HOW MUCH DO YOU REMEMBER?

Q. Who was this James, the writer of this epistle?

Q. To whom did he write the letter, primarily?

Q. What is the main message of the Book?

Q. What part of the body is so difficult to control?
How should we use it?

YOUR ASSIGNMENT FOR NEXT WEEK
1. Read the Book of First Peter (5 Chapters) twice.
2. Review your notes on the Book of James.
3. Mark your Bible from your notes.
4. Be present next Lord's Day for I Peter — a great study.

Lesson 48
"The Book of I Peter"

(Where lines are provided, please look up Scriptures and fill in the entire Scripture or the main Truth of the passage.)

1. **The Book**

   The Apostle Peter was originally named Simon (a common Greek name), the Hebrew equivalent being Simeon (Acts 15:14). Jesus gave him a new name, Cephas (Aramaic), or Peter (Greek). So the name Simon Peter means the same person. The name "Peter" means "a little rock." The "Rock" which the Church is built upon is the "Rock," Christ Jesus (Matt. 16:18). Peter was the son of a Jew named John or Jonas. Peter had one brother whose name was Andrew. They lived on the north shore of the Sea of Galilee in Bethsaida. They were fishermen.

   Peter has been called the *apostle of hope;* Paul, the *apostle of faith;* John, the *apostle of love.*

   The Book of I Peter was written to the "sojourners of the dispersion." This was a term used for those Jewish believers who were scattered to that part of the world we now know as Asia Minor (V-1). Its purpose is to encourage and strengthen during a time of conflict and trial. Therefore, the book is relevant for our day.

2. **The Central Message**

   "Blessed be the God and Father of our Lord Jesus Christ, which according to His abundant mercy hath begotten us again unto a lively hope by the resurrection of Jesus Christ from the dead . . ." (1:3).

3. **The Structure of the Book**

   THE LIVING HOPE — Chapters 1 to 2:10
   THE CHRISTIAN LIFE — Chapters 2:11 — 4:11
   THE LORD'S RETURN — Chapters 4:12 — 5

4. **The Living Hope — Chapters 1 through 2:10**

   (1) Immediately after the salutation Peter gives a marvelous doxology — (V-3) — which is the Central Message of the Book. This is praise to God for "His abundant mercy has begotten us again unto a LIVING HOPE, by the resurrection of Jesus Christ." This wonderful Hope is expanded in V-5, "KEPT by power of God through faith;" in V-7, 8, 13, we see other benefits of the living hope through testing, rejoicing, hope to the end.

   The Old Testament prophets did not understand about the coming and work of the Messiah (Matt. 13:17). The angels desired to look upon the things concerning Christ (V-10-13). In V-13-17 is our high calling in Christ and how we should live.

   How we were redeemed (saved): underline V-18 and write V-19:

   _____

   _____

   (2) At V-20 we find the word *"fore-ordained"* which is *"foreknowledge"* as in V-2. A subject hard to comprehend for most people but let us explain it in easy terms:
   "Foreknowledge, election and predestination are in that order. The

213

foreknowledge determines the election, or choice (1:2) and predestination is the bringing to pass of the election.

"Election looks back to foreknowledge; predestination looks forward to the destiny. The foreknown are elected, and the elect (those who accept Christ of their own free will) are predestinated, and this *election is certain to every believer by the mere fact that he believes.*" (Scofield Bible)

Look up Romans 8:28-29. We are predestined to be conformed to the image of His Son.

(3) In V-22; 2:3 — THE LIVING WORD. We have been "born again" by the Word of God. It will never pass away.

Notice the, "Wherefore" of 2:1 continues the subject of the Living Word. Memorize and write 2:2: _____

_____

_____

(4) In 2:4-10 we see the "LIVING STONE." We are also *living stones* in a spiritual house. In V-6 the chief cornerstone is Christ.

So in this first section Peter speaks of:

- THE LIVING HOPE
- THE LIVING WORD
- THE LIVING STONE

We are now priests of God — having access to God. It is a birthright of *every* believer (V-9).

5. **The Christian Life — Chapters 2:11 — 4:11**

The section begins with, "Dearly beloved." We sense a change here. Peter begins to tell us about:

(2) THE CHRISTIAN LIFE AND HOW TO LIVE IT.

We are to refrain from fleshly lusts — V-11.

- to be aboveboard — V-12
- to be obedient — V-13
- to do well — V-15
- to honor, love, fear God — V-17

We are to act right on the job — V-18-20.

We are returned sheep (if we believe) to the *Shepherd* and *Bishop* of our souls — because of the sufferings of Christ on the Cross — V-21-25. (V-24 is a good definition of atonement.)

(2) THE CHRISTIAN LIFE IN THE HOME — 3:1-7.

A wife can often win her husband by her conduct. Inward adornment wins the lost husband. Husbands are to love and honor their wives. The ideal marriage is one based on Christ.

(3) THE CHRISTIAN IN THE CHURCH — 3:8-17.

Be of one mind, love each other, have compassion, shun evil, "be ready always to give an answer to every man that asketh you a reason of the hope that is in you" — V-8-15. Be willing to suffer for well doing — V-17.

(4) CHRIST SUFFERED FOR OUR SINS — 3:18-22.

We come now to one of the most difficult of all the passages of the Bible.

Read from V-17 through 22 again, slowly.

What does that mean. Dr. W. A. Criswell says, and I agree, "our problem begins with the words, 'By which spirit he went and preached to the spirits in prison.' What does that mean? Christ was put to death in the flesh, but was quickened in the Spirit. *His* spirit was quickened, and in *that* spirit He went and preached to the spirits in prison. He did not go to preach to the spirits in prison when

He was raised from the dead, as the King James Version seems to imply. Let me go over that again. It was *not* when Christ was raised from the dead in His new resurrection body He went down to Hades and preached to the spirits. The text says that being put to death He was quickened in the spirit, in which spirit He went down into hell to preach to the spirits in prison. Before Christ was incarnate, He was pure spirit and He was glorious in spiritual majesty. When Christ was separated from His body, His spirit was quickened (made alive). When our Lord suffered and died He went down where, in the days of His flesh, He could not have gone. Read Ephesians 4:8-9. When you study these verses closely you will come to the same conclusion I have come to. Paul says our Lord in His death descended into the lower parts of the earth and to a Jewish people. This means that when He descended into the lower parts of the earth, it was another world, Hades. Both Paul and Peter wrote the same thing. Jesus was quickened by the Spirit, in which spirit He went and preached to the spirits in prison *before* He was raised from the dead. Why does the apostle speak only of those in the days of Noah? What about all the other spirits who were no less disobedient in other periods? We may suppose these are excluded because they are not named, but that is not so. Peter was deeply impressed by the Flood of Noah. In II Peter 2:5 he speaks of the Noahic Flood and in 3:5, 6 he speaks of it again. So the flood made a great impression on his mind. When Christ went down to Hades, He went to herald, to proclaim" — (Criswell, *Sermons On Peter,* pp. 77-79).

There are scores of interpretations. I think He proclaimed the news of a *finished redemption* — spelling *doom* in torment and *glory* in paradise. See Luke 16:19-31.

We are identified with Christ in baptism.

(5) THE CHRISTIAN LIFE ENDURES SUFFERING — 4:1-11.

It gives victory over the old nature. We can no longer be satisfied to live in the flesh — V-1-3.

The coming of the Lord inspires Christian living — V-7.

We are to love the brethren and be kind to them — use the gift God has given us — and all of us have a gift — V-9-10. Note Peter's doxology in V-11.

6. **The Lord's Return — 4:12 through 5**

Peter is concerned about the tribulation, which was yet future but was surely coming upon Christians. He begins (V-12) — "Beloved think it not strange concerning the fiery trial which is to try you." As the rest of the book indicates, Peter was thinking of the "great tribulation." This concurs with Paul's teaching that the second coming of Christ is to be preceded by a fiery period of tribulation. Note the emphasis of Peter on the second coming of our Lord:

Note 4:13 _____

_____

5:1 _____

_____

5:4 _____

_____

Did you notice the "crown of glory?" This is one of five rewards for the Christian:

(1) INCORRUPTIBLE CROWN — (conquer old nature) — I Cor. 9:25-27.

(2) CROWN OF REJOICING — (for soul winners) — I Thess. 2:19.

(3) CROWN OF LIFE — (martyrs crown) Rev. 2:10.

(4) CROWN OF RIGHTEOUSNESS — (Love the Lord's appearing) — II Tim. 4:8.

(5) CROWN OF GLORY — (faithful teachers and preachers) — I Peter 5:2-4.

Peter says that we should not worry but, "casting all your care upon Him; for He careth for you."

What a glorious Book! Read it again.

HOW MUCH DO YOU REMEMBER?

Q. What was Peter's other name?

Q. Can you name three LIVING *things mentioned?*

Q. How did Christ preach to the spirits in prison?

Q. Out of the five crowns (or rewards), how many can you claim?

YOUR ASSIGNMENT FOR NEXT WEEK

1. Read II Peter — (only 3 Chapters — read twice).
2. Review your notes on I Peter.
3. Mark your Bible.
4. Be present next Lord's Day for II Peter.

Lesson 49
"The Books of II Peter and Jude"

(Where lines are provided, please look up Scriptures and fill in the entire Scripture or the main Truth of the passage.)

1. **The Two Books**

   These two Books, II Peter and Jude, are very similar to each other. There is such a similarity, that one would suppose that they were both inspired from the same background. This is especially true of II Peter, Chapter 2 and the book of Jude.

   There is much controversy over the authorship of II Peter. The New Testament canon of Scripture was formed from a basic rule — "shall be written by an apostle or an amanuensis of an apostle." An amanuensis is a "secretary" or "writer." The Council of Carthage said, "Nothing shall be read in the churches except the recognized canon," and then listed the 27 Books of the New Testament. The authorship of II Peter has been questioned because of the difference between the style and writing of I and II Peter. I Peter was written elegantly — Greek flows perfectly — but II Peter sounds as though it were written by a man using a Greek dictionary; Peter spoke Aramaic, he was grown when he followed Jesus. I Peter was written by Peter through his secretary, an amanuensis, who was Silvanus (I Peter 5:12). II Peter was written by Peter himself or one who could not write Greek like Silvanus. This is the reason for the difference in style between the two Books. Peter wrote the epistle! (3:1).

2. **The Central Message of II Peter**

   "The knowledge of God and of Jesus our Lord, according as His divine power hath given unto us all things that pertain unto life and godliness through the knowledge of Him that hath called us to glory and virtue:" (1:2-3).

   (The main thought is *Apostasy.* There is no mention of the Lord's death, resurrection, ascension, prayer.)

3. **The Structure of the Book**
   - THE GREAT CHRISTIAN GRACES — 1:1-14
   - THE AUTHORITY OF THE SCRIPTURES — 1:15-21
   - THE APOSTASY — FALSE TEACHERS — Chapter 2
   - THE RETURN OF THE LORD — Chapter 3

4. **The Great Christian Graces — 1:1-14**

   There is danger in the Christian life without growth. There is also the danger of knowledge without practice. With a "like precious faith" (V-1) and "precious promises" (V-4), the partakers of His divine nature can "escape the corruption that is in the world through lust."

   There are seven Christian graces added to "faith." These should be a part of our way of life — (V-5):

   To faith add:
   - VIRTUE, and to virtue,
   - KNOWLEDGE, and to knowledge

NOTES

through the Bible in one year

- TEMPERANCE (self-control), and to temperance
- PATIENCE, and to patience
- GODLINESS, and to godliness
- BROTHERLY kindness, and to brotherly kindness
- CHARITY — meaning love.

If these be a part of your life, you will not be idle nor unfruitful in the knowledge of our Lord Jesus Christ (V-8). The Christian who becomes "sterile" forgets that he was purged from his old sins (V-9).

Peter reminds us of our calling and he stirs us to remember (V-10-14).

5. The Authority of the Scriptures — 1:15-21

The approaching death of Peter was on his mind. His main teaching here is the fact of the coming of the Lord based upon his own eyewitness account of the transfiguration (V-15-16). The next verses explain. Read V-17-18. Look up:

Matthew 17:5: _____

_____

The verses 19 through 21 contain the most profound statements about the Word of God:

"A more sure word of prophecy" — (V-19) — (more sure than Peter's eyewitness account of the transfiguration).

"No prophecy of the Scripture is of its own interpretation" — (V-20 — *we must teach Scripture with Scripture*).

"Holy men of God spake as they were moved by the Holy Spirit." (V-21). See II Timothy 3:16-17.

6. The Apostasy — False Teachers — Chapter 2

False prophets were heretics for Israel. False teachers shall also be in the Church denying the redemption of Christ. False followers will go after false teachers (V-1-3). Peter lists three types of apostates of the past who will appear in the future:

(1) "ANGELS WHO SINNED" — (V-4). Rebellion against God.

(2) "THE UNGODLY" of Noah's day — (V-5) — (Matt. 24:37-39).

(3) "IMMORALITY," like that of Sodom and Gomorrah — (V-6) — Romans 1:24-32).

"The Lord knoweth how to deliver the godly out of temptation —." (V-7). Isn't that great? Look at I Cor. 10:13 again.

The remainder of the Chapter is a vivid but awful description of apostasy. Angels would not presume to do such things (V-11); these apostates (false teachers) are like animals (V-12); they're lustful (V-14); following Balaam for worldly gain (V-15); they have head knowledge (V-20); they are as hogs returning to the pig pen (V-22).

Jesus had much to say about apostasy: Matt. 15:14; Matt. 12:43-45; Luke 12:47-48.

The lesson for us today, in the Church, is never allow compromise. False doctrine should never infiltrate the classroom or pulpit under the guise of "easy going kindness."

7. The Return of the Lord — Chapter 3

Peter wrote this letter (V-1) to cause them to remember that in the last days scoffers would be present to ridicule the second coming of Christ. They will say that nothing has changed since the creation (V-1-4).

Peter reminds them and reminds us in V-5-7. The reminder was "the world that then was" was destroyed by water. Jesus says His coming will be like that. Look up Matthew 24:37-38. Write in Verse 37:

_____

_____

3:10 gives a vivid description of the destruction of the earth:

- "heavens pass away with a great noise" —
- "melt" — elements dissolve —
- "elements" — all material in the earth —
- "fervent heat" — is energy.

In view of these facts of Scripture about the future, the believer should be serious, set apart for the Master, winning the lost (V-11 and 14).

Now read V-13 — Note: *we,* according to His promise, look for . . ."

Peter concludes the epistle by saying that Paul wrote the truth in depth. The former rebuke of Paul toward Peter did not ruin their relationship. (See Galatians 2:11-14.)

Note V-18 — "But *grow* in grace and in knowledge." We grow only through the Word of God.

"THE BOOK OF JUDE"

1. **The Book**

Jude was the brother of James, the beloved pastor at Jerusalem, and half brother of our Lord. Along with his brother, Jude did not believe in the Lord until after the resurrection (John 7:3-8). Between the resurrection and the ascension, both were saved and they were present in the Upper Room just prior to Pentecost (Acts 1:13 — note "Judas the brother of James" is Jude).

Jude is the only book devoted entirely to the apostasy which is to come upon Christendom before the Lord Jesus returns. Jude brings all the teachings about apostasy to a climax — going all the way back to the Garden of Eden and on through His people Israel, right up to the present day.

The Book is very similar to II Peter. Peter placed the false teachers in the future (II Peter 2:1); whereas Jude saw them as already present.

2. **The Central Message**

"Ye should earnestly contend (strive) for the faith which was once for all delivered unto the saints" (V-3b).

3. **The Structure of the Book**

- Why We Should Strive For the Faith — V-3-16
- How We Can Contend For the Faith — V-17-23

4. **Why We Should Strive For the Faith — V-3-16**

(1) In Verses 3 and 4 we see the apostate teachers creeping into the fold unnoticed. They were probably even known as "good men."

They hold to two basic denials of the faith —

- "turning the grace of God into lasciviousness" and
- "denying the only Lord God, and our Lord Jesus Christ."

(2) Certain doom on these false teachers in V-5-7 is foretold and illustrated by *three* historic examples of apostasy from the past:

- EGYPT — "afterward destroyed them that believed not" — V-5.
- ANGELS — "kept not their first estate" — V-6.
- SODOM AND GOMORRAH — "are set forth for an example" — V-7.

(3) In V-8-11, Jude describes in harsh terms the character and conduct of these false teachers. He compares them with three historic figures remembered for ungodly acts and attitudes:

- CAIN — the natural man, having his own way.
- BALAAM — making merchandise of their type of "a gospel."
- KORAH — denying the authority of Moses as God's spokesman.

(4) In V-12-13 there are six metaphors describing the apostate teachers:
  (a) "SPOTS" (V-12) — are "hidden rocks" in the love feasts, referring to the Lord's Table in I Cor. 11:17-30.
  (b) "FEEDING THEMSELVES" (V-12) — false shepherds feed their own desires without fear.
  (c) "CLOUDS WITHOUT WATER" (V-12) — describing the false promises of apostasy.
  (d) "TREES WITHOUT FRUIT" (V-12) — describing the barren profession of apostasy.
  (e) "RAGING WAVES OF THE SEA" (V-13) — describing the wasted effort of apostasy.
  (f) "WANDERING STARS" (V-13) — describing the aimless purpose of all false teaching.

(5) The Enoch prophecy of coming destruction — V-14-15.

Enoch predicted the second coming of Christ before our Lord came the first time. Enoch announced two great events:
  • "The Lord cometh with ten thousands of His saints" — V-14.
  • "To execute judgment upon all ungodly" — V-15.

Look up Col. 3:4 _____

_____

I Thess. 3:13 _____

_____

II Peter 3:7 _____

_____

5. **How We Can Contend For the Faith — V-17-23**

Apostasy has been foretold — we have been warned — V-17-19.

We are to build up ourselves in faith; to pray; to keep ourselves in God's love; to look for the Lord Jesus Christ; and we are to win the lost V-20-23.

Verses 22 and 23 we could describe with the following examples:
  • V-22 can be illustrated by those who need tender firm care because of things such as alcohol or drugs (V-22).
  • The first part of V-23 could be illustrated by an unsaved person being strongly influenced to join a perverted cult group.
  • The second part of V-23 could be illustrated by a Christian man dealing with a beautiful woman concerning immorality in her life.

The closing doxology of Jude is one of the sublime statements of the New Testament:

"Now unto him that is able to keep you from falling, and to present you faultless before the presence of his glory with exceeding joy, To the only wise God our Saviour, be glory and majesty, dominion and power, both now and ever. Amen."

(JUDE 24-25)

HOW MUCH DO YOU REMEMBER?

Q. Why was the authorship of II Peter questioned?

Q. What is the main emphasis of II Peter and Jude?

Q. Can you tell how the Bible was given to us? (Look at II Peter 1:21)

Q. Who was Titus?

YOUR ASSIGNMENT FOR NEXT WEEK
  1. Read I, II, III John — (7 short Chapters).

2. Review your notes from this study.
3. Mark your Bible.
4. Be present next Lord's Day for the study of the three little Books of John.

An Added Note

In Jude 9 there is a reference to the contention between Michael and the devil over the body of Moses. Why did Satan want the body of Moses? Because Satan wanted the body to be worshipped by Israel as a sacred relic.

Look up Deut. 34:5-6:_____

_____

_____

The *"he"* in this Scripture is a reference to the archangel Michael, the hero of this statement.

Lesson 50
"The Books of I, II, III John"

(Where lines are provided, please look up Scriptures and fill in the entire Scripture or the main Truth of the passage.)

1. **The Book of I John**

   John, the same who wrote the Gospel of John and the Revelation, is the author. This first epistle of John is often referred to as the "Epistle of No Compromise." In the Gospel of John, he describes us as sheep in His fold — in this epistle, as members of his family.

   John gives the reason for his writing in each of the three types of revelation:

   > In the Gospel — John 20:31 — "But these are written, that ye might believe that Jesus is Christ, the Son of God; and that believing ye might have life through His name."

   > In the Epistle — I John 5:13 — "These things have I written unto you that believe on the name of the Son of God, that ye may know that ye have eternal life —."

   > In the Revelation 1:19 — "Write the things which thou hast seen, and the things which are, and the things which shall be hereafter."

2. **The Central Message**

   > "We know" (over 30 times). Examples: 2:3, 5, 21, 29; 3:2, 5, 14, 19, 24, etc.

   (This is a Book that gives assurance of salvation. Read it and underline the word "KNOW.")

3. **The Structure of the Book**

   A BOOK OF SEVEN CONTRASTS

   (1) Light versus darkness — 1:5 — 2:11.

   (2) God the Father versus the world — 2:12 — 2:17.

   (3) Christ versus the Anti-Christ — 2:18 — 2:28.

   (4) Good works versus evil works — 2:29 — 3:24.

   (5) The Spirit versus the spirits — 4:1 — 4:6.

   (6) Love versus pretense — 4:7 — 4:21.

   (7) The New Birth versus the world — 5:1-21.

   Another simple Structure of the Book is:

   - GOD IS LIGHT — 1:1 — 2:2
   - GOD IS LOVE — 2:3 — 4:21
   - GOD IS LIFE — Chapter 5

   (We shall not study this rich Book by the above. They are self-explanatory but we shall highlight the Book.)

4. **Highlights of Chapter 1**

   (1) John again goes back to "from the beginning" as in John 1:1 (eternity past). V-1 of this epistle sets forth:

   - *"We have heard"* — John heard Jesus speak (eargate)
   - *"We have seen"* — John saw Him — (eyegate)

- *"Looked upon"* — to look saves
- *"Handled"* — he had felt the Master's heartbeat — John 13:23; 21:20, 24

(2) He is the source of fellowship — 1:3.

Christian fellowship means sharing in the things of Christ. Paul used the word "KOINONIA" when speaking of praying, teaching the Word, the Lord's Supper and giving.

We have fellowship if we "walk in the Light" — V-5-7. Jesus is the Light.

We retain fellowship by confession of sin — 1:9. Memorize this. It is the Christian's bar of soap.

5. **Highlights of Chapter 2**

(1) Christ is our advocate (our attorney) if we sin. He has paid for our sins; as we confess, he restores us to full fellowship — V-1-2.

(2) Obedience to the Lord and His Word is evidence that we belong to Him, which in turn produces love for the brethren — V-3-11.

This is one of the best tests one can apply to the question:

"How can I be sure I am a Christian?"

J. Vernon McGee says, "The Christian life is like a triangle:

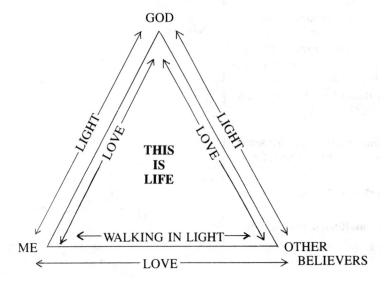

(3) We must not love the world — V-15-17.

Note V-16: "Lust of the flesh"
"Lust of the eye"
"Pride of life"

These are the things of the world. Every sin can be placed under one of these.

(4) Note the emphasis on "many Anti-Christs" — V-18-28. This is in reference to the last days (and we are in them) and much false teaching by false teachers. There will be a departure from the doctrine of God (V-19) denying the deity of Jesus, yet calling themselves "Christians" — (V-22-23).

6. **Highlights of Chapter 3**

(1) The Father's love for us — (V-1). We do not *expect* to be the Sons of God — WE ARE!

We are *now* the sons of God, but we shall be like Him — V-2.

(2) In V-8 and on we see good versus evil works, but the climax is V-24 for the Christian. "Hereby we *know* that He abideth in us, by the Spirit which He (Jesus) hath given us."

7. **Highlights of Chapter 4**

(1) "Try the spirits." Don't believe everything that *seems* sincere and

good. There are false spirits ready to try us every day.
Underline 4:1.

The Holy Spirit indwells every believer — V-4.

The Christian will always hear the Word of God — the preacher, the teacher — but the unsaved will not hear — V-6.

(2) The great passage on love by John is found in V-7-21. Read and underline the many times you find the word "love" (27 times — find them).

Write here V-18: _____

_____

_____

8. **Highlights of Chapter 5**

(1) Faith produces victory over the world — faith in Christ — V-1-4.

(2) V-6 seems to be a hinderance to scholars. There are three that bear witness to the truth of salvation by faith in Christ:

- WATER — the Word of God (See John 19:34-35)
- BLOOD — the death of Christ for our sins (See Eph. 1:7)
- SPIRIT — truth (See Acts 1:4, 8)

V-7 — Is the Father, Son (Word), Holy Spirit?

V-8 — The Holy Spirit works in our hearts when we are born again; He takes the Word and applies the shed blood of Christ to our hearts.

(3) The key of the epistle is found in V-11-15. Underline this section in red — *remember it!*

9. **The Seven Tests of Our Walk With God**

They begin with the words, "If we say," and "He that saith."

Here they are: • 1:6 — False fellowship
- 1:8 — False sanctity
- 1:10 — False righteousness
- 2:4 — False allegiance
- 2:6 — False behavior
- 2:9 — False spirituality
- 4:20 — False speech

THE BOOK OF II JOHN

1. John, identifying himself only as "the elder," is the author. He wrote this brief letter to a lady — "the elect lady." The contents of V-5, 10 and 12 indicate that the letter was a personal note to a real person (not to a local church, as some writers indicate). The letter was written from Ephesus about A.D 90.

2. **The Central Message**

"For the truth's sake" — V-2.

3. **The Structure of the Book**

Walk in Truth and Love — V-1-6

Guard the Doctrine of Christ — V-7-13

4. **Walk in Truth and Love — V-1-6**

Truth is the theme of this epistle. The truth John speaks of is the doctrine of the Scriptures. The reference in V-4 is an answer to a letter John had received.

V-5 — the truth John refers to is not a new thing, but that which they had received from the Father from the beginning — that we love one another.

Look up Galatians 6:2:_____

_____

The love is the love of the "new law of Christ" brought about by the Holy Spirit in the heart of every believer (see Romans 5:5).

We should love each other and the proof is in our walk — V-6.

5. Guard the Doctrine of Christ — V-7-13

"He that abideth in the doctrine of Christ, he hath both the Father and the Son" — V-9.

Many false teachers were traveling among the churches (V-7-11) who would not confess that Jesus Christ was here in the flesh. These were deceivers and anti-christs. (See I John 4:1-2). They did not believe in the humanity of Christ and denied His incarnation.

We are not to support anyone preaching and teaching a false doctrine. There are so many cults and "isms" in our day. John says, if we support them, we become partakers of that evil doctrine — meaning we share in spreading a false doctrine (V-10-11).

THE BOOK OF III JOHN

1. This third epistle of John deals with personalities — three men. These three teach us some basic truths.

2. The Central Message

"Beloved, I wish above all things that thou mayest prosper and be in health, even as thy soul prospereth" — V-2.

3. The Structure of the Book

- GAIUS — Walking In Truth — V-1-8
- DIOTREPHES — Loves Pre-eminence — V-9-11
- DEMETRIUS — Good Report of All Men — V-12-14

4. Gaius — Walking In Truth — V-1-8

John calls Gaius "the beloved" four times. This man of God was a source of great joy for John. He had cared for all of "the fellows — helpers of the truth." The "truth" in this good man was the Lord Jesus Christ.

5. Diotrephes — Loves Pre-eminence — V-9-11

This man wanted all the praise and glory. Notice that he was guilty of:

(1) Not receiving John — (V-9)

(2) Making malicious statements against John — (V-10)

(3) Refusing to entertain the brethren (missionaries) — (V-10)

(4) Excommunicating the ones that "put up" the missionaries in their homes from the church — (V-10)

6. Demetrius — Good Report of All Men — V-12-14

There is only one verse about this man; it gives us a good lesson in Christian character. His name indicates that he was a convert from paganism. He spoke only good of all men and of the Gospel itself. He adorned the doctrine of Christ. Others testified of his faithfulness to Christ.

We can be a Gaius, helping spread the Gospel — or we can be a Diotrephes, hindering the work for personal attention — or a Demetrius, adorning the Gospel of Jesus Christ.

HOW MUCH DO YOU REMEMBER?

Q. How many Books did John write?

Q. Can you name them?

Q. What is the Central Message of I John?

Q. Can you quote from memory I John 1:9?

Q. II John was written to _____.

Q. III John was written to _____.

YOUR ASSIGNMENT FOR NEXT WEEK
1. Read the first 11 Chapters of Revelation.
2. Review your study of the three epistles of John.
3. Mark your Bible.
4. Be present next Lord's Day for the first of two lessons on Revelation.

Lesson 51
"The Book of
Revelation" — Part I

(Where lines are provided, please look up Scriptures and fill in the entire Scripture or the main Truth of the passage.)

1. **The Book**

    Our study of this, the last Book of the Bible, shall be in two parts — two lessons. It is impossible to cover all of the teachings of the Revelation, therefore, we shall try to grasp the high points which —

    - God gave to Christ
    - Then Christ sent by the angel
    - Then the angel gave to servant John
    - And finally John gave to the seven churches

    This authenticates every word found in the Book of Revelation.

    John, the Apostle, wrote the Revelation. He had already written four other New Testament Books: The Gospel of John, I John, II John, III John. In the Gospel of John, he reached farther back into eternity than any other Bible writer (John 1:1-3). In Revelation he reaches farther into eternity future than any other writer (Revelation 21 and 22).

    Man writes history – God writes prophecy. Revelation is prophecy from God. The importance of the Book is in V-3, and there we find *three beatitudes* of the Book:

    (1) "Blessed is he that *readeth*

    (2) And they that *hear* the words of *this prophecy*

    (3) And keep those things which are written therein."
    John wrote this prophecy from the Isle of Patmos.

2. **The Central Message**

    "The Revelation of Jesus Christ" — V-1.

    (The word Apocalypse is compounded from a verb and a preposition: *"APO"* means "away from." *"KALUPTO"* means "to hide, to cover." "Apokalupsis," therefore means "to unveil, to reveal." The Revelation then reveals, unveils the coming triumph of Jesus Christ.)

    Before we give the structure of the Book, it may help you to understand the Revelation by knowing some of the interpretations of the Book. In V-3 we read, *"now* the time is at hand." However, if we group every theory and idea ever written about this Book we can group them under four general headings.

    They are briefly:

    (1) THE PRETERIST INTERPRETATION.

    Preterist is from the Latin word "praeter" meaning "past." So they are the group who look upon the Revelation as having already been fulfilled in the years and generations of the past.

    (2) HISTORICALLY CONTINUOUS INTERPRETATION.

    These believe that the Revelation is a panorama of the history of the church from the days of John.

(3) THE SPIRITUALIZERS — IDEALISTS.

These interpret the Book as a symbol of the great struggle between good and evil. They do not accept the Book as actual — only symbolic.

(4) THE FUTURIST INTERPRETATION.

This is the group that believes that beginning at the fourth Chapter of Revelation, an unveiling of the consummation of the age is described. Most of us who are called "evangelicals" believe this basic interpretation — that most of the things in the Book are still to come to pass. Nothing in history can compare to the judgments depicted in this Book.

Now you can decide which theory you might agree with – only after you have finished these two lessons, please.

So what does God mean when He says, "For the time is at hand?" He means that the return of our Lord is always imminent — always.

3. **The Structure of the Book**
   - "Write the things which thou hast seen" — Chapter 1.
   - "And the things which are" — Chapters 2 and 3.
   - "And the things which shall be hereafter" — Chapters 4-22.

(This is the outline of God to John in 1:19.)

4. **"Write the Things Which Thou Hast Seen" — Chapter 1**

In obedience to that command, John wrote the things which he had seen. He saw the glorified Lord, the Alpha and Omega, the beginning and the ending. He had seen the seven golden candlesticks (lampstands) and in the midst of the seven candlesticks he saw One like unto the Son of God. John described the vision of the Living Lord: His garments, eyes, head, hair, feet, voice. John saw in the right hand of the Lord "seven stars" (V-16). What were these "candlesticks" and "stars" (V-16)? John tells us in V-20, the seven stars *are* the "angels" — messengers actually pastors of the "seven churches." "The seven candlesticks *are* the seven churches."

5. **"And the Things Which Are" — Chapters 2 and 3**

(1) "The things which are" — are the seven churches. In 1:20 "the seven candlesticks are the seven churches." He doesn't refer to a riddle or an enigma. The message was clear that John was to write in a book what he saw and send that message to the seven churches which *are* in Asia.

The seven churches represent all of God's churches. The divine arithmetic in the Revelation is significant because the number *"seven"* means "fulness," "complete" — the complete household of God. The seven churches represent all the churches of all ages. John lived in the same dispensation, same age that we live in today — the day of the Church Age.

(2) Christ speaks to the seven churches in a definite order. He follows a definite pattern as you will see as we study each of the seven churches. The pattern in each is:
   - First Christ identifies Himself
   - Then He commends the church (all but Laodicea)
   - Next He condemns the things that are wrong. (He had no condemnation for Smyrna and Philadelphia.)
   - Then He warns the church
   - And finally He challenges the church

(3) EPHESUS — "Unto the pastor of the church at Ephesus, write . . ."

This was the church of the Apostles. Note now the pattern of our Lord to Ephesus:
   - HE IDENTIFIES HIMSELF: 2:1 — "Things saith He that

holdeth the seven stars in His right hand who walks in the midst of the seven golden candlesticks."

- HE COMMENDS THE CHURCH: V-2-3, "I know thy works, thy labor, thy patience, etc."
- HE CONDEMNS: V-4, "Nevertheless I have somewhat against thee, because thou hast left thy first love."
- HE WARNS: V-5-6, "Remember — repent or I will remove the candlestick —."
- HE CHALLENGES: V-7, "He that hath an ear, let him hear what the Spirit saith unto the churches; to him that overcometh will I give to eat of the tree of life which is in the midst of the paradise of God."

(4) SMYRNA — "Unto the pastor of the church in Smyrna, write . . ."

This was the church of persecution.

- HE IDENTIFIES HIMSELF: 2:8, "These things saith the first and the last which was dead and is now alive."
- HE COMMENDS: V-9-10 — (Read these verses). This was the church of the martyrs and persecution. There were ten distinct attempts by imperial rulers to crush the infant church. These are historical events from the days of Nero to the days of Diocletian.
- HE CONDEMNS: none.
- HE WARNS: V-10, "Fear none of these things — Be thou faithful."
- HE CHALLENGES: "I will give thee a crown of life" (see James 1:12).

(5) PERGAMOS — "Unto the pastor of the church at Pergamos, write . . ."

This church was married to the state — a church of the world.

- HE IDENTIFIES HIMSELF: 2:12, "These things saith He which hath the sharp sword with two edges."
- HE COMMENDS: V-13, "I know thy works — thou holdest fast my name and hast not denied my faith."
- HE CONDEMNS: V-14-15, "But I have a few things against thee" (Read these verses).
  They were practicing false doctrine.
- HE WARNS: V-16, "Repent, or else—"
- HE CHALLENGES: V-17, "To him that overcometh—"

(6) THYATIRA — "Unto the pastor of the church in Thyatira, write . . ."

This church is the church under the government — a state church.

- HE IDENTIFIES HIMSELF: V-18, "These things saith the Son of God."
- HE COMMENDS: V-19, "I know thy works — love, service, faith, patience."
- HE CONDEMNS: V-20-23 — They were allowing the ministry of a false prophetess, Jezebel.
- HE WARNS: V-24-25 — (Read the warning).
- HE CHALLENGES: V-26-28, "And he that overcometh—"

(7) SARDIS — "Unto the pastor of the church at Sardis, write . . ." (3:1.)

This church period is the church of the Reformation:

- HE IDENTIFIES HIMSELF: V-3:1, "These things saith He that hath the seven Spirits of God and the seven stars." Don't forget the divine arithmetic. There are not seven different spirits of God; here in 3:1 Jesus says "these things saith He that hath the seven Spirits (the fulness, complete, total spirit) of God."

- HE COMMENDS: V-4, "Thou hast a few names even in Sardis — they are worthy."
- HE CONDEMNS: V-1, "Thou hast a name that thou livest, and art dead."
- HE WARNS: V-2-3, "Be watchful and strengthen the things that remain — remember — repent."
- HE CHALLENGES: V-5-6, "I will confess his name before My Father—." (Look up Luke 12:8-9.)

(8) PHILADELPHIA — "Unto the pastor of the church in Philadelphia, write . . ." (V-7.)

This church means "open door." It represents the great missionary movement.

- HE IDENTIFIES HIMSELF: V-7, "These things saith He that is holy, He that is true, He that hath the key of David, He that openeth and no man shutteth," etc.
- HE COMMENDS: V-9, "Thou hast kept my Word and hast not denied my name."
- HE CONDEMNS: He has no condemnation.
- HE WARNS: V-11, "Behold I come quickly, hold that fast which thou hast—."
- HE CHALLENGES: V-8-12, "I have set before thee an open door — I will subdue your enemies — I will keep thee."

(9) LAODICEA — "Unto the pastor of the church of the Laodiceans, write . . ." (V-14.)

This church represents the church of the last days before the coming of Christ.

- HE IDENTIFIES HIMSELF: V-14, "These things saith the Amen, the faithful and true witness, the beginning of the creation of God." This is a true description of our Lord in His own words.
- HE COMMENDS: Nothing good!
- HE CONDEMNS: V-15-17, "Thou art neither cold nor hot — because thou art lukewarm — I will spue thee out of my mouth. Thou sayest, I am rich, etc."
- HE WARNS: V-18 (read).
- HE CHALLENGES: V-19, "As many as I love, I rebuke and chasten" (see Hebrews 12:5-8). Then a personal challenge at the close of the Church Age is given in V-20-21 (write these verses).

_____

_____

_____

_____

6. **The Third Part of the Outline**

"And the things that shall be hereafter" — will make up the second lesson for next week.

Notice, however, that at the end of the "things which *are*" — the churches — John writes in 4:1, "I looked and behold a door was opened in *heaven;* and the first voice which I heard was as it were a trumpet talking with me; which said, COME UP HITHER and I will show thee things which must be hereafter" (META TAUTA — after these things of the churches).

So, just as the seven churches take us through the church periods in history, now at Chapter 4 that church period is over. We are called "up hither" — raptured. The Church is not mentioned again until Chapter 19:7.

7. **Compare Your Church**

In the study of the churches, compare your church with the seven. You will also find individual members in most churches who will have the characteristics of one or more of the seven churches, i.e., some have lost their first love, some mission oriented, some lukewarm, etc.

This first lesson in the Book of Revelation merely sets the stage for the lesson next week.

HOW MUCH DO YOU REMEMBER?

Q. Name the Books John the Apostle wrote.

Q. What is the Central message of Revelation?

Q. Where is the outline of the Book found?

Q. Can you name the seven churches?

YOUR ASSIGNMENT FOR NEXT WEEK
1. Read the last 11 Chapters of Revelation (12 through 22).
2. Review your notes on this lesson of Revelation.
3. Underline and mark your Bible.
4. Be in class for the last lesson in "Through The Bible In One Year" — next Lord's Day.

Lesson 52
"The Book of Revelation — Part II"

(Where lines are provided, please look up Scriptures and fill in the entire Scripture or the main Truth of the passage.)

This is the second part of our study of the Book of Revelation. It is a continuation of the last lesson wherein we took up the first two points of God's outline to the Apostle John in the writing of this Book. They were:

1. **"Write the things which thou hast seen" — Chapter 1.**

2. **"And the things which are" — Chapters 2 and 3.**

    In this lesson we shall take up the third point of the outline — therefore, the Central Message shall be the same as that of Lesson 51 and the "Structure of the Book" shall be the same as that lesson.

    John wrote what he had seen: he had seen the glorified Lord and he described Him magnificently in Chapter 1. Then he wrote about the things which *are,* namely — the churches.

    Now we come to the last part of the outline and that is today's lesson.

3. **"And the Things Which Shall Be Hereafter" — Chapters 4-22.**

    (1) FOURTH CHAPTER. Here we come to the third part of the outline God gave to us — the things after these things. The Greek phrase is *"meta tauta"* meaning "after these things." After what things? After the things of the churches. So John delineates from this point on the magnificent outline of God.

    You will notice in Chapter 4, Verses 1 and 2 say: "After this I looked and behold, a door was opened in heaven: and the first voice which I heard as it were of a trumpet talking with me, which said, *come up hither,* and I will show thee things which must be hereafter."

    John is raptured up to heaven, a harbinger of the rapture of the Church at the end of the Church Age. When do you see the Church again in the Revelation? It absolutely disappears from the earth. It disappears until you get to the 19th Chapter when the Lord comes with His saints. The reason it is not seen? The Church is in heaven.

    (2) What happens from the fourth Chapter to the nineteenth Chapter is the tribulation, the judgment of God upon the earth after the saints are taken away. That is the same thing that the angels said to Lot in Genesis 19:22 — "Haste thee, escape thither; for I cannot do anything till thou become thither." Judgment cannot fall until God's children are taken out. Was it not that way in the days of Noah? As long as Noah was in the earth, judgment could not fall. God put him in an ark, and who shut the door? God shut the door. That was the judgment of God upon the people outside of the ark. The judgment could not fall until Noah was safe on the inside. It is the same way in this world, as it was in the days of Lot, as it was in the days of Noah. The judgment does not fall, it cannot fall until God's children be taken out. But the very minute they were taken out, the judgment fell; Sodom and Gommorah were destroyed with fire and brimstone.

Here in the Revelation after the Church is raptured, after it is taken out of the earth, immediately the judgment begins to fall. After the Church Age, after the Church is raptured, Chapters 4 through 19 tell us exactly what happens down here when the Church is taken away.

Now there are many theories and many ideas by many theologians and teachers. I am merely trying to present what is so naturally visible here in the Scriptures.

(3) The fourth Chapter of Revelation is the beginning of this glorious opening from heaven. "The seven lamps which are the seven spirits of God" in Verse 5 does not mean that there are seven spirits; the word *"seven"* refers to the fulness, the completeness of the Spirit of God.

That there were four *beasts* is the wrong translation; it should be four *living* ones — "zoa" — the root word from zoology meaning "living creatures." These are the cherubim of the Old Testament. They represent all of the creation of God, north, south, east and west. Then you have the twenty-four elders, representing the twelve tribes of the Old Testament and the twelve apostles of the New.

(4) FIFTH CHAPTER. We have here the vision of the little book sealed with seven seals, with only Christ, the Lamb of God able to open it. This opening of the seven seals is the *beginning* of the judgments of God.

(5) SIXTH CHAPTER — the six seals are opened. The *first seal* is the revelation of the man of sin — Chapter 6, Verse 2. You look at those four horsemen of the apocalypse. The white horse, the conqueror, is the *first seal*. The *second seal* is the red horse, war and death. The *third seal,* the black horse, is famine. The *fourth seal* is the pale horse of death. The *fifth seal* is those that are slain, the martyrs. The *sixth seal* is the great judgment of God upon the earth when they cried for the rocks in the mountains to fall upon them.

(6) SEVENTH CHAPTER — Chapter 7 is an interlude. The sixth Chapter is that awesome judgment of the sixth seal. Then the seventh Chapter is that interlude. When things are at their darkest, we have our greatest revival. So it will be in the Great Tribulation. The greatest revival the world has ever seen will be in the days of the Great Tribulation. John says, "I don't know who these people are dressed in white robes and where they are from." The elder said to him, "These are they which came out from great tribulation, and have washed their robes and made them white in the blood of the Lamb." — V-14. In that day, you are going to have a lot of people saved and a lot of people martyred.

(7) The seventh seal is the opening of the seven trumpets. You have those seven trumpets in Chapters 8 and 9. The trumpet judgments are more severe than the seal judgments.

(8) TENTH CHAPTER — You have the little book which you saw at the beginning. It says here, "In the days of the voice of the seventh angel . . . the mystery of God shall be finished." — Rev. 10:7. Here in the tenth Chapter it says that the little book is to be eaten and it will be in your mouth sweet; it will be in your stomach bitter. The Bible becomes great bitterness if there is judgment in it for any individual. It is sweet if the person is saved.

(9) ELEVENTH CHAPTER — This Chapter gives to us the consummation of this age. Look at Verse 15: "And the seventh angel sounded and there were great voices in heaven, saying, the kingdom of this world are become the kingdoms of our Lord and of His Christ; and He shall reign forever and ever." The revelation is done. It seems to close at this point. In the Book of Daniel, it is divided also into two parts, right in the middle. So it is with the

Revelation. The Revelation comes to a close with the eleventh Chapter. It splits right in the middle.

(10) TWELFTH CHAPTER — God, through John, reveals some of the personalities and some of the epochs in that final judgment. We start over again. The Revelation seems to close and the mystery of God is finished in Chapter 11. Now in Chapter 12 we start over again. First in Chapter 12 is the great wonder in heaven. The woman is Israel giving birth to the Christ child. Then a struggle between Israel and Satan. They overcame Satan by the blood of the Lamb, by the word of their testimony. Read V-1-7.

(11) THIRTEENTH CHAPTER — The first part of it is the description of the beast rising out of the sea. That is the political leader — the man of sin — the Anti-Christ. The last part of Chapter 13 is the beast that comes out of the earth. That is the false prophet — a religious false prophet. You have those three personalities in those two Chapters. Chapter 12 is Israel giving birth to Christ; Chapter 13 are the beasts who shall be the Anti-Christ known as the man of sin; and beginning at Verse 11 you have the false prophet.

(12) FOURTEENTH CHAPTER — This is an interlude. Here we see the same 144,000 (Verse 1) that we saw in Chapter 7. There in Chapter 7 the 144,000 Jews were seen in their ministry upon the earth. Here in Chapter 14 the 144,000 are seen on Mt. Zion (Read Verse 3).

(13) FIFTEENTH CHAPTER — This is the introduction to Chapter 16 and the pouring out of the vials of wrath upon the earth — all seven of them. Here you have a description of the final battle — look at Verse 16, Chapter 16: "And he gathered them together into a place called in the Hebrew tongue Armageddon."

(14) SEVENTEENTH CHAPTER — You have the revelation of the scarlet woman. In Verse 3, "I saw a woman sit upon a scarlet colored beast — the woman was arrayed in purple and scarlet and decked with gold and precious stones — having a golden cup in her hands — upon her forehead was a name written, mystery, Babylon the great, the mother of the harlots and abominations of the earth." In the last part of the Chapter 17, Verses 8-18, you have a description of the head of the religions of the earth. There is so much here that could take lesson after lesson but this must remain an overview.

(15) EIGHTEENTH CHAPTER — We see here the judgment of God upon mercantile Babylon, the natural world, the financial world, the merchandizing world of materialism. Look at Verse 12 and on down, describing those things in which Babylon traffics: silver, gold, linen, purple, scarlet, ivory, wood, brass, iron, marble, cinnamon, frankincense, wine, oil, flour, wheat, sheep, horses, chariots, slaves, and *the souls of men*. Isn't that an amazing thing? That's merchandizing Babylon, which also will be judged. It is a world that know not God — the materialistic world.

(16) NINETEENTH CHAPTER — Here is the great battle of Armageddon. It is a war. In the 19th Chapter we see Jesus and the Church in heaven at the marriage supper of the Lamb.

In Verse 11 you see the actual second coming of Christ to the earth, "I saw heaven open, and behold a white horse, and he that sat upon him was called Faithful and True . . . his eyes were as a flame of fire, and on his head were many crowns . . . his vesture was dipped in blood; and his name is called the Word of God. And the armies which were in heaven followed him upon white horses." I think the Lord is coming during the Battle of Armageddon.

(17) TWENTIETH CHAPTER — We see here the Millennium. The Millenium *means a thousand years*. At the end of that Millennium is the Great White Throne Judgment. This is the resurrection of the

ungodly who are judged as to whether one is saved or not. This White Throne Judgment is for the unsaved people only. All of us who are in Christ shall stand before the "judgment seat of Christ" to receive the things done in the flesh which are called rewards. The wicked shall stand at the White Throne Judgment to receive their reward of damnation. No Christian shall take part in this judgment.

(18) TWENTY-FIRST AND TWENTY-SECOND CHAPTERS — Here is John's vision of the new heaven and the new earth. I want to point out just one thing and then we must close this lesson. Notice Chapter 21, Verse 1: "and I saw a new heaven and a new earth; for the first heaven and the first earth were passed away; and there was no more sea." What does he mean by that? Always in the Bible the sea was a monstrous thing. The sea separated John from his beloved disciples and his friends and people at Ephesus. To John, the sea was a symbol of loneliness, exile and separation.

He closes the Revelation with that beautiful benediction. Quoting the Lord: "He which testifieth these things saith, surely I come quickly." — Rev. 22:20. His answering prayer is, "Even so, come, Lord Jesus." That closes the apocalypse; it closes the Revelation and it closes the Bible.

There is so much that needs to be taught in reference to this blessed Book. There are so many questions in your mind right now that I hope you will study the Book of Revelation, not as a complicated work, but as a message from God the Father, to Christ, to the angel, to John, to us.

Now as we come to the conclusion of "Through The Bible In One Year" it is my prayer that this study will have made the Bible a Book of "Living Hope" and an exciting adventure in the Christian life. May the Holy Spirit teach all of us now — as we continue to teach the Word of God.